Cyber Smart

Cyber Smart

Five habits to protect your family, money, and identity from cyber criminals

Bart R. McDonough

WILEY

Cyber Smart: Five habits to protect your family, money, and identity from cyber criminals

Published by
John Wiley & Sons, Inc.
10475 Crosspoint Boulevard
Indianapolis, IN 46256
www.wiley.com

Published simultaneously in Canada

ISBN: 978-1-119-55961-0
ISBN: 978-1-119-55963-4 (ebk)
ISBN: 978-1-119-55964-1 (ebk)

Manufactured in the United States of America

V10006857_121118

For general information on our other products and services please contact our Customer Care Department within the United States at (877) 762-2974, outside the United States at (317) 572-3993 or fax (317) 572-4002.

Wiley publishes in a variety of print and electronic formats and by print-on-demand. Some material included with standard print versions of this book may not be included in e-books or in print-on-demand. If this book refers to media such as a CD or DVD that is not included in the version you purchased, you may download this material at http://booksupport.wiley.com. For more information about Wiley products, visit www.wiley.com.

Library of Congress Control Number: 2018963005

I dedicate this book to my mother, Kaye "Gigi" McDonough. My intelligent, thoughtful, caring, and beautiful mother—your unconditional love and encouragement coupled with your unwavering demand of excellence propelled me forward in my life and career. THANK YOU, Momma!

About the Author

Bart R. McDonough is CEO and founder of Agio, a hybrid managed IT and cybersecurity services provider specializing in the financial services, healthcare, and payments industries. Bart has deep institutional knowledge of the investment world, with more than 20 years of experience working in cybersecurity, business development, and IT management within the hedge fund industry. His core strengths are assessing, defining, advocating, and driving the adoption of risk management strategies, controls, and models, which enable organizations to advance cybersecurity resiliency while successfully complying with evolving regulatory requirements and behavioral transformations.

Harnessing his expertise in alternative investments, Bart and his team of more than 240 employees have developed cybersecurity and managed IT tools tailored to protect financial businesses' most precious assets: money and reputation. Just one example of Agio's industry-changing work included finding and repairing a Bloomberg Professional Services setting that could have compromised more than 300,000 subscribers. As CEO, Bart has grown Agio's roster of clients to exceed 300, spanning hedge funds, private equity firms, asset managers, investment banks, and healthcare providers.

Bart is a board member of several cybersecurity companies. Prior to founding Agio, he worked at SAC Capital Advisors, BlueStone Capital Partners, OptiMark Technologies, Sanford Bernstein, and American Express. Bart attended the University of Oklahoma and received his undergraduate degree from the University of Connecticut. He is married to the two-time Emmy Award–winning television producer Cheryl McDonough, and he has three incredible children: Russell, Ava, and Kya.

Credits

Associate Publisher
Jim Minatel

Project Editor
Gary Schwartz

Production Editor
Barath Kumar Rajasekaran

Copy Editor
Kim Wimpsett

Production Manager
Katie Wisor

**Content Enablement and
Operations Manager**
Pete Gaughan

Marketing Manager
Christie Hilbrich

Business Manager
Amy Knies

Project Coordinator, Cover
Brent Savage

Proofreader
Nancy Bell

Indexer
Johnna VanHoose Dinse

Cover Designer
Marina Mirchevskaya

Cover Image
© blackred/Getty Images-Gold
Skeleton Key, © monsitj/Getty
Images-Background

Acknowledgments

I'd like to start by thanking the team that helped me get this book published and ultimately distributed: Jim Minatel, Gary Schwartz, and Barath Kumar Rajasekaran at Wiley.

I'd also like to thank the thousands of Agio clients who kept asking me questions at my Cybersecurity Awareness Seminars, which led me to writing this book. I can't wait to share it with all of you.

A huge thank-you to my researcher, Kelly Eley, for all of your valuable time on this project—you were simply a delight to work with, and I can't wait to collaborate with you again. In addition, I'd like to thank Kimberly Peticolas for all of her coaching and advice on getting this idea into a published book.

Next, I have to thank so many of my amazing colleagues at Agio (https://agio.com/) for refining so much about what I know about cybersecurity, management, and life. I have to give a big personal shout-out to Ray Hillen for coining the phrase "Brilliance in the Basics." A special thanks to Lori Rabin for her amazing editing capabilities. Others I want to thank personally include Chris Harper, Mark Fitzner, Miten Marvania, Garvin McKee, Kate Wood, Nick Mancini, Jessica Golle, Heather Matthews, Josh Bentley, Greg Blattner, Marina Mirchevskaya, Kaitlin Boydston, Jason Price, Andrew Werking, Eva Lorenz, Laurie Leigh, Emily Ellis, Carrie Bowers, Donato Lalla, Tim Steiner, Steve Foster, Joe McCusker, and the rest of the amazing organization at Agio (#OneAgio).

A few clients and colleagues I'd like to thank are David Berger, Danny Moore, Avi Gesser, Barry Ko, Ramin Safai, and especially Chris Corrado.

I have to thank my lawyer and great friend Kevin Malek (well, at least I think we are friends) for all of his assistance in this project and so many others in my life.

I have to thank so many of my "brothers" for all their candid (and, yes, sometimes dumb) questions: Troy Bailey, Neil Berkeley, Travis Warford (no Travis, it's not cheese), Johnny O'Fallon, Brendhan Fritts, Chris Nichols, and Ryan Ball. Troy and Neil, I'd especially like to thank you for yelling at me one night over drinks to just "write the damn book" and giving me the courage to fail.

Everyone who knows me knows Gina Peterson is the engine who keeps me going, and without her, none of the meetings that took place to get this book published would have been possible. A huge thank-you to Gina, and her husband Nate, for allowing our family to interrupt hers constantly. Andrea Duarte, while joining us late, has been amazing at helping to smooth out our days and lives and giving this book its final polish.

I've been fortunate to have the most loving and caring parents in the world who have always encouraged me to do more and be better and have always supported me along the way. Education, especially the ability to read and write, were always valued in our home. My father has always been such a rock and a great example of hard work. Your work ethic and your devotion to your family continues to inspire me, Poppy! While I didn't appreciate it at the time and it may have led to some tears, I can't thank my wonderful mother enough for never taking the easy way out and letting me turn in terrible writing. Thanks for always pushing back on me (with your red pen!) and making me better, Momma.

Finally, my immediate family. Thank you for supporting me in everything I do. Kya, thank you for always asking the hard, right questions. You always get to the heart of the matter and helped me clarify and simplify my recommendations in the book. Ava, thank you for first calling me "Tech God"—flattery will get you everywhere. Seriously, thank you for allowing me to understand better the teen viewpoint in using the Internet. Russell, you don't know how much your calm demeanor helps me in life. Thank you for insisting on using correct grammar in texts, thank you for putting up with all the test devices I install and use at the house, and thank you for always being so patient and helpful. You are the rock of this family and occasionally are funny too.

Cheryl, my love and my talented superstar, thank you for being patient with me while I took the time to put this book together. Thank you for working tirelessly to keep our lives running while personally working so hard to make the world a better place through your documentaries and not take life too seriously. Thank you for being my best friend—always making me laugh and not to take life too seriously. Finally, thank you for being the audience to all my ridiculous cybersecurity stories; for always perfectly playing the part of the "normal person" (while we know you aren't really normal!), and keeping me in check. And yes, love, you do have to update your computer and phone now.

Contents at a Glance

Contents

Foreword

Statement of Purpose

Cybersecurity is one of the most important, and most disregarded, aspects of our daily responsibilities. Technology has overtaken our lives—the pervasiveness of the Internet has affected how we do almost everything—from communicating to banking. Drawing on his extensive work with hedge funds, private equity firms, celebrities, hospitals, and more, Bart McDonough accurately and thoroughly describes the cybersecurity threat landscape—the who, what, when, where, why, and how—and then helps readers understand how to perform proper "use, care, and feeding" of accounts and devices to avoid exposure in many areas of daily life. Just as people must tend themselves to maintain their health, so too should they practice proper "cyber hygiene" with websites, software, and devices to protect themselves and their families in a world of cyber threats.

As an expert in the cybersecurity field, McDonough has traveled around the world speaking at conferences for the FBI, Goldman Sachs, JP Morgan, Morgan Stanley, Citibank, Credit Suisse, Jefferies, Bank of America, and others, where he addresses crucial cybersecurity recommendations for businesses. However, the most common question he receives from the attendees at these conferences is "How can I protect myself at home, on a personal level, away from the office?" Addressing this very question in this book, McDonough combines his extensive industry knowledge with real-world examples of cyberattacks and how to prevent them as well as how to recover from them.

The idea of identity theft and other forms of cyberattacks can be daunting to the average person in today's society; however, it does not have to be that way. With the proper knowledge, outlined as the five "Brilliance in the Basics" habits in this book, everyone can learn better practices to help prevent bad actors from taking advantage of their money, personal information, and devices. Moreover, the more people who protect themselves, the better off everyone is. While there are several books out there that address the topic of cybersecurity, the majority of these focus on security for businesses and corporations. Few are intended to teach individuals in the general public how properly to protect their money, identities, personal information, devices, networks, and online experiences.

Cyber Smart focuses exclusively on this audience. Written in plain English and using everyday relatable examples, McDonough helps readers easily understand how they can personally update their approaches to Internet and device safety, and he does this through a positive, proactive style. While other comparable titles focus on fear-based conditioning, *Cyber Smart* focuses instead on maintaining the idea that while these technological advances have risks, there is no reason not to take advantage of them as long as you do it with open eyes and an awareness of how to keep your information safe.

Introduction

A s technology advances and we adopt new cloud-based services, wearables, fitness trackers, smart home appliances, and cars, we need to balance our rapid consumption of technology with vital knowledge of how safely to use, maintain, and protect these Internet-connected products.

Protecting our identities from the onslaught of endless cyber scams and hackers has become an exhausting effort. It can feel like we need a technical degree to defend ourselves and our families from cybersecurity attacks and ensure we're secure in our day-to-day personal and professional lives. Since we don't hear these cyberattacks knocking at our door or receive real-time evidence of our sensitive information circulating the underbelly of the Web, it's hard to grasp how vulnerable we are at any given moment. In this book you learn how to find your exposed information on the Internet—and discover you've been breached—it can feel like there's nothing you can do to protect your and your family's leaked Social Security numbers, passwords, and more. I am here to tell you there is hope. In this book, you'll learn to practice the essential cybersecurity habits to protect your family from bad actors.

Technology advancement brings opportunities, but it also creates risk, making it necessary to teach ourselves proper "use, care, and feeding" of our devices. If we don't, we risk significant exposure in many areas of our life. Similar to caring for ourselves, we must practice proper "cyber hygiene" with websites, software, and devices.

We know we spend a ton of time online, but we may not realize how our heavy Internet usage can increase our risk of falling victim to cybercriminals. It's as easy as visiting a website with infected ads that harvest our computer's CPU power, so bad actors can "mine" highly profitable Bitcoin cryptocurrency, typing credit card numbers into legitimate-looking, spoofed websites, or accidentally downloading ransomware from a linked "Funny Cat Video" our "friend" sent us. We devote a lot of time and energy to these online interactions. If we neglect the "use, care, and feeding" of technology and our presence in cyberspace, we risk letting bad actors run rampant—infecting and sabotaging our cyber comforts, wiping out years of family photos and personal files to ransomware demands in the thousands of dollars, or repeatedly using and abusing our identity.

If we lived in a "bad" neighborhood with a high level of crime, we would take the necessary precautions to protect ourselves, our family, and our belongings. We are mindful of our surroundings—we lock our doors, install extra locks, don't carry loads of cash on us, and so forth. However, when we are in a good neighborhood with low crime, we tend to be more relaxed around our physical safety precautions.

When it comes to our cyber lives—we all live in a bad neighborhood. And we *all* need to practice essential cyberhygiene precautions, or else we play a risky game of cyber roulette to see how much we *think* we can get away with before the neighborhood bad actors succeed in their cyberattacks against us. Then it's game over—or, at the least, we experience a lot of unnecessary frustration, embarrassment, expense, and cleanup.

This is not said to scare you—it is to help prepare you to have the right mind-set when you are online. My primary goal is to share real stories of people like you—victims of common cyberattacks—and then provide specific recommendations you can use to protect yourself against cyberattacks and scams. The secret to practicing cybersecurity is what I call "Brilliance in the Basics"—five crucial cybersecurity habits that I recommend you perform regularly.

Brilliance in the Basics habits

1. Update Your Devices
2. Enable Two-Factor Authentication
3. Use a Password Manager
4. Install and Update Antivirus
5. Back Up Your Data

Performing these five basic, recurring cyberhygiene principles will work to prevent cyberattacks and serve as a cure for prevalent cybersecurity issues. I will show you how to manage your Internet presence safely, as well as your technology usage, so you can continue to enjoy the pleasures and opportunities that come with the cyberspace you love. You'll discover more about the "Brilliance in the Basics" cyberhygiene habits in Chapter 7.

Debunking Cybersecurity Myths

I will also address and dispel popular cybersecurity myths throughout the book. Recognize any of these?

Hacking Myths

- "Why bother doing anything? If a hacker wants to get me, they will. I mean huge companies and the U.S. government get hacked. I can't do anything to protect myself—it's a lost cause."
- "Bad actors aren't interested in my data. I'm not a celebrity or public figure. I don't have anything of value to them."
- "Websites wouldn't steal my computer's CPU power to 'mine' crypto-currency, like Bitcoin, just by visiting them."
- "The applications in the Apple App Store or Google Play store are safe. I can't download 'bank account–stealing' malware from a simple cross-word puzzle app, can I?"
- "I'm not worried about ransomware. Law enforcement will catch the adversary and get my files back, right?"

File Storage and the Cloud Myths

- "I don't store my information in the cloud because it's not safe."
- "I store my files in the cloud already, using Apple iCloud and Google Drive. They back up my files, right?"
- "I perform backups to an external hard drive that's always plugged into my computer. My files are protected."

Password Management Myths

- "Remembering and keeping up with fancy passwords is too difficult. There's no way I can do it for every site I use."
- "Two-factor authentication takes too long. As long as I have a strong, unique password for each account, I am secure."
- "Cloud-based password managers aren't secure."

Web Browsing Myths

- "Websites with the lock symbol in the URL are safe to use."
- "Public Wi-Fi is secure if it requires a password."

Email Account Myths

- "It's not necessary for me to create a separate email just for banking if I have a strong password for my bank account, even if I use the same password for my email account too."
- "I don't have anything of interest to the adversary in my email account. Good luck reading all my boring emails."
- "Email providers like Google or Yahoo aren't making money from my email conversation with my spouse."

Identity Theft Myths

- "Credit monitoring and fraud alerts will protect me from identity theft. I don't need to activate a security freeze."
- "My child doesn't have a credit history. Their identity won't get stolen, and their credit score won't be damaged."
- "I don't shred sensitive documents when I throw them out. No one would sift through my garbage to steal my identity."
- "I connect with anyone who sends me a friend request on LinkedIn. We're all professionals here, not scammers."
- "I trust my doctor's office with my Social Security number when they request it. They need it for vital reasons, right?"
- "I can't be denied critical medication at a hospital just because someone stole my identity and tampered with my medical files, can I?"
- "I trust retailers and gas stations to protect their card swipe, or dip, machines from skimmers that steal card numbers."

By learning the facts, you can set the record straight and safeguard yourself and your family. Cyber awareness will be like second nature.

In fact, let's dive in and dispel one myth right now.

Myth   "Why bother doing anything? If a hacker wants to get me, they will. I mean huge companies and the U.S. government get hacked. I can't do anything to protect myself—it's a lost cause."

Fact   You can safeguard yourself from the vast majority of threats. It takes only a few steps, which I list in the ensuing chapters. By learning to protect yourself, you will take a "bite" out of cybercrime. You'll emerge a newfound "Brilliance in the Basics" expert and be ready to share your learned cyber-security hygiene basics with others.

We need to work together to defend our privacy, security, money, and peace of mind. It's our right to enjoy what technology and the Internet have to offer. The last thing we should do is to admit defeat and compromise these fundamental liberties by surrendering our security and, along with it, our personal information, assets, and identity.

Protecting our security does not necessarily mean we have something to hide; it's the preservation of our identities and those of our loved ones. This includes our money, medical records, credit files, devices, online presence, and more. Cyber threats influence every part of our lives. We must implement proper cyberhygiene habits accordingly. And that starts here.

How to Use This Book to Outsmart Bad Actors

This book gives a detailed portrayal of the current cybersecurity landscape and its threats, and it explores how we, as adult professionals, can protect ourselves and our families as more of our life duties move online via Internet-connected devices.

Throughout my experience providing cybersecurity training to thousands of business professionals, I observed a growing need among the participants to learn how they can secure themselves on a personal level in addition to safeguarding business operations. It became apparent the cybersecurity community was focusing primarily on business executives and overall business security, leaving a shortage of cybersecurity guidance made available to us as individuals. We are the fabric making up a business, and we are the ones sitting on the other side of the company computer. The focus in this book will be on closing the personal cybersecurity guidance gap. I will share the basic cybersecurity habits you need to protect your and your family's online assets and identity—personally *and* professionally.

I designed this book in two parts: Part I, "Setting the Stage," and Part II, "Specific Recommendations."

Part I: Setting the Stage

In this part, I define some common cybersecurity terms and provide an overview of cyber risk that poses a threat to our families and ourselves. After that, we learn more about who is the adversary, their main goals and targets, and their attack methods and weapons of choice.

Next, I cover the "Brilliance in the Basics"—the five core habits that serve as an ounce of cyberattack prevention worth a pound of cybersecurity cure.

Finally, I touch on some grave mistakes we can make without realizing we've made them, like an accidental data breach. I conclude Part I with detailed incident response steps you can take if you encounter the unfortunate—ransomware, spam, email compromise, and more.

Part II: Specific Recommendations

In this part, you'll find helpful, straightforward steps to begin protecting your identity, money, email, files, social media, website access, passwords, computers, mobile devices, home network, Internet of Things (IoT) devices, as well as your information while traveling.

Throughout each chapter, you will notice a few features: accounts of cyberattack and scam victims, segments on popular cybersecurity myths, and straightforward and practical cybersecurity recommendations.

These accounts are real stories about attacks, scams, or methods of defense. While I include quite a few, they are just the tip of the iceberg. Many dangers are lurking in cyberspace, waiting to pounce on unsuspecting targets who don't know how to protect themselves adequately.

In addition to these real-world stories, I include specific, actionable recommendations outlining how you can stay safe in the midst of frequent and severe cybersecurity attacks. By actively applying the handful of key, learned, defense techniques to your day-to-day personal and professional life, you will be practicing what some of the most secure people in the world do.

I also address popular cybersecurity myths to which we've all fallen prey, believing at one time or another. We've already tackled the first of these myths in this introduction. Going beyond just addressing these myths, in this book I provide the facts on which you'll need to focus to protect yourself and your loved ones with clarity and efficiency so you can continue enjoying all that the Internet has to offer.

How to Contact the Author

You can contact Bart McDonough by visiting his personal website—www
.Bartmcd.com—where you will find his latest thoughts and links to the most
current social media posts.

Download

Go to www.wiley.com/go/cybersmart to download a brief reminder of
"Brilliance in the Basics" habits you can keep with you everywhere.

Cyber Smart

Setting the
Stage

1 Overview of Cyber Risks

William and Nancy Skog had cherry-picked an impeccable, perfect, river-front residence in Wilmington, Illinois. Exhilarated by the thought of moving into their dream home, the Skogs could practically see their new lives—watching the tranquil riverboats cruise by and listening to the water birds sing. There was one final step needed to finalize their purchase—wire $307,000 in closing costs to their real estate attorneys. Having received an email with payment instructions sent from what looked like a legal assistant at the firm, William and Nancy wired over their entire life savings—$307,000. Their new life was about to begin. Days later, however, the couple sat across from their lawyer at the closing table and learned their payment never arrived. The Skogs immediately panicked. If their attorneys didn't get the money, who did?

Let's take a closer look at the details of the wire transfer scam. All $307,000 of the Skogs' hard-earned cash had vanished without a trace. Fraudsters, impersonating their real estate attorneys, had pocketed the entire wire transfer. Almost everything in the closing cost email the Skogs had received looked genuine. The email signatures appeared authentic (because the bad actor copied and pasted the real one), the file attachment had the attorney's actual letterhead, and the details of the real estate transaction were accurate.

How could a bad actor obtain all of this information? A variety of attack methods and vectors could have been used: including compromising one or more email accounts of those involved in the transaction, pretending to be a prospective client and emailing the firm to obtain a response and thus an email signature, or finding the attorneys' letterhead via an Internet search.

Bad actors use automated hacking software that scans data breach dumps for email addresses of people working in a specific industry, such as real estate. Once they collect a list of email addresses, they send *phishing* emails (an email-based, social engineering attack) to obtain the victim's email account password fraudulently. Once they have the password and successfully gain access, they research and monitor real estate transactions in flux. When the timing is right, bad actors send an email to home buyers with "new" wire transfer instructions.[1] It can be easy for victims to believe the malicious email is legitimate, since it can actually be sent from the authentic (hacked) account of one of the real parties involved.

WARNING   The best method of protection is to not trust email and to be extremely cautious when receiving emails requesting money.

Despite the scam's convincing elements, there were indicators something was wrong. The fraudulent email used unorthodox sentence structure, such as ". . . and have us set ready your closing." Notice anything yet? But beyond suspicious grammar, what could have tipped the Skogs off to the fake email sent by the bad actor? The sender's email address and links might have contained clues. Hovering over any links in the email could have produced red flags, like different or similar-looking URL addresses (for example, `RealEstate.com` versus the malicious URL `RealEstate-co.com`).

Next, the circumstances themselves were reason enough to be wary. Cyber-attackers and scammers target their victims in moments of heightened emotion. People are often distracted and/or overwhelmed when scared or elated. In the case of the Skogs, the adversary recognized an opportunity when the Skogs were buying their dream home—a scary and thrilling life event. It was the perfect storm of emotions to render the Skogs vulnerable and allow the scammers to steal the couple's hard-earned life savings successfully when they least expected it. The couple's only saving grace was their daughter, who purchased the home for them.

The Skogs' tremendous loss to real estate wire transfer fraud is indicative of a growing epidemic. In 2016, the FBI found that $19 million in real estate transactions were "diverted or attempted to be diverted" by bad actors, and that amount increased to practically $1 billion in 2017—a 5,163 percent increase in just one year.[2] The cruelest part of real estate wire transfer fraud is the rare chance of ever recovering stolen funds. According to James Barnacle, chief of the FBI's Money Laundering Unit, "I don't want to set false expectations for consumers. The chance of recovery here is slim."[3]

Real Estate Wire Transfer Fraud Prevention Steps

Now that you've learned the life-shattering reality of real estate wire transfer fraud, here are some essential prevention steps:

- Before performing a wire transfer, confirm the exact closing instructions with your real estate broker, attorney, or both, in-person, over video or on the phone. (Remember to validate their phone number first.)
- Verify all emails received are genuine. Look out for red flags indicating a phishing email attack, and be suspicious of clicking any email links or opening any file attachments. (You will learn more about phishing email attacks in Chapter 4 and Chapter 5, as well as how to protect your email in Chapter 12.)
- Review other payment options that can potentially provide more protection than a wire transfer, like a cashier's check.
- Initiate a test wire transfer for $100 and confirm the intended receipent received the wire transfer.
- Don't use insecure Wi-Fi to access or send email communications about sensitive transactions. (See Chapter 15 for safe web browsing practices when using public Wi-Fi.)
- Secure your email account with two-factor authentication, and use a strong and unique password for each of your accounts. (See Chapter 15 for details on protecting web access and passwords.)
- Consider using a secure method of file transfer and storage. Use a paid version of Box.com or similar trusted cloud environment. This will allow you to transfer files securely and control which email addresses can access the files.
- Check to see whether your financial institution has insurance available for purchase to protect you from wire transfer fraud liability. Banks are just starting to sell policies for wire transfer fraud protection up to a certain amount. Because there's no standardized, one-size-fits-all policy, check the fine print for variations among banks.[4]

If You're a Victim of Wire Transfer Fraud

If you've fallen victim to a real estate wire transfer scam, here are immediate incident response recommendations:

- Call the bank that sent the transfer to discuss your options.
- Alert the bank on the receiving end to discuss your options.
- Notify local law enforcement, and file a police report.
- Notify your local FBI field office, and file a complaint.
- Visit the FBI Internet Crime Complaint Center (IC3) and file a complaint online at https://www.ic3.gov/default.aspx.

Real estate wire transfer fraud is just one example of the many common and devastating cyber risks we face. Cyberattacks are growing and evolving at a staggering rate, but by continually practicing the handful of basic protection techniques you'll soon learn, you can strengthen your cybersecurity with ease.

Cyber-Risk Statistics

Serving as a testament to the increase in cyber risk and the need for easy-to-understand, personal, cybersecurity guidance, Verizon published the following statistics in its 2017 "Data Breach Investigations Report," sourced from 65 organizations:[5]

- 51 percent of data breaches involved organized crime groups.
- 1 in 14 people were tricked into clicking a malicious link or email attachment.
- 66 percent of malware was installed by opening malicious email attachments.
- 43 percent of all data breaches used social media attacks.
- 81 percent of hacking-related breaches used stolen and/or weak passwords to gain access.
- 93 percent of social engineering used phishing techniques.
- 14 percent of breaches were caused by mistake.

Why do attackers have such a high success rate in wreaking havoc and causing breaches? One possible explanation is that people rely solely on technology to protect them. In reality, antivirus and firewalls can only do so much, and they don't provide any protection against "legit" emails from compromised counterparties, such as your lawyer, real estate agent, or banker. It takes individual awareness and implementation of proper cyberhygiene practices to defend oneself holistically.

Throughout the book, you will learn about how to defend yourself against the vast majority of threats. There are a set of fundamentals, which when practiced together will dramatically increase your cybersecurity posture. I simply call this collection of activities and technology "Brilliance in the Basics."

Brian Krebs, a well-known cybersecurity researcher and investigative reporter, put together a "Cybercriminal Code of Ethics," to convey "immutable truths" depicting how bad actors benefit from a lack of investment in personal cybersecurity.[6]

- If you hook it up to the Internet, we'll hack at it.
- If what you put on the Internet is worth anything, one of us is going to try to steal it.
- Even if we can't use what we stole, it's no big deal. There's no hurry to sell it, and we know people.
- We can't promise to get top dollar for what we took from you, but hey—it's a buyer's market. Be glad we didn't just publish it all online.
- If you can't or won't invest a fraction of what your stuff is worth to protect it from the likes of us, don't worry: you're our favorite type of customer!

Another reason cyberattackers are successful is individuals don't necessarily have the proper cybersecurity knowledge to detect cyber threats. (You will obtain that knowledge reading this book!) Scotland Yard found in every month London citizens lose $36 million and report around 3,500 cases of cyber fraud. The most common offenses include phishing emails and malware such as ransomware. Bad actors are aware of this lack of understanding when it comes to cyberattacks. Instead of attempting to compromise a company's firewall directly, these scammers target individuals via their personal lives. The hope is this approach will provide a path to a company's network and thus multiple victims. From here, these bad actors can steal personal information, money, and computing resources.[7]

Breaches, Cyberattacks, and Hacks—Oh My!

Now you've read a bunch of statistics about breaches, cyberattacks, and hacks—what do they actually mean, and what's the difference between the three?

A *breach* is an incident where sensitive, private, or confidential information is accessed or leaked without authorization. The types of information valued by bad actors include Social Security numbers, credit card and bank account numbers, billing addresses, tax returns, medical information, usernames and passwords, and more.

A breach can be a result from a cyberattack, a hack, or simply a mistake. Each week, bad actors break into networks and systems and steal people's information, sometimes amounting to tens of millions of data elements or more. Most of the time, this stolen data is used to commit fraud. At other times, it can be used as blackmail, such as the case with the Ashley Madison breach, which leaked names and credit card numbers of customers of the extramarital affair website. Bad actors got ahold of the leaked information and threatened Ashley Madison customers into paying a fee; or else they would divulge their activities to their spouses and the general public.

Companies nowadays store massive amounts of personal information about their users for the purposes of its services, ease of access, data analysis, or the convenience of automated payments. Data can be seen as a toxic asset—the more it's accumulated and the longer it sits in storage, the higher the stakes if the information gets into the wrong hands.[8]

A *cyberattack* is when attackers (that is, individuals, criminal organizations, nation states, terrorist organizations, and so on) carry out malicious attacks, such as social engineering against people with the primary objective of accessing, modifying, disclosing, or selling stolen information. Cyberattack targets can include individuals, businesses, government agencies, national infrastructure, and more. A cyberattack doesn't necessarily involve the act of hacking or even the direct use of computers.

A *hack* is a simple or complex act of malicious intent that involves using automated or manual technology to crack a code or break into a target's computer systems or network. It is simply digital trespassing.

Hacking can be a component of a cyberattack, which can lead to a *data breach*, but a cyberattack doesn't necessarily require hacking skills or computers at all. A data breach can occur without a cyberattack or a hack. A data breach can happen by mistake; as an example, someone sends an email to the wrong person or list of people, resulting in a data breach. Have you ever written an email, attached a sensitive file, and then accidentally sent it to the wrong person? Yep—we've all done it. This is considered a data breach since you didn't intend to send the information to those recipients.

Now that you've read about the main differences between a breach, a cyberattack, and a hack, in the next chapter you will learn who the adversary is, what they want from you, and how you can protect yourself and your family from their cyberattacks and scams.

Notes

1. https://youtu.be/ToUEr4X1WgU
2. www.chicagotribune.com/classified/realestate/ct-re-1105-kenneth-harney-20171030-story.html
3. https://www.cnbc.com/2017/10/19/scammers-are-conning-home-buyers-out-of-their-down-payment.html
4. http://insurancesidebar.com/Home/tabid/427/entryid/158/Make-Sure-to-Read-Fine-Print-with-New-Wire-Transfer-Fraud-Insurance.aspx
5. www.verizonenterprise.com/resources/reports/rp_DBIR_2017_Report_execsummary_en_xg.pdf
6. https://krebsonsecurity.com/2017/01/krebss-immutable-truths-about-data-breaches/
7. https://www.standard.co.uk/news/crime/cyber-crime-costs-londoners-26-million-a-month-police-warn-a3784706.html
8. https://www.schneier.com/essays/archives/2016/03/data_is_a_toxic_asse.html

2 Attackers

At 22 years old, Albert Gonzalez was one of the most valued cyber-crime informants working for the U.S. government—an expert in social engineering, cybercrime, and financial fraud. Years before assuming this role, Gonzalez was just another troublesome teen—and then some. At the age of 14, Gonzalez hacked into NASA. The stunt resulted in a slew of FBI agents showing up at the South Miami High School he attended. Buoyed by his own success, Gonzalez moved on to more complicated hacks. Obtaining credentials from Internet service providers to access "free" broadband service, Gonzalez was able to collect sensitive personal information, network diagrams, and business documents from the companies. Gonzalez recalled, "I would learn about the system architecture. It was as if I was an employee." Wielding these same skills, Gonzalez later convinced a New Jersey Internet company to hire him as a cybersecurity professional after hacking into their network—a creative alternative to an interview. All that came to an end in 2003. Gonzalez was arrested for using forged credit and debit cards to make a sizable withdrawal from a local ATM.

After his arrest, the then 22-year-old Albert started working as an informant for the Secret Service's Electronic Crimes Task Force. They had been investigating credit and debit card fraud in Gonzalez's area without much success. Their target? Members of Shadowcrew.com, a website notorious for trafficking stolen payment card information and selling tools to create fraudulent credit and debit cards for "cashing out" at ATMs. As it happened, Albert Gonzalez was the website's moderator. When threatened with 20 years in prison, Gonzalez *reluctantly agreed to help the Secret Service take down Shadowcrew. A jail cell is a powerful motivator: Gonzalez helped the Secret Service indict 19 Shadowcrew members, people who had trusted him and had followed his leadership.*

After his cooperation in what was dubbed "Operation Firewall," Gonzalez stayed on as a paid informant. Unbeknownst to the agency, however, Gonzalez was back to his old tricks. During his tenure with the Secret Service, Gonzalez carried out some of the most shocking cyber heists in U.S. history—all behind the backs of the federal agents who gave him a second chance. Gonzalez and his group of hackers orchestrated attacks against numerous corporations, stealing around 180 million payment card accounts from T.J. Maxx, Marshalls, OfficeMax, BJ's Wholesale Club, and Dave & Buster's restaurants. In addition to these cyber heists, Gonzalez's crew hacked into Target, Barnes & Noble, JCPenney, Sports Authority, Boston Market, and the ATM network at 7-Eleven stores. Some of you may remember these attacks or, unfortunately, may have been a victim of them.

Gonzalez's double life was unveiled in 2008, at the age of 27, when he received two 20-year jail terms for the cyber heists he and his international crime syndicate had unleashed. The judge handed down the lengthiest-known sentence for computer crimes at the time, commenting, "What I found most devastating was the fact that you two-timed the government agency that you were cooperating with, and you were essentially like a double agent."

"I've been asking myself, why did I do it?" Gonzalez told Time Magazine *reporter, James Verini, over the phone from prison. There wasn't just one answer. While serving as a paid informant, Gonzalez continued to hack because his salary wasn't enough. Even when he was eventually content with the money, he couldn't stop himself— he'd already gone too far and was in too deep. But even beyond the money and his inability to leave the syndicate, Gonzalez hacked for the intellectual challenge and the thrill of stealing.*

Albert Gonzalez is set to be released from prison in 2025 at the age of 44, pending good behavior as well as time served.[1]

The Adversary

Who is the adversary, our cybersecurity "enemy"? You'll probably recognize this popular visual description of a hacker: a hooded figure with a mask, typing on a computer in the shadows of a basement with lines of computer code furiously racing by on the screen. Sounds pretty scary—if it were only true.

The truth is, the adversary can be anyone from a polite neighbor who gardens to a teenager at your kid's high school. Most commonly, the adversary is an international criminal and terrorist organization. According to the HackerOne study "Who Are Hackers," which surveyed hackers who helped businesses find system vulnerabilities (for example, bug bounty programs), 90 percent of hackers are under 34 years of age, 97 percent are male, and 45 percent are employed full-time and hack in their spare time.[2] These cybercriminal and terrorist organizations are well-oiled machines conducting themselves as businesses to target your money and resources. Today's cyberattackers can be compared to a corporate employee; they have performance reviews, are measured against their peers for how effective they are, and are encouraged to develop sophisticated processes that are repeatable and scalable.

So, who are the targets? Are bad actors singling out individuals? With the exception of some high-profile personalities—such as government officials, wealthy individuals, and celebrities—bad actors aren't targeting you specifically. But they aren't exactly removing you from their attack zone either. They are certainly targeting aspects of you—your job title, your college alumni, the type of credit card you have, etc.

The adversary is performing drive-by attacks anywhere and everywhere. It's like a typical car thief walking around a parking lot lifting door handles, seeing whether any of them will open. If a door is unlocked, they'll quickly look for items they can steal—an iPhone, a handbag, money in the glovebox, or the actual car. By practicing the "Brilliance in the Basics," the handful of cybersecurity habits that you'll soon learn in Chapter 7, you'll keep your personal information secure, or "your car doors locked," and get the adversary to move on.

What are an adversary's motives? Albert Gonzalez's hacking incentives— starting at age 14—included money, the thrill of the theft, and an intellectual challenge. The majority of bad actors are after your money and anything they can monetize. Their targets include your credentials, holding your locked files for ransom, stealing your wire transfers, and accessing your computing resources to carry out wide-scale hacking attacks (for instance, as part of a botnet).

While money is a powerful incentive, the adversary has additional cyber-attack motivations. While 72 percent of hackers do it for the money, 71 percent do it for fun, 66 percent hack for the thrill of a challenge, and 51 percent hack to "do good in the world." The 2016 HackerOne study also states that 57 percent of hackers who participated in bug bounty programs did it for free.[2] These generous hackers are defined as *white hat* because they perform hacks to help strengthen the cybersecurity of businesses. *Black-hat* hackers, on the other hand, perform hacks to destruct, monetize, and deplete your computing resources.

What does an adversary do with the credentials and personal information they have accessed? After bad actors gather databases of credentials and information from vulnerable systems and websites, they either keep it to themselves, post it publicly on the Internet, or sell it on the Dark Web. On the *Dark Web*, which is an anonymous form of web browsing that requires a unique Tor web browser to access, compromised information, like your Social Security number, date of birth, and billing address, sells for the low price of $1 to $8, while your credit card number sells for $20 to $60.[3] Bad actors use purchased personally identifiable information (PII) and protected health information (PHI) to assume someone's identity, make purchases and perform financial fraud, obtain health insurance, receive payments for faked medical treatments, and open credit card accounts.

The adversary can also steal intellectual property for economic gain (for example, nation-state attackers), perform illegal acts of cybercrime (for instance, criminal organizations), and carry out terrorism and political agendas (for example, terrorist organizations). While these are serious threats, most "normal" people are not in the direct line of fire.

Nation-State Attackers

Nation-state attackers focus on targets of national interest or individuals and companies that possess highly sensitive information that can be used to the attackers' economic advantage. You frequently hear about nation-state adversaries in the news—they hack and influence political elections and leak information taken from high-profile government agencies. Nation-state hacking groups, such as APT1 (also known as PLA Unit 61398 in China), are more interested in economic gain and technological advancement through the theft of intellectual property, such as military fighter jet blueprints, than making a profit. Other nation-state hacking groups, such as Russia-based Fancy Bear, perform politically focused cyberattacks. Fancy Bear is connected with Russian efforts to influence the 2016 U.S. presidential election and attacking the Democratic National Committee (DNC). The preferred attack methods of Fancy Bear include spear phishing and spreading false information by hacking into target organizations and feeding altered data to journalists.[4] A federal indictment from Robert S. Mueller III unveiled how Russian agents used spear phishing attacks to con Democratic party workers into sharing their login credentials. The Russian agents used real-looking email addresses to send messages with malicious links designed to collect sensitive information, which then allowed them to access the Democratic Party computer networks. Once inside, Russian bad actors installed malware and stole sensitive political documents—later releasing them to the public for the purposes of interfering with the 2016 U.S. presidential election. The bad actors used the spear phishing attack method against election administrators across different U.S. states to gain access to polling networks. Election officials are increasingly worried about the potentially devastating effects of a phishing email. "It's shockingly easy to compose a spear phishing email that is targeted, that is seemingly genuine, that is loaded with the kinds of personal details that would lure someone into clicking onto an attachment that they shouldn't," said Democrat Minnesota Secretary of State Steve Simon. Thomas Rid, a professor at John Hopkins University, who helped identify Guccifer 2.0, a Russian hacking identity, warned, "As long as people make simple mistakes, even the most sophisticated adversary will use very simple methods." In one attack scenario mentioned in the indictment, bad actors sent a fake Google security notification to John Podesta, chairman of Hillary Clinton's campaign, which resulted in Podesta's assistant clicking the link and typing in his login credentials. Election offices nationwide are beginning to roll out two-factor authentication for their employee accounts, in addition to cybersecurity training.[5]

Nation-state attackers also focus on stealing state secrets and the personal information of government employees. In June 2015, the U.S. Office of Personnel Management (OPM)—essentially, the government's HR department—was targeted by nation-state attackers, compromising 21.5 million current, former, and prospective government employee records. The compromised employee records included sensitive information needed to perform background verifications (such as Social Security numbers) and the intimate details of government workers' security clearance levels.[6]

Nation-states attackers target victims in their home country and abroad. Take additional cybersecurity precautions before traveling, especially to any hostile nation states. You'll learn more about protecting your information when traveling in Chapter 21.

Criminal Organizations

Cybercrime organizations operate like highly organized businesses. Cybercriminal organizations go after your money by holding your files for ransom, installing spyware on your computer to steal and sell your personal information, stealing banking information, and pocketing wire transfers.

Each cybercriminal "employee" helps their "employer" by obtaining your money, personal information, and computing resources. As you saw earlier, most hackers are 34 and younger, and they choose to be a professional cybercriminal as a career. In fact, 80 percent of black-hat hackers are connected to a sophisticated criminal organization.[7]

In May 2017, WannaCry became the most significant ransomware outbreak in history, spreading across the world like wildfire. Cybercriminals from the Shadow Brokers gang used the leakage of powerful U.S. NSA cyber weapons to spread devastating ransomware—incapacitating hospital systems, businesses, and individuals' computers worldwide.

The U.S. government, specifically the CIA, kept a secret Windows operating system vulnerability to themselves, intending to create a cyber weapon to fight terrorism by exploiting a nonpublicized security hole. In doing so, they risked the destructive cyber weapon getting into the wrong hands—and it did. The result? More than 300,000 computers across the world were infected with the WannaCry ransomware strain. The Shadow Brokers gang demanded a ransom of $300 to $600 per compromised system.[8]

As long as you update your devices on a regular basis—one of the core "Brilliance in the Basics" cybersecurity habits—you help safeguard your systems from known vulnerabilities. It's when these vulnerabilities are unknown that you are at risk. We rely on the manufacturer to create security updates for, or *patch*, security holes in our devices. It's crucial that you install these once they're made available.

Terrorist Organizations

Terrorist organizations and hacking activists (*hacktivists*) want to create fear and terror through the use of cyberattacks. Their motivation is to advance their religious and political agendas. They'll perform cyberattacks to spread propaganda and use your computing resources to further their large-scale botnet attacks, turning your devices into "bots" that perform commands the bad actor gives behind the scenes.

One day, Cheryl E. Holdren, wife of the former White House official John P. Holdren, received an email from her "husband" asking for their Xfinity home cable service password. Quickly replying without looking more closely at the spoofed phishing email, Cheryl handed over the family's home network password to the cyberterrorist and political hacking group Crackas with Attitude. Gaining access to the Holdren network, the group redirected the Holdren's home phone to the Free Palestine Movement headquarters.

This redirect wasn't the group's first hack. Crackas with Attitude, a "hacktivist" group promoting Palestinian statehood, had previously hacked into the email accounts of other former U.S. government officials, including CIA Director John Brennan, FBI Deputy Director Mark Giuliano, and James Clapper, along with a number of other high-profile victims.[9] Even officials trained to be on guard and practice caution have fallen prey to the adversary. The threat is real. The consequences are devastating.

Bad Actors Who Got Caught

We hear about all of the ways bad actors carry out cybercrimes against us but not as much regarding the adversary getting caught, prosecuted, and handed a jail sentence. Law enforcement has been doing its best to keep up with the rapidly evolving cyber landscape by working with global law enforcement Bad actors are being held accountable for their cybercrimes carried. out against innocent individuals and businesses. The following are stories of some big-time bad actors who learned the repercussions for their illegal actions.

GRANT WEST: A ONE-MAN CYBERCRIME WAVE

Grant West, 26, called the "One Man Cybercrime Wave," received a 10-year sentence in May 2018 for hacking into more than a dozen organizations, stealing payment card information, carrying out phishing attacks against 100 businesses, and selling PII on the Dark Web and hacking "how to" guides to other aspiring bad actors. West, from Sheerness, England, pleaded guilty to conspiracy to commit fraud and computer misuse. West's case was the first situation where authorities seized Bitcoin cryptocurrency—more than $659,000 of it—in addition to $33,000 in cash. Authorities also seized an SD storage card owned by West, which held 63,000 credit and debit card numbers, 78 million email addresses and passwords, and proprietary data stolen from 500 businesses. Judge Michael Gledhill, who handed down West's sentence, claimed there was still $2.1 million unaccounted for.

The damages caused by West, or "Courvoisier," as he was known on the Dark Web, were enormous—Barclays was left with $400,000 in cleanup expenses after West stole $112,000 from customer accounts; British Airways was left with a $533,000 remediation price tag after West compromised its Avios reward program; and Just Eat, an online food takeout and delivery service, was left spending $266,000 to correct the exposure of 165,000 individuals' names, addresses, and payment card information.

In response to West's actions, Judge Gledhill gave a warning to those with improper cybersecurity defenses, "When such inadequate security is confronted with a criminal of your skills and ambition, it is totally unfit for purpose and worthless. This case should be a wake-up call to customers, companies, and the computer industry to the very real threat of cybercrime."[10]

BARATOV YAHOO BREACH

In May 2018, Karim Baratov, 23, a Canadian hacker-for-hire originating from Kazakhstan, received a five-year prison sentence by a U.S. judge for his indirect role in a hard-hitting Yahoo breach affecting 500 million user accounts. Baratov's sentence was considerably lower than what he could've faced—20 to 30 plus years in prison. In the investigation led by the San Francisco FBI field office, Baratov admitted to working with Russian intelligence officers by providing them with email passwords. The alleged

Russian Federal Security Service (FSB) officers used the information Baratov provided to hack into Yahoo's network. In addition to the five-year sentence, Baratov was mandated to pay a fine equal to all of his remaining assets, or $2.25 million. Baratov began his career as a paid email hacker, taking payment from anyone who wanted to hack into an email account. Now Baratov will be serving his time in jail for his role in computer hacking and economic espionage by working with Russian FSB officers to breach Yahoo.[11]

GAMMELL DISTRIBUTED DENIAL-OF-SERVICE ATTACK

John Kelsey Gammell, 55, from New Mexico was handed down a prison sentence of 15 years for launching distributed denial-of-service (DDoS) attacks against his previous employers, business competitors, and law enforcement, as well as being in possession of a firearm as a convicted felon.

Gammell purchased ready-to-go DDoS attacks from public DDoS-for-hire websites using payments in cryptocurrency. Similar to Baratov, Gammell's goal was to become a DDoS entrepreneur and sell "stress test" services on Craigslist and Facebook to anyone who wanted to perform a DDoS attack against a designated target.[12] The FBI Cyber Crime Squad of Minneapolis obtained probable cause of Gammell's DDoS attacks while looking into a year-long DDoS attack against Gammell's former employer, the Washburn Computer Group. The company received harassing emails alongside the DDoS attacks that sarcastically inquired (Gammell always attached a photo of a mouse laughing) how everything was going at the company and whether they needed any IT help. With the help of the FBI's investigation, including their search warrant for Gammell's Gmail account, evidence was found to charge Gammell for his DDoS attacks against organizations such as Wells Fargo, Enterprise Rent-A-Car, Hong Kong Exchanges and Clearing, JP Morgan Chase, Verizon Communications, and more.[13]

SELEZNEV—WIRE FRAUD AND AGGRAVATED IDENTITY THEFT

Roman Seleznev, 33, a Russian native, participated in a cyberattack against RBS Worldpay, a credit card processor in Atlanta, and acted as the head merchant on a black-market website that sold stolen credit card information, among other cybercrimes.

Seleznev was handed a 14-year jail term by a federal judge in Atlanta, Georgia. This term will be served concurrently with a 27-year sentence he was already serving—the longest sentence given in relation to cyber-crime charges—for wire fraud and aggravated identity theft. The 14-year jail sentencing was imposed because of evidence exposing Seleznev's role in exploiting $50 million worth of PII and payment card information.

Seleznev is appealing the previous 27-year prison sentence given to him by a Seattle court, which holds Seleznev accountable for 38 counts of cyber-crime charges. If he successfully appeals the 27-year sentence, he will still serve the 14-year sentence due to his guilty plea and the waiving of his right to appeal.

Federal authorities worked together with Maldivian government offi-cials to apprehend Seleznev. The Maldives serve as a popular vacation spot for Russian cybercriminals because of the belief they would be immune from the grasp of Western law enforcement agencies. When U.S. author-ities arrested Seleznev, they found 1.7 million stolen credit card numbers on his laptop, along with a password cheat sheet that connected him to a decade's worth of cybercrime activity. Seleznev earned tens of millions of dollars by defrauding more than 3,400 financial institutions. Now, he will be serving 14+ years in jail.[14]

OPERATION WIREWIRE

Operation WireWire, a six-month investigation led by the FBI, Department of Homeland Security, Department of Treasury, and the U.S. Postal Inspection Service, culminated in the arrest of 74 individuals across the globe who were involved in *email account compromise (EAC)* ploys to inter-cept and steal wire transfers from businesses and individuals (for example, prospective home buyers). The 74 arrests made consisted of 42 bad actors in the United States, 29 in Nigeria, and 3 in Canada, Mauritius, and Poland. Operation WireWire successfully seized close to $2.4 million and disrupted and recovered around $14 million in fraudulent wire transfer payments.

These federal recovery efforts, working closely with international government agencies, helped mitigate the growing issue of EAC—also known as *cyber-enabled financial fraud*—which has grown to more than $3.7 billion total financial losses, according to the U.S. Department of Jus-tice's Internet Crime Complaint Center (IC3).[15] In a public statement on the

74 arrests, Attorney General Sessions commented on the dangers of wire transfer fraud, "Fraudsters can rob people of their life's savings in a matter of minutes. These are malicious and morally repugnant crimes." FBI Director Christopher A. Wray also stated, "[Operation WireWire] demonstrates the FBI's commitment to disrupt and dismantle criminal enterprises that target American citizens and their businesses."

The Department of Justice indicated that EAC is a prevalent scam in which they will proceed to investigate and prosecute the involved bad actors, as well as money mules, regardless of their location around the globe. Bad actors use money mules, who may or may not be aware of the fraudulent activity, to transport money from victims to designated bank accounts. Bad actors recruit money mules by posting "work-at-home" job scams where an "employee" transfers the fraudulent money and keeps a portion of it as payment. Federal law enforcement executed more than 51 domestic actions to carry out the 74 arrests of bad actors involved in financial fraud. These actions included search warrants, money mule warning letters, and asset seizure warrants. Of the 47 arrests, 15 alleged money mules were charged for their malicious role in defrauding victims and transporting their life savings to hard-to-trace locations.[16]

Now that you've gotten a taste of who the adversary is and what they're after and why, you're ready to delve into the next chapter. In the coming pages, you'll learn more about the adversary's specific attack targets and goals.

Notes

1. www.nytimes.com/2010/11/14/magazine/14Hacker-t.html

2. https://www.hackerone.com/sites/default/files/2017-06/The%20Hacker-Powered%20Security%20Report.pdf

3. https://www.pcmag.com/news/357382/heres-how-much-your-identity-goes-for-on-the-dark-web

4. https://www.darkreading.com/attacks-breaches/8-nation-state-hacking-groups-to-watch-in-2018/d/d-id/1331009?image_number=2

5. https://www.washingtonpost.com/news/powerpost/paloma/the-cybersecu-rity-202/2018/07/17/the-cybersecurity-202-russia-hacking-tactics-exposed-in-mueller-indictment-still-a-threat-election-officials-say/5b4cc4fd1b326b1e646953dd/?utm_term=.65fb9c559a71

6. https://www.opm.gov/cybersecurity/cybersecurity-incidents/

7. http://deloitte.wsj.com/cio/2015/05/12/security-expert-marc-goodman-on-cyber-crime/

8. www.telegraph.co.uk/news/2017/05/13/nhs-cyber-attack-everything-need-know-biggest-ransomware-offensive/

9. https://motherboard.vice.com/en_us/article/mg7ex8/teens-who-hacked-cia-director-also-hit-white-house-official

10. https://www.bankinfosecurity.com/hacker-who-sold-financial-data-receives-10-year-sentence-a-11038?rf=2018-05-30_ENEWS_SUB_BIS_Slot6&mkt_tok=eyJpIjoiTURJd0lqWXpOOR05pWkRVMiIsInQiOiJTWXN EaXkyM1F1WHhzNFFiaWhUaGpwUGZIdzZwZ3VRMmZMOXA2blAyY nR0dksrdlwvVWs5NWZCS3QwZlZZczVwXC9WZG52eGJva0tYRXphVk RQSXFcL2hIZE0zK2pCeUYrNm9QVjFEMlwvRU1sZFNYaDVXaFEyQjV QdHVMSXZFZ1R5dVYifQ%3D%3D

11. https://www.bankinfosecurity.com/canadian-hacker-jailed-for-5-years-following-yahoo-breach-a-11041

12. https://www.bankinfosecurity.com/ddos-attacker-targeted-banks-police-former-employer-a-10604

13. https://dd80b675424c132b90b3-e48385e382d2e5d17821a5e1d8e4c86b.ssl.cf1.rackcdn.com/external/john-kelsey-gammell-complaint-jan2018.pdf

14. https://krebsonsecurity.com/2017/12/carding-kingpin-sentenced-again-yahoo-hacker-pleads-guilty/

15. https://www.fbi.gov/news/stories/international-bec-takedown-061118

16. https://www.justice.gov/opa/pr/74-arrested-coordinated-international-enforcement-operation-targeting-hundreds-individuals

3 Attack Targets and Goals

Debbie Davis, of Idaho, noticed her bank account was frozen due to suspicious activity. There was no money left in the account. Inquiring further, a Wells Fargo security officer informed Davis her card was used to purchase $1,500 in gas at three gas stations dispersed among three states. Debbie realized this happened after she visited a certain truck stop to get gas.[1] Debbie would later find out that Vachik Babayan, the bad actor behind the fraudulent scheme, would spend a year in prison for pleading guilty to installing credit card skimmers at gas pumps in Idaho. Babayan, of California, traveled to Idaho to install the skimmers. He rented a large U-Haul truck to block the view of the security cameras so that he could install the skimming devices. After installing the skimmers, he tested them with his own credit card to make sure that they worked. What he didn't realize was that by doing this, the Secret Service, as well as local authorities, would use this information to pinpoint him as a suspect. Babayan's skimmers had collected the credit, debit, and PIN numbers of around 160 individuals.[2]

You'll uncover more harrowing details of adversarial cyberattack methods and how to protect yourself from becoming a victim in upcoming chapters.

As mentioned in the previous chapter, the bulk of bad actors are after your money with the goal of monetizing anything they can find (like a common car thief). Their attack targets include obtaining your account login credentials and personally identifiable information (PII), holding your files ransom, stealing your money via wire transfers, and abusing your computing resources to perform global hacking attacks (or, more recently, to help the adversary mine precious cryptocurrencies).

Next, we dig deeper in attackers' targets and goals to obtain an overall understanding of how they steal your information and resources and what they do with these assets once stolen. You may recall from the car thief analogy that the adversary takes the "path of least resistance." By applying the "Brilliance in the Basics" mentioned in Chapter 7 of this book, bad actors will see your information is protected and unattainable and thus move on to an easier target.

How Attackers Get Your Money

Bad actors get your money and steal your banking information through a variety of attack methods. These include ransomware, traditional extortion (that is, if they find "dirt" on you through data breaches and refuse to turn over your data until you pay for it), scams, credit card number–stealing skimming devices, and intercepting your wire transfers. Remember the couple who lost their entire life savings when attempting to buy a home in Chapter 1? These methods are all too common. Remember, for the most part, bad actors aren't attacking anyone specifically—they're merely putting the line out to see who will take the bait.

What Attackers Do with Your Money

Bad actors are looking to get rich off the attacks they perform. Whether they're a lone wolf or part of a large cybercrime ring, it's mainly about the profits. On a wider scale, cybercrime organizations use their profits to make cyberattacks more efficient, and cybercriminals are professionals who want to do a "good job."

Even so-called retired attackers are in it, at least in part, for the money. Kevin Mitnick, considered one of the most famous black-hat hackers of all time, now runs a cybersecurity consulting and white-hat hacking business that provides zero-day exploits to companies for the small price of $100,000 a piece—no questions asked.[3] Hackers who've gotten caught and did time in prison, like Gonzalez and Mitnick, sometimes end up as white-hat hackers who help the government and everyday businesses protect themselves against cybercrime, finding a way to monetize their services, legally.

How Attackers Get Your Credentials

Attackers aren't targeting you specifically or patiently waiting for you to give them your password. They're sending out massive amounts of automated phishing attacks to see if you'll be tricked into giving them your credentials. Besides phishing attacks, the adversary primarily obtains your credentials through the "back door," or exposed databases, via a data breach. It is less common to see bad actors stealing your username and password at the "front door," such as at a website login screen.

Password databases taken from data breaches either get publicly posted on the Internet or sold on the Dark Web, and they're usually not very expensive to purchase. The credential reselling business has grown substantially, with bad actors competing to sell their stolen offerings.

Carder's Paradise is a popular service on the Dark Web that sells sought-after website account credentials. In just a few short months in 2017, one bad actor sold more than 35,000 credentials to Carder's Paradise, making $288,000 in commissions, with each stolen credential bringing in an average of $8.19 in profits.[4]

PayPal credentials go for the highest price on the Dark Web—$274 per account. Below that, bank account credentials sell for around $160, and Western Union accounts fetch $101. After that, Apple ID login credentials cost about $15 apiece. A bundle of stolen credentials, matched to one person, can earn a bad actor $1,200. Stolen credentials are easily obtainable through phishing attacks, which you'll read more about in the upcoming chapters.[5]

What Attackers Do with Your Credentials

Once the adversary has your credentials, they attempt to use them to compromise as many other accounts as possible.[6] As mentioned before, bad actors lease out access or resell your credentials. However, this technique doesn't work if you use a unique password for each individual account and enable two-factor authentication. By practicing the basic cybersecurity hygiene techniques I discuss in this book, like two-factor authentication, you'll make it increasingly difficult for attackers to gain access to your accounts, and they'll set their sights on the "weakest links" instead.

How Attackers Get Your PII

The way that attackers steal your PII, essentially your identity, is similar to stealing your account credentials. Bad actors obtain your PII (for example, Social Security numbers, billing addresses, birth dates, or drivers' license numbers) through mass-executed phishing attacks or by stealing sensitive consumer databases from organizations through the "back door." Stolen databases found on the Internet and the Dark Web provide you and your family members' PII to the highest bidder. The aforementioned Dark Web credential selling service Carder's Paradise also sells people's PII and whole identities, priced by their FICO credit score. The identity of someone with a flawless credit score of 850 goes for around $150. Carder's Paradise also allows bad actors to obtain credit reports on targeted identity theft victims, before they purchase the PII, for a $35 processing fee.[7]

Here's another eye-opener—medical information goes for ten times more than credit card numbers on the black market.[7] Anthem, the second largest health insurer in the United States, experienced a breach of 78.8 million patients' PII in 2015. The information exposed to bad actors included names, birthdates, medical ID numbers, Social Security numbers, street addresses, email addresses, and employment and income data.[8] With such exposure, it is even more imperative for patients to track, maintain, and protect their data and where it's being stored and circulated. Read on to learn what attackers do once they purchase or steal your PII, such as valuable medical information.

What Attackers Do with Your PII

Once attackers purchase your PII from services on the Dark Web, they'll attempt to open up credit and utility accounts in your name, apply for loans, and gain access to healthcare benefits.

The $3 trillion U.S. healthcare industry is a treasure trove for bad actors, from crooked doctors who bill Medicaid for treatments that were never performed to bad actors who impersonate you with your Social Security number and medical information to receive treatment and then send you or your insurer the bill.

There are numerous ways that medical information can be lucrative for fraudsters. For instance, bad actors use medical information found on the Dark Web (including Social Security numbers, policy numbers, diagnosis codes, and billing information) to generate counterfeit medical IDs. These sought-after IDs allow fraudsters to gain access to healthcare treatment, prescription drugs, and medical equipment. Fictitious "doctors" combine stolen medical information, a patient number, and a fake provider number to file fraudulent claims with insurers. In Chapter 10, "Protecting Your Identity," you'll discover methods to protect yourself from the ever-growing threat of medical identity theft and other identity theft schemes.

How Attackers Get Your Computing Resources

Bad actors obtain your computing resources through a couple of different methods. The first is to implant malware on your devices when you visit a malicious website, click a link, or open an infected attachment in an email. The second route is to gain access by scanning the Internet for vulnerable Internet of Things (IoT) devices with weak or default "admin"/"admin" username and password credentials. Most IoT devices come with default credentials that can be searched on the Internet and exploited if you do not change them to a strong, unique username and password combination.

What Attackers Do with Your Computing Resources

One of the adversary's goals in exploiting your computing resources is to implement large-scale, botnet attacks using a large number of device bots. The adversary harnesses the computing power of the devices under their control to perform distributed denial-of-service (DDoS) attacks against a designated target. Any IoT device connected to the Internet is susceptible and could be used in a global attack against a specific target.

Take a visual survey of your house—how many IoT devices do you have? These can be smartwatches, fitness trackers, video cameras, streaming devices, smart cars, refrigerators, appliances, thermostats, light switches, light bulbs, and so on. These seemingly simple devices are lucrative targets. First, it is difficult for manufacturers to keep up with the latest threats and provide firmware updates that would protect these products from attacks. Second, individuals often fail to reset the default login credentials, leaving these IoT devices vulnerable.

In October 2016, Dyn, a Domain Name System (DNS) service that acts as a large Internet "phone book provider" to ensure you arrive at the website you type into your browser's address bar, was targeted by a DDoS attack. The attack shut down popular websites like Reddit, Spotify, and Twitter. Bad actors pointed more than 10 million IoT devices at Dyn, causing its services to shut down from the overload of Internet traffic sourcing from the DDoS attack. How could attackers gain control of tens of millions of IoT devices? Malware, called Mirai, searched the Web for vulnerable IoT devices with default or weak login credentials. Once infected, Mirai turned the device into a bot, which was now under the control of a bad actor or *botmaster*. To perform the DDoS attack, the botmaster pointed the 10 million devices at the designated target, which in this case was Dyn.[9]

Now bad actors are spreading more mature IoT malware, such as IoTroop, to collect as many IoT bots as they can. Even though it is unclear what the adversary will do with the increasingly infected IoT device "troops," researchers believe that the adversary will shift from using IoT attacks to disrupt services, like Dyn, to monetizing their attacks.[10] In Chapter 20, "Protecting Your IoT Devices," you'll learn how to shield your IoT devices effectively and safeguard them from becoming infected bots.

Bad actors also want your computing resources for mining cryptocurrency. Cryptocurrency is a secure and anonymous form of digital money some of which require "mining" to create and authenticate transactions. Mining cryptocurrency involves cracking difficult cryptographic algorithms and requires massive amounts of computing power. Because of the dramatic Bitcoin price increase in 2017—one Bitcoin that was valued at $1,000 in early 2017 rose to $10,566 in December of that same year—bad actors are flocking to mining cryptocurrency.[11] But to do so, they need loads of computing resources. If bad actors can't buy the resources needed, they'll steal them from your computers. Smominru, a piece of global cryptocurrency mining botnet malware, has infected more than 526,000 Windows computers since 2017. Smominru exploited its computing power to mine Monero cryptocurrency, earning $3.6 million (about 8,900 Moneros) in rewards. Cryptocurrency miners receive compensation for cracking cryptography and keeping the market transactions flowing.[12] We'll talk more about protecting your computer in Chapter 17, "Protecting Your Computer," so hang tight.

Coming up, you'll discover more about adversary attack methods and how they're brought about. You'll be able to pinpoint common attack methods and techniques, such as social engineering (such as pretexting and phishing), malware (for instance spyware and ransomware), and scams (for example, fake technical support and phony IRS calls).

Notes

1. www.instakey.com/currentnews/man-indicted-in-idaho-card-skimming-scheme/

2. www.localnews8.com/news/kifi-top-story/man-sentenced-for-installing-credit-card-skimmers/58522552/

3. https://www.wired.com/2014/09/kevin-mitnick-selling-zero-day-exploits/

4. https://krebsonsecurity.com/2017/12/the-market-for-stolen-account-credentials/

5. https://9to5mac.com/2018/03/07/apple-id-logins-sell-for-15-on-the-dark-web-the-most-valuable-non-financial-credentials/amp/

6. https://www.wordfence.com/learn/brute-force-attacks/

7. https://www.reuters.com/article/us-cybersecurity-hospitals/your-medical-record-is-worth-more-to-hackers-than-your-credit-card-idUS KCN0HJ21I20140924

8. https://www.csoonline.com/article/2880352/disaster-recovery/anthem-confirms-data-breach-but-full-extent-remains-unknown.html

9. www.bbc.com/news/technology-37738823

10. https://www.darkreading.com/vulnerabilities---threats/6-cybersecurity-trends-to-watch/a/d-id/1331103?_mc=rss_x_drr_edt_aud_dr_x_x-rss-simple

11. https://www.nytimes.com/2017/12/07/technology/bitcoin-price-rise.html

12. https://thehackernews.com/2018/01/cryptocurrency-mining-malware.html

4 Attack Methods

Chances are you have a LinkedIn account and routinely receive emails from the popular professional networking site notifying you when someone wants to "connect" with you. Imagine one day that you get an email with a "connection" request from a senior executive at one of your employer's competitors. The thoughts start circling. "Are they interested in hiring me?" "What could they possibly want to discuss?" You click the link in the email to view the request on LinkedIn, which then asks you to log in to your account. After you type in your credentials, a system error comes back, "Incorrect Password." "Well, that's strange," you think, "could it be my other password?" After typing in your second password, the website comes back with a duplicate error. You then think, "Ah, it must be my "super-secret, super-secure, not-even-my-spouse-knows banking password." After your third password attempt, you get the same "Incorrect Password" error. You finally get frustrated and leave the website.

Does this sound like a LinkedIn technical issue? It's not. You were tricked into clicking a phishing email link that took you to an identical-looking spoofed LinkedIn website specifically designed to steal your account credentials. Not only did you give up your actual LinkedIn password, but you gave the bad actor three of your password variations for other websites. What happened next? A bot (you may recall, most cyberattacks are automated) recorded your entered credentials and, with one try, attempted your credentials on more than 1,000 websites. If you reuse a single password on multiple websites, a bad actor can compromise your accounts in a few minutes or less. By following the "Brilliance in the Basics" techniques mentioned in this book, such as enabling two-factor authentication and creating a strong, unique password for each account, the bad actor wouldn't be able to compromise your accounts without a long and hard fight. This means instead of pursuing your credentials, they would move on to easier targets that use the same password for all of their accounts.

Phishing emails are just one method of attack. In this chapter, you will learn the details of email compromise, social engineering, pretexting, malware infections, Wi-Fi network hacking, and scams.

Social Engineering

Bad actors use a range of attack methods, but some are "cash cows" and are therefore utilized over and over again. Social engineering is one of those schemes. Social engineering is a broad attack method used in more than 66 percent of all cyberattacks[1] and includes many detailed attack approaches— email phishing (that is, mass-produced spear phishing, whaling, email, and email compromise), voice phishing (vishing), SMS phishing (smishing), and pretexting attacks. Bad actors can also manipulate the population's perception by spreading false news.

REBECCA'S FAKE NEWS DILEMMA

Rebecca, communications director at MCorp, was getting ready for her usual day of work and skimmed through the news. When she saw this morning's top headline, her stomach dropped, "MCorp's CEO Steps Down After Found Using Company Funds to Pay Off Victims of Office Sexual Misconduct." Rebecca froze in terror. She did not approve this press release.

What Rebecca didn't know was hours before a bad actor had used public Wi-Fi, with the added protection layers of a virtual private network (VPN) and the anonymous Tor browser, to publish a fake press release using a compromised MCorp communications department employee account. By retrieving the employee's account credentials through a phishing attack using information obtained on LinkedIn and typing up a fake press release, the attacker caused MCorp's reputation to falter and their stocks to plummet.[2] With a Word document, stolen credentials, lack of two-factor authentication protection, and the click of a button, bad actors can manipulate perceptions globally.

With social engineering, a bad actor manipulates a victim into giving them access to privileged information. Attackers use your information, collected from social media sites, to make their social engineering attacks even more believable. We are empathetic animals; we want to help others and want to believe the best in people—and that's precisely what social engineers bank on. Instead of trying to break into a firewall or a computer, bad actors, using social engineering, just ask for the information. And people give it to them, repeatedly, at an alarming rate.

Bad actors use fear tactics over the promise of rewards because they know their threats will pique our curiosity and potentially scare us into acting. We have an innate "fight or flight" response, which fuels the impulse to react quickly to perceived dangers, such as phishing emails that threaten the immediate shutdown of our email account or a warrant for our arrest citing unpaid parking tickets that require a payment—right now.

Even though the types of social engineering attack methods vary, the attacker's goals remain the same—they want your money, credentials, PII, computer resources—all of it.

Phishing

Phishing is an attack method where a bad actor sends out a lure to trick you into "biting," or handing over valuable information.

Phishing Attacks

Phishing attacks vary by the attack vector used, such as email or the phone, and by the sophistication of the attack, where phishes are customized for a specific target. Phishing attacks are the most common way you will be hacked; it's the first step in the attack path.

MARK FALLS FOR A BAD APPLE

Mark was scrolling through his email inbox when he saw a new email, "Your Apple Invoice No. 3589216143." Mark was slightly confused because he didn't purchase anything from Apple recently. "I hope my account wasn't hacked," he thought. Upon opening the email, he saw charges for two movies and five music albums. He found a link at the bottom of the email that said, "If you did not authorize this purchase, click here to 'Manage your refunds.'"

Worried a bad actor compromised his Apple account, he followed the instructions and clicked the link to request a refund and investigate further. Landing on an Apple login page, he entered his Apple ID and password and awaited the next step. Instead of loading his account page, the website displayed an error, "404 Page Not Found." Within a few minutes, his iPhone made a loud alarm sound, locked him out, and displayed the following pop-up, "Hacked by Omir Floo. Send $100 to this address to unlock your device." Mark's face flushed when he realized he'd been fooled into thinking the Apple email invoice was real. By falling for the phishing email, bad actors had Mark's Apple login credentials, held his iPhone for ransom, and were making multitudes of Apple Store and Apple Music purchases while Mark was locked out of his account and device.

Email Phishing

Email phishing is the infamous attack method where a bad actor sends an email to you and hopes you will click a malicious link or open an infected file attachment. They're mass-producing these emails and automating the send-off. If you have a Gmail account, you may not get frequent phishing emails because of their efficient spam filter; just don't go rifling through the Spam folder—it won't be a pretty picture.

Would you click a "Restart Membership" link if you received an email from Netflix confirming an account cancellation request? How about "Click here to Verify Your Information" from Bank of America, claiming they've witnessed invalid login attempts? What about responding to an urgent request in an email from your "boss"? Bad actors rely on two key ingredients when crafting a phishing email—impersonating an authority figure and urging immediate action. This immediacy lessens our ability to detect malicious content because we are laser-focused on getting the task out of the way to continue on with our day.

Other common phishing emails include fake social media requests, UPS package undeliverable notices, prize-winning notices or free product offers, and tactics that create a sense of urgency (for example, pay this bill or it'll impact your credit; confirm your email account details or else it'll be shut down, and so on). As stated earlier, scare tactics are more effective than reward-based lures because bad actors know that we feel the need to respond rapidly to perceived threats because of the fight-or-flight response hardwired into our brain.

Spear Phishing

Spear phishing is a more targeted phishing attack involving customized email messages. Bad actors search the Internet for facts about you and then use them against you. This tactic is automated and done in mass quantities. Attackers harvest lists of people with similar characteristics. For example, they might collect information from LinkedIn and other social media accounts to create a customized attack targeting everyone who attended a specific school. This is common. In fact, I bet each of you reading this book has received a phishing attack using your former school as a means to trick you into clicking a link, maybe via a fake alumni site or newsletter.

Because bad actors know I am the CEO of Agio (based on information pulled from LinkedIn and Agio's website), I receive spear phishing emails claiming to be from our finance department, trying to trick me into approving wire transfers. Luckily, I can detect the red flags of a malicious phishing email. And now, you will spot them too.

Do you post any of the following information publicly? Or, when you do a Google search for yourself, do any of these come up in the results?

- Schools you've attended
- Current and previous employer names
- Job titles and detailed responsibilities
- Family member names
- Home addresses
- Phone numbers
- Email addresses
- Pet names
- Charities you donated to
- Shopping "wish lists" or Pinterest accounts
- Personal blogs, websites, and social media accounts

If you've answered yes to any of these, a bad actor can harvest this information in bulk quantities to make crafted email attacks more believable, preying on our innate curiosity to click and open things. What's more, they can do this quickly with automated hacking tools.

LANA IMPRESSES THE WRONG "CEO"

Lana's Not-So-Good First Impression

Lana, having just been hired as an HR employee at 365Capital, was excited to update her LinkedIn profile with the details of her new position. After setting her corporate email account on her mobile device, she received notification of a new email from the CEO, Bob Farin. When Lana saw the subject line, "Need Employee W-2 Forms ASAP," her adrenaline started pumping. She thought to herself, "I need to make a good impression and do this right now." She opened the email, read Bob's W-2 request, and went to work. After sending over the W-2 forms of 365Capital's entire workforce, Lana sat back with a smile, pleased with her proactive work ethic.

Eric's Vacation Plan Goes Awry

With tax season arriving, Eric and his 365Capital co-workers were thrilled for their tax refunds. "I'm going to take a weekend trip to Iceland," Eric said, "What are you all going to do with your refund check?" Eric went home and worked on his tax return. When clicking Submit, he received an error from the IRS stating he already filed a tax return. Eric texted his friends at work and told them the perplexing news. "Let me know if you can file your tax returns successfully," he said, "I am going to let my manager know about this weird error." The next day at work, Eric emailed his manager, Sue, to let her know of the tax return issue in case the information was wrong on his W-2 form. Eric was called into Sue's office, "Eric, I need to talk to you about a serious event that occurred last weekend." "Okay," Eric said, nervously, "What happened?" "Unfortunately, a new HR employee was targeted in a spear phishing attack that pretended to be Bob Farin, asking for all of the 365Capital employee W-2 forms. "Did the HR employee send the W-2 forms?" Eric asked. "Yes," Sue replied, "we are investigating right now, but it looks like we are dealing with fraudulently filed tax returns and refund checks that already cleared." Eric, aghast, said, "Will we be able to get our money back?" Sue, with a disheartened look, replied, "It's not looking good Eric, I am sorry."

After $5 million in legal fees and identity theft monitoring services, 365Capital's massive privacy breach caused its reputation to falter, and its employees and customers alike were having a tough time trusting the corporation again. Because of a simple update to LinkedIn and a new hire falling for a spear phishing email, thousands of employees lost out on a tax refund.

This type of "CEO" phishing attack is particularly effective, as it combines authority and a sense of urgency. You don't want to challenge your CEO's request, but you sense there's something a bit off. Always make sure to verify requests for sensitive information in person or over the phone before acting.

Whaling

Whaling is another phishing attack technique. To an attacker, a *whale* is a high-profile target, someone with a great deal of access to valuable information, money, and computer systems (such as business executives and politicians). Because of the size of the target, the adversary may perform background research and personally customize the whaling attacks instead of mass-producing them; it all depends on the attacker's motive and methodology.

In August 2014, more than 500 private celebrity photos, most of them nude, were leaked on 4Chan message boards. (4Chan is considered the "dark corner" of the Internet.) Because of speculation, sources believed the leak was caused by an Apple iCloud vulnerability since the celebrities used iPhones. However, Apple stated that the photo leak, dubbed "The Fappening," was caused by targeted phishing attacks. Bad actors obtained the celebrities' usernames, passwords, and security verification answers by searching fan pages and other informational resources. Once cyberattackers obtained enough publicly available information, they compromised celebrity email and iCloud accounts, leaking the highly personal photos. In response to the celebrity photo leak, Apple unveiled two-factor authentication for its iCloud users, providing a secondary layer of protection.[3] You'll learn more about two-factor authentication and other crucial cyber hygiene practices in Chapter 7, "Brilliance in the Basics."

Phishing is a frightening form of cyberattack. Separating myth from fact is an important step in arming yourself against this type of scam.

Myth   "I'm not a celebrity; no one is going to try to hack me."

Fact   The scary reality is that targeted phishing attacks are not limited to celebrities, as in the iCloud photo leak; these attacks happen to every one of us. If we can find publicly available information about ourselves on the Internet, it can and will be used against us. As we learned earlier, bad actors automatically collect this information in bulk and send out phishing emails in mass quantities, not just to celebrities, high-profile individuals, or big businesses. Bad actors experience less risk by targeting individuals. Large companies have employees dedicated to monitoring and defending their cybersecurity. This increases the chances of a bad actor getting caught and put in prison. By practicing "Brilliance in the Basics," we can protect ourselves and families from cyberattacks like phishing and email account compromise.

Email Compromise

Email compromise involves a bad actor compromising a target's email account via a phishing attack, allowing them to access the victim's email login credentials. Once an attacker enters the targeted email account, they look around for useful information to send more phishing attacks to the victim's contacts.

JANE FALLS FOR FEAR OF DELETION

Jane Corbin, a filmmaker, was up against a deadline; she had just an hour left to complete and turn in her latest work, a documentary film. With less than 60 minutes left on the clock, she heard the ding of an email. "Yahoo" claimed Corbin needed to confirm her account details immediately or they would shut down her email account (again, a fear-based tactic).

Panicked by having less than 60 minutes to hand in her work, she clicked the email link and typed in her credentials on the spoofed Yahoo website. Suddenly, Corbin's screen turned blank, and she couldn't use her computer. To add insult to injury, the bad actor immediately sent out an email to thousands of her contacts stating she had been robbed while out of the country and needed money right away.

In just a matter of minutes, Jane became another cyberattack victim. More specifically, Jane Corbin was a victim of a spear phishing attack. The bad actor had enough information about her Yahoo account to make the email wording and design look believable. As we've discussed previously, bad actors like to target you when you're on the more extreme sides of the emotional spectrum—terrified or blissful. Corbin, frenzied and in the final stages of a huge project, was more vulnerable. Banking on her heightened emotional state, the bad actor timed their attack well; Corbin was distracted as she finalized the script, talked with researchers abroad, and watched multiple video editing TV monitors.[4] Cybersecurity was the last thing on her mind.

Myth "I don't have anything of interest to the adversary in my email account. Good luck reading all my boring emails."

Fact Your email account is a goldmine. Do you have any of the following in your inbox, sent, or trash folders?

- Password reset links
- Order confirmations
- Travel and flight itineraries
- Personal communications and photos
- Tax documents
- Emails from websites you use (for example, health or car insurance, banking, credit cards, and so forth)
- Contracts, or scanned documents with your Social Security number, credit card numbers, driver's license, or photo IDs

The list goes on, but the simple fact is bad actors can and will perform a variety of malicious acts with just one hack of your email account. Consider the "Reset Password" emails currently sitting in your inbox. Attackers will click the "Reset Password" button on all of the websites you commonly visit, and since the email account they compromised will probably receive the resulting password reset codes, they will then access your accounts across multiple sites. A way to safeguard against this particular threat is to use multiple email addresses for different purposes (such as, banking, social media, shopping).

Or, as we've discussed previously, email compromise is a technique commonly used in real estate wire transfer fraud. The Skog couple in Chapter 1 lost their entire home-buying savings of $307,000 to a fraudster who targeted individuals involved in their real estate transaction. In that instance, the attacker likely compromised the real estate attorney's email account to send out a "clone phishing" email that added "new" instructions for the Skogs' wire transfer.

Clone Phishing

Clone phishing is when a bad actor finds a lucrative-looking email in a compromised email account, copies the email signatures and wording, and sends out a duplicate clone phishing email that looks almost identical. Usually, the attacker will insist their email is authentic by saying it is a "resend" with corrected "mistakes, updates, or changes." They'll send the duplicate email from a spoofed address that looks similar to the real one. Instead of the genuine email, such as `jill@ABCRealEstate.com`, they'll swap out, add, or remove a letter or number to create a spoofed email. Look at `jill@ABCRealEstate.com`. Did you notice the spoofed email domain? The bad actor used the number 1 in place of the letter *L*. Bad actors register web domains that look similar to authentic ones to create email addresses that'll look identical at a quick glance. These fraudsters like to catch victims when they feel rushed and panicked, such as at the end of the work week or in a heightened emotional state, like you are when buying a new home.

By following the "Brilliance in the Basics" tips—enabling two-factor authentication on all of your accounts—you will frustrate a bad actor and prevent them from gaining access to your email. Even though you might be squeaky clean in your cyberhygiene practices, be mindful of the emails you receive from others and look for any red flags. When partaking in any transactions, be cautious every step of the way; always confirm wire transfer instructions in person or over the phone, and be wary of clicking on email links and opening attachments. If you're buying a home, check out the recommendations on staying safe in Chapter 1—if you haven't done so already.

Voice Phishing

Another tactic is *voice phishing*. Known as *vishing*, this scam consists of a bad actor using a phone call as an attack vector to get information from you. Have you ever received a call from the "IRS" claiming you have accumulated "late debt" and need to make a payment via wire transfer immediately? Or have you received a vague voicemail like, "We've tried to call you several times now, and we really need to speak with you about that time-sensitive matter we discussed. We'll wait a couple more hours to hear from you"? Other vishing attacks can involve an automated robocall claiming to lower your debt, asking you to verify the last four digits of your Social Security number, credit card number, and more, to see whether you qualify, or it can be something as simple as "Say 'yes' or press 1 to accept a prize offer."

A well-known vishing attack is the "Can You Hear Me?" scam. In January 2017, the Better Business Bureau (BBB) warned that attackers were sending out recorded calls asking if you could hear them clearly. If you ended up saying "yes," the bad actor would identify you as a live target for additional vishing calls (since you answered this one) and would go on to use the audio recording of you saying "yes" as proof that you'd "signed" up for products and services. Then, they would demand payment for those products and services.[5]

A good way to defend against vishing attacks like the "Can You Hear Me?" scam is to simply not answer calls from phone numbers you don't recognize, even if it's in the same area code. And never hand over information to people you don't know personally.

SMS Phishing

SMS phishing, known as *smishing*, is when a bad actor uses text messages as an attack vector to gain valuable information. Popular smishing tactics include impersonating your bank, impersonating the IRS, and stealing your two-factor authentication passcodes.

CLAIRE GOT SMISHED

Thirty-eight-year-old expecting mother, Claire Pearson, lost her entire life savings, $90,000, to a smishing attack that claimed to be her UK bank, Santander. The attackers spoofed the bank's mobile number and sent Pearson a smishing text claiming suspicious activity had occurred on her account and that she needed to call the phone number provided immediately. Frightened, Pearson called the number and spoke to a kind "customer service representative" who took her bank account login credentials and assured her the issue would be solved once she told him the one-time passcode (OTP) she had received in a text. While she was still on the phone, the bad actors gained access to her account and amended a previous payment she made, effectively draining her life savings. Because Pearson was the one who "consented" to giving the bad actors her OTP, her bank's policy claimed that they were not at fault.[6] Pearson was left without recourse and forced to face motherhood without the hard-earned savings she'd set aside for this next chapter in her life.

Remember banks or any company for that matter, will never ask for your password or two-factor authentication code over the phone. You only type your password and two-factor authentication code on the verified website login screen or mobile app. Always locate your bank's customer service number on the back of your card and be cautious of links or phone numbers mentioned in a text message. One final warning: bad actors can spoof phone numbers using voice over IP (VoIP) technology easily. This can include calling you from anywhere, even the "White House," just by using caller ID spoofing services readily available on the Internet. Bad actors simply type in the phone number they want to show up on your caller ID, even though the call originates elsewhere. Be on guard if you receive any alarming or suspicious-looking messages (remember, fear and scare tactics are the most effective methods bad actors use), and don't hand over personal information to anyone, except when you are certain the recipient is valid and there is an absolute need for it.

While phishing emails are an effective means of cyberattack, they can be avoided by following the "Brilliance of the Basics" tips outlined in this book. Moreover, now that you know what to look for, you can apply your newly trained eye to potential phishing email scams, protecting yourself and your family from the pitfalls we've discussed here.

Pretexting

Pretexting is a technique used in phishing attempts that gives some pretext to a conversation to get information from you (for instance, someone pretends to be your friend, family, spouse, employer, location, or a government official). Pretexting attacks rely on building a false sense of trust and security with you. The attacker works to craft a convincing story that will be hard to second-guess later.

Pretexting is a key ingredient in phishing attacks and scams. Here is one example of how pretexting was used to steal thousands of dollars from hopeful romantics looking for love online.

A BAD PRETEXT FOR LOVE

A woman from Castro Valley, California, reported to the BBB that a man on Match.com named James Stevenson—an "engineer and business owner of JS Urban Engineering"—scammed her out of $72,000. How did he manage such a momentous scam? The fraudster built up pretext with the victim, gaining her trust. Over a month of email dating, Stevenson claimed he had an accident on a job site and needed money to fix it so he could keep his "million-dollar contract." The unsuspecting woman wired him the money, over and over again. She thought she was helping a man she had grown to care about. The straw that broke the camel's back was a surprise rendezvous gone wrong. After finally deciding to meet face to face, the optimistic lover flew to Dallas, Texas, ready to surprise her beau in person—but he never showed up. The bad actor later sent her a text message apologizing and explaining he had been lying the entire time. Heartbroken and out tens of thousands of dollars, it was a far cry from a fairytale ending to the woman's cyber fling.[7]

Malware

Malware is another common attack method that includes ransomware, spyware, scareware, adware, Trojans, viruses, and worms. Malware is short for "malicious software," which is any type of software that is intended to disrupt or harm your computer. Listed next are the common types of malware that users face today.

Cryptomining Malware and Cryptojacking

Bad actors are increasingly stealing computer power to mine cryptocurrency. For some cryptocurrency, mining is necessary to produce, secure, and verify digital currency transactions. After transactions are validated and approved, they get added to a blockchain—a public ledger of digital transactions—and crypto miners receive cryptocurrency as compensation.

Cryptomining

Cryptomining is entirely legal at its core, as it solves complex mathematical equations to help manage in-demand, decentralized digital currency and transactions. Because cryptocurrency values are increasing, along with the compensation incentive for helping to mine it, bad actors are racing to harness computing power any way they can—they steal your computer's power when you visit an infected website (known as *cryptojacking*) and install cryptomining malware on your computer. Cryptomining malware, like WannaMine and Smominru, can be tricky for antivirus programs to detect because it doesn't need to download any files to your system. Crypto miners use legitimate Windows programs to engrain persistent, permanent background processes on your PC. Unpatched PCs are particularly vulnerable to cryptomining malware. Any discovered vulnerabilities can be exploited by crypto miners to propagate and spread their mining malware to other devices on your network.[8] The second way cryptomining occurs on unsuspecting victims' computers is through cryptojacking.

Cryptojacking

Cryptojacking is the act of exploiting a website visitor's CPU computing resources to mine cryptocurrency. On a large scale, bad actors infect thousands of websites simultaneously by infecting a single content provider with cryptomining code, therefore affecting any website utilizing the targeted content provider's resources.[9] Anyone with a computing device is subject to cryptojacking attacks—even smart fridges and TVs, in addition to computers and mobile devices. According to Avast, cryptojacking cases rose globally from 146,704 in September 2017 to 22.4 million in December of the same year and to 93 million by May 2018.

The rise in cryptojacking attacks can be attributed to these three reasons:

- Cryptojacking code doesn't require much skill to use.
- The attacks are more difficult to detect on the target device, and the act is anonymous.
- The reward the bad actor receives in exchange for mining cryptocurrency (while using your CPU) goes directly to the bad actor's encrypted cryptocurrency wallet.[10]

Website administrators are even using cryptocurrency mining plug-ins on their websites to take advantage of visitors' computing power to supplement their ad revenue. The worst part is, even after you close your web browser, cryptomining processes can still run on your computer without your knowledge—crypto miners hide a tiny browser window behind a PC taskbar.[11] You will learn more about cryptojacking attacks and how to protect your devices—and your electricity bill—from bad actors in Chapter 17, "Protecting Your Computer."

Follow these steps to protect your devices from crypto miners:

- Use antivirus that can block cryptocurrency mining.
- Monitor your CPU levels and computer processes.
- Use a verified browser plug-in that blocks crypto mining.

Unlike cryptomining attacks, where money goes straight into the bad actor's wallet, ransomware interacts with the device user in the hopes of getting a ransom paid for unlocking down a target device.

Ransomware

Ransomware is a type of malware that holds your files for ransom. This malicious software is frequently installed via a phishing email with a malicious link or attachment, or by "drive-by download," when a victim visits an infected website. Ransomware encrypts your files and demands a ransom be sent in cryptocurrency on the Dark Web for the decryption key. Every 10 seconds, someone gets infected with ransomware.[12] The average ransom cost is $1,000.[13]

> **MY PHD THESIS HAS BEEN KIDNAPPED!**
>
> It's a couple of days before your final dissertation submission date. You're utterly exhausted, and the PhD is so close you can taste it. In your rush to the finish line, you've been working at coffee shops using their public, insecure Wi-Fi.
>
> One day, you come home, turn on your PC, and notice it's running slow. You can also see that your filename extensions have changed to `Mary's Dissertation.xyz`, in place of `Mary's Dissertation.docx`. You open up your web browser to look at computer troubleshooting guides, and a black web page with bright red text opens up and leaves you alarmed. It reads, "Your files have been encrypted. To regain access, pay $1,000 in Bitcoin cryptocurrency to have them unlocked." The terror sets in. You've worked for years on this 200-page dissertation—it's practically a book!
>
> What do you do now? Do you take the chance and pay the ransom in the hope they'll release your files? Should you call the police? Did you perform a recent backup of your files? Do you have $1,000 set aside to pay the ransom? Do you know how to get Bitcoin? In the blink of an eye, that degree you've worked so hard for is in jeopardy.

Take a look at these myth versus facts to help you better understand and protect yourself against this type of scenario:

Myth   "I'm not worried about ransomware. Law enforcement will catch the adversary and get my files back, right?"

Fact   In most cases, no. That is why ransomware has such a high success rate of getting people to pay a ransom for the (potential) release of their encrypted files. It's a challenge to track down the bad actor behind the ransomware, and since most ransomware cases are low on the cost scale in the eyes of the FBI, they don't spend millions of dollars on ransomware defense. Instead, they rely primarily on open source tools to attempt file recovery.

Nevertheless, even with the FBI's small chance of obtaining restitution and file recovery for the victim, the FBI still warns people not to pay the ransom unless all other options are exhausted. They say this for a few reasons. First, ransomware attack kits sell for $100 on the Dark Web. Any person with a little hacking knowledge can send out malicious ransomware attacks.[14] These amateur attackers may not have the tools to release your files. Or, even if they do, they might choose not to do so. Either way, now you're out files and ransom money. A second reason for the FBI's warning is that paying the ransom encourages the bad actors to continue their malicious campaigns. Handing over money is a positive reinforcement to keep launching attacks.[15]

Even with the FBI advising people not to pay the ransom, many individuals, organizations, and law enforcement officials still end up doing so.[16] If you don't have your files backed up in a separate, secure location, you may need to come to terms with losing your data for good—or consider paying that average ransom cost of $1,000.

Practice "Brilliance in the Basics" to avoid losing your files and gain peace of mind. This includes regularly backing up your files in a secondary, cloud location and enabling antivirus and anti-malware on your devices. If you do experience the unfortunate, you'll learn detailed response steps in Chapter 9, "Incident Response."

Spyware

In addition to ransomware, *spyware* is another form of malware that serves the purpose of spying on the passwords you type, looking through your computer's camera, and snooping through your files for personal information. FruitFly, a Mac-specific spyware program developed by 28-year-old, now-indicted voyeur Phillip Durachinsky, allowed him to snoop through personal information and remotely access the video cameras of many, unaware victims. For 13 years, Durachinsky, a resident of North Royalton, Ohio, spied on individuals, businesses, schools, police departments, and federal agencies using his program. FruitFly steals files, passwords, and remotely turns on computers' cameras and microphones. The visual and audio breach makes FruitFly and similar software especially invasive and personal.[17]

To avoid spyware and other types of malware, it's essential to enable anti-virus programs on all of your devices and keep them up-to-date. This is a "Brilliance in the Basics" essential. Remember to remain wary of suspicious-looking emails and malicious websites as well.

Scareware

Scareware is malicious software that tries to convince you that there's a virus on your computer. This scare-based tactic tricks you into clicking a deceptive pop-up that states, "You've downloaded a virus." This pop-up leads to the real malware infection. Once the scareware downloads its malware onto your computer, another pop-up will appear, advising you to pay to upgrade your antivirus to stay protected. Now the bad actors have your credit card number and can continue to install even more malware on your computer.

On top of that, scareware victims lose their files if they don't have a secure, secondary backup that's not infected. To avoid becoming a victim of scareware, follow the "Brilliance in the Basics" tips, enable your antivirus, and perform regular backups. Additionally, you can enable the Block Pop-up Windows setting on your web browsers and install ad-blocking browser extensions. A word to the wise, bad actors frequently create malicious browser extensions that look similar to popular add-on programs, so do your research before downloading.

Adware

Adware, another version of malware, shows up as pop-up advertisement windows (some being difficult or impossible to close), automatic redirection from a safe website to a malicious one, and more. Once infected, adware can sometimes be difficult to remove from a computer and can do some severe damage.

A CAREER RUINED

In 2007, Julie Amero, a substitute teacher in Connecticut, found herself facing up to 40 years in jail for "exposing students to pornographic images" on her classroom computer. Did Amero do such a horrific thing? No—Amero was a victim of adware and spyware, and she was completely unable to stop it from spreading. At the time Amero was tried, however, the U.S.

court system couldn't wrap their heads around the sophisticated behavior of adware. It was incriminating, making it appear that Amero had visited the pornographic sites herself when, in fact, malicious software was the real culprit.

Their testimony initially unheeded, computer scientists paid for a newspaper advertisement to spread the word that Amero was the victim, not the criminal. Their bold strategy worked, and the scientists were finally heard. It was concluded that this incident occurred because of malware, and the school didn't have proper firewall protection—their antivirus was unlicensed and out-of-date. While Amero's conviction was vacated in 2008, the teacher still forfeited her teaching credentials and faced a $100 fine.[18] Amero's career completely stalled, all because her computer didn't have up-to-date antivirus software.

Trojans

Trojans are pieces of malware hidden inside of a "Trojan horse." They look innocent, but they are the exact opposite. Trojans most commonly arrive via phishing emails with malicious links, attachments, or both.

One example of this type of malware is Kronos, a banking Trojan discovered in 2014 and allegedly created by 23-year-old security researcher Marcus Hutchins. Kronos spreads through malicious file attachments and is designed to pilfer bank account credentials and then, as a result, money. Interestingly enough, Kronos was not Hutchins' only claim to fame. Hutchins, otherwise known as MalwareTech, became famous when he stopped the crippling WannaCry ransomware from continuing its devastating global spread in 2017. Registering a URL found in the WannaCry's source code, he activated a kill switch, effectively stopping the ransomware in its tracks. Unfortunately for Hutchins, he is currently awaiting trial and faces a maximum of 40 years in prison for his cybercrimes related to Kronos.[19]

Later, in November 2017, a new strain of the BankBot banking Trojan was discovered in innocent-looking apps in the Google Play store for Android devices. What individuals thought was a solitaire game or a cool flashlight actually held vicious malware that overlaid the interface of real banking apps with the goal of stealing victims' banking credentials.[20]

Wi-Fi Network Hacking

Wi-Fi network hacking is when a bad actor takes advantage of insecure wireless networks with weak encryption protocols or passwords, especially default passwords already configured on the router. For a long time, WPA2 was considered the best security encryption protocol for wireless networks. Older protocols, such as WPA and WEP, were obsolete and extremely vulnerable to hacks.

In October 2017, a security researcher found a way to exploit the gold standard WPA2 and released the details to the public, calling it the Krack vulnerability. As alarming as it sounds for the strongest Wi-Fi network protection protocol to be exploitable, an attacker needs to be in proximity to your home network to take advantage of it. While bad actors discover new attack methods, it is important to keep your router and devices updated with the latest security patch releases. Otherwise, you may be vulnerable to publicly available cyberattack exploits, like the Krack vulnerability.[21]

WHEN A PIRATE ISN'T A PIRATE

Barb Angelova, an Illinois graphic artist, switched Internet service providers (ISPs) and was given a cheap router with limited configuration options and no instructions on how to set it up securely. A year went by without incident. Then, Angelova received a letter from her ISP claiming she'd been illegally downloading content.

Specifically, her ISP accused her of stealing a movie called *The Man of Tai Chi* and warned the Motion Picture Association of America (MPAA) could come after her in a legal battle. Angelova was alarmed, "When my account is flagged and I'm held responsible for someone else's activity, that's terrifying." How could she prove she wasn't the pirating culprit? The incriminating home IP address was hers.

Angelova was lucky. While she could've had her bandwidth throttled or her account suspended, her ISP refrained, recommending that she change her router's password to a strong and secure one.[22]

Wi-Fi network hacking tactics range from accessing and downloading illegal content to performing incriminating acts using your IP address. As you learned with the teacher who was nearly sentenced to 40 years in prison for a pornographic spyware infection on her classroom's computer, it can be difficult for investigators to differentiate you from the bad actor when they find convincing evidence on your network's IP address. You will learn how to safeguard your and your family's network from becoming a Wi-Fi hacking crime zone in Chapter 19, "Protecting Your Home Wi-Fi."

Scams

Scamming is a popular attack method where cybercriminals use social engineering to get you to hand over your money, personal information, and even access to your computing devices. While scammers tend to target the trusting younger or older crowds, they don't discriminate—setting their sights on everyone in between. The primary goal of scamming is to make money. So, where's there's money, there are scammers.

Myth "I will never fall for a scam; they are incredibly obvious."

Fact Even those who claim to be foolproof can get pulled into a scam. Getting swindled can happen so quickly you may not realize it at first. Scammers are professionals too; it's their job to scam you.

Have you ever gotten a friend request on Facebook or LinkedIn and thought you were already connected to that person? Let me guess what you did—you added them and simply assumed they removed themselves from your friend list at some point in time or they made a new account. Did you stop to think that this might be a scammer duplicating your friend's account to gain access to your personal information? Well, that's a common tactic scammers use. Once you've accepted their request, they'll scrape any valuable details about you that can be used to answer your accounts' security questions, send you malicious links and attachments, and more. If you do get an unexpected friend request, look at the profile and verify it is the genuine person. Don't add or accept people you don't know personally, and make sure you are careful about what you're posting on social media. You'll learn more about protecting your social media presence in Chapter 15, "Protecting Your Social Media."

Common cyber scams include fake technical support services, IRS impersonation, spoofed communication from a "loved one" in jail who needs bail money, virtual kidnapping, and fake online romance, also known as *catphishing*. Let's break these scams down in more detail.

Fake Technical Support

Oh, fake technical support, how we loathe you. Most everyone reading this book will relate to the call from "Microsoft" or "Apple" claiming they located a virus on your computer that needs to be eradicated—and the money you need to hand over for them to "remove" that malware. Even though Microsoft or Apple would never call you to inform you of a computer infection, people fall for this scam and pay bad actors big bucks to remove "viruses," which in turn allows for actual viruses and spyware to infect victims' computers. And the vicious loop continues.

THE KOOBFACE GIFT CARD SCAM

One victim of an Apple technical support scam lost $22,000 in Target gift cards. After searching for Apple's tech support hotline, the victim called a fraudulent one, which had appeared in the top search results. Once on the phone, the victim detailed their computer problems. The scammer diagnosed the issues as a Koobface malware infection. The scammer then transferred the victim to Joseph, an "Apple security professional," who offered to help the victim remotely. As per Joseph's instructions, the victim downloaded AnyDesk, a remote desktop connection software, and gave Joseph access to their computer via the program. Once inside the victim's computer, the scammer "verified" Koobface was indeed in the system. Joseph explained that he could remove the virus for a $15,000 fee, only to be paid in Target gift cards (claiming he earned a commission off of card sales). Joseph went on to assure the victim they would receive the entire amount back, except for a few hundred dollars for Apple's services.

It worked. After the victim handed over the $15,000 in gift cards, "Apple Technical Support" claimed the victim's refund check was getting held up in customs and, later, state tax verification. To process, they required an additional $6,200. Finally realizing this was a scam, the victim was unsure of how to proceed. Desperate to get their money back, the victim kept paying the extra fees, in hopes the money would return. It never did.

While we may see a number of red flags in this set of circumstances, the victim found the scam believable because of the details: the authentic-sounding Apple hold music, the scammers' professionalism, and the scammers' availability—they were always reachable at the same phone number.[23]

To prevent falling for a technical support scam, always remember that no legitimate company can detect viruses over the phone, and they do not call to warn you of infection. Only your computer's antivirus program can do that. If you receive a call claiming to be Apple or Microsoft, hang up. Locate and call the real technical support number on the actual Apple or Microsoft website. Or submit a help desk ticket directly through that verified website.

If you've fallen victim to a tech support scam, don't feel embarrassed. Follow these incident response recommendations:

- Notify local law enforcement, and file a police report.
- Notify your local FBI field office, and file a complaint.
- Visit the FBI Internet Crime Complaint Center (IC3), and file a complaint online at www.ic3.gov.

Government Agency Impersonation

Scammers also love to impersonate the IRS. Their latest technique consists of depositing a large sum of money directly into your bank account or sending you a check and then placing a threatening call from the "IRS collection agency" to explain they made a mistake and need the refund sent back to them ASAP. They even threaten the victim with fraud charges and an arrest warrant. Scammers enjoy this scheme because the money is actually in your account or behind the check mailed to you. If you receive an unexpected large deposit from the IRS, don't go out and spend it! Contact your bank's automated clearinghouse department to have the refund sent back to the actual IRS. Then, go to `https://www.identitytheft.gov/` to follow additional action steps. If you receive an unexpected check from the actual IRS, visit `https://www.irs.gov/taxtopics/tc161` for specific action steps to return erroneous funds.[24]

Remember, the IRS will never call or email you—they only send letters in the mail. And they won't harass you over debts and threaten legal action. If you receive a threatening call claiming to be the IRS, even if it looks believable because the scammer spoofed the caller ID to show "911," it is not real. Remember to slow down, take a breath, and always contact the IRS, or designated party, through their direct phone number.

Bad actors can also pretend to be from U.S. Citizenship and Immigration Services. Scammers based out of India were indicted by the U.S. District Court for the Southern District of Texas for threatening victims with arrest, prison terms, and deportation if they didn't cough up a fee to the "government." Once the victims agreed to pay, the India-based scammers worked with U.S. co-conspirators to obtain the fraudulent funds, usually through wire transfers and prepaid cards, and funnel the cash back to India.[25]

The Grandparent Scam

Sometimes, scammers take their attacks to the next level by pretending to be a family member in jeopardy. The *grandparent scam* is a wildly common tactic where grandparents receive calls from their "grandkid," stating they're in jail and need bail money. Scammers find out how family members are related through online obituaries or "people search" websites like Radaris. Once they understand the familial ties, scammers call the grandparent and share their emotional story, hoping to obtain thousands of dollars in fraudulent wire transfers. Unfortunately, the "grandparent scam" works because the victims focus on the "emergency" at hand and don't think to hang up on the scammer and directly call the grandchild.

Virtual Kidnapping Extortion

Virtual kidnapping is similar to the grandparent scam. Here, the scammer pretends to be a kidnapped family member who needs thousands of dollars in ransom money.

VIRTUAL KIDNAPPING SCAM

Arran Collins was at his day job when a call came in from what sounded like his 10-year-old daughter, Victoria. "Daddy! Help. They got me in a van." A man got on the phone next, demanding $50,000, or else the kidnappers would kill Collins' daughter.

Luckily, Collins had the presence of mind to make a call to his daughter's elementary school and found out that Victoria was safe and sound. What Collins experienced was a virtual kidnapping scam, an attempt to extort money from him. Usually, virtual kidnappers try to keep the victim on the phone to prevent them from checking with the kidnapped family member in question.

To avoid becoming a victim of scams that rely on fake family emergencies, educate your loved ones about the "grandparent scam," as well as virtual kidnapping schemes. The FBI recommends hanging up the phone if you receive a suspicious phone call from someone demanding money in a time-sensitive manner. If you do stay on the line with the scammer, use a secondary form of communication, such as a text message, to check in with the family member in question. If you do receive a "grandparent" or virtual kidnapping scam phone call, notify local law enforcement and your FBI field office.[26] Don't feel embarrassed if this happens to you; reporting the scam to the authorities helps law enforcement agencies prosecute the scammers behind the scheme. In the long run, you're helping decrease the chances family emergency scams will happen to someone else.

Unpaid Utility Bill Scams

Unpaid utility bill scams use scare tactics found in common phishing scams, such as threatening to shut down access to a critical service and attempting to relay a feeling of heightened urgency. Scammers call claiming to be billing representatives from your utility company but are actually crooks looking for a quick payoff. During the phone call, scammers will state, "To avoid an immediate shutoff of your electricity, you need to settle an overdue bill by providing me the number of your credit or prepaid debit card." Scammers often prefer a prepaid card since it means fast cash and will direct you to a Western Union, or a similar wire transfer service, and provide instructions on how to set up the card. Scammers tend to give all sorts of details to keep the story going but will be sketchy when asked about your utility account details.

Online Dating Scams

Online dating scams, commonly known as *catphishing*, involve a scammer pretending to be someone else on a dating website. If you've watched the hit MTV series *Catfish*, then you know what I'm talking about—two people connect on the Internet, sparks fly, and, finally, the show's producers unveil the real, shocking identities behind the online personas when the two people meet in person. Some individuals who were featured on the show still end up dating, even after finding out their online beau was pretending to be a fictional person. Sometimes, catphishing is more harmful. As we read earlier, one woman from

Castro Valley, California, lost $72,000 to an "engineer and business owner" she thought she loved. Her "beau" turned out to be a fraudster and only admitted it when she flew down to Dallas, Texas, to meet him as a surprise.

THE HIGH COST OF ROMANCE

An online romance imposter stole $300,000 from a woman named "Amy." Amy talked with "Dwayne/Duane" (he spelled it two ways—red flag, yet?) through text messages and long, dreamy phone calls every day for three months.

After a couple of months of Dwayne making Amy swoon with his copied and pasted romantic quotes from the Internet, Dwayne started requesting loans. He needed help to "get through customs" and "pay his workers."

Even after Amy took off the rose-colored glasses and realized she was in the middle of a con, she continued to talk to Dwayne, intent on catching him in the act. Amy went as far as offering Dwayne a $50,000 bribe in exchange for real documents identifying himself in the hope that she could turn them over to the FBI and incriminate him. After sharing her story with the FBI, Amy learned of a woman in the next town over who had lost $800,000 in a similar scheme.

Why do these victims take so long to realize they've been scammed? Steven Baker, director of the FTC's Midwest Region, explains the victim's denial, "Once people are invested in these [scams], it's extremely difficult to convince them they are not dealing with a real person. People want to believe so bad." To help keep these scams alive, scammers use a psychological technique called *confirmation bias*. Dwayne used this strategy with Amy. One night, Amy texted Dwayne, demanding him to take an immediate picture of himself. Dwayne sent her a photo of "him" lounging on a bench in the sun. This single photo verified Amy's confirmation bias—Dwayne was real and, was indeed, in love with her. Little did she know, scammers like Dwayne use a script, complete with photos and starry-eyed phrases, that's crafted well in advance and even shared among scammers.[27]

Catphishing is popularly known as "419" scams because most of the fraudsters reside in Nigeria or are West African expatriates living in European countries. 419 is the name of the Nigerian government's criminal code for dealing with fraud, and it was enacted to help minimize Nigeria's massive scam culture. And it is massive— Nigerian scam victims lost $220 million in 2016, according to the U.S. FTC, and online dating scam reports to the FBI have tripled since 2012.[28]

The following are specific recommendations from the FTC concerning prevention and response to the online dating scam epidemic.[29] To prevent falling victim to an online dating scam, the FTC warns the public to watch out for these signs of a potential scammer:

- The scammer wants to talk via email or text messaging right away, instead of the dating website message service.
- The scammer claims to be from the United States but is traveling extensively for work or is overseas in the military.
- The scammer attempts to win over the victim by claiming they feel an immediate love connection from the start.
- The scammer sends romantic messages that sound like they came from an illustrious poetry collection—and they probably did.
- The scammer tells victims they plan to visit them but gets held up by customs, a failed business deal, a traumatic situation, or all three.

If you find yourself in the midst of an online dating scam, the FTC recommends doing the following:

- Don't wire money to the scammer, no matter how severe the story sounds (for instance, mugging, hospital bills, and so forth).
- Don't make online purchases or forward packages to another country for the scammer.
- Report online dating scams to the dating website, the FTC, your local FBI field office, the FBI's IC3 Crime Complaint Center, and your State Attorney General.

Job Scams

Job scams can come in the form of those Craigslist postings luring people to "work from home and make $10,000 a month." Some victims have even been lured into buying supplies from a designated vendor for imaginary childcare jobs. Job scams can come in more elaborate forms, where victims believe the scammer is an employee at a well-respected "company."

A COSTLY JOB SCAM

A recent college graduate, let's call him "John," was a victim of a job scam and lost $25,000 he could've used toward paying off his student loan debt. Like most graduates, John posted his résumé on popular job-listing sites.

One day, John got an email from "Genesis Venture Capital," where a woman named Lisa Thompson offered him an opportunity to interview for a project management position. Sounds good so far, right? After a month-long interview process and filling out employment forms, GVC gave John his first project—find the lowest-priced store to purchase four sets of three laptops. A man named Charles Payne at GVC gave John the Wells Fargo bank account details that would be used to reimburse John's credit card purchase of $25,000 in Best Buy gift cards. (Payne said it had to be done that way since John was a new "employee.")

John, a bit suspicious at this point, decided to verify. Visiting the Wells Fargo bank from which the routing number originated, John inquired about the account's legitimacy. The bank representative confirmed. John, still a little wary, asked the representative to reach out to the account owner and ensure they were the initiators of the impending transaction. The representative declined; that wasn't in line with protocol.

John decided to proceed with caution. Making a smaller, $500 purchase of the gift cards, John requested the reimbursement transfer. He got the funds, as promised. Feeling confident, John proceeded with the instructions he'd been given by GVC; $25,000 in gift cards later, his reimbursement payments were suddenly flagged as fraudulent, coming from a compromised Wells Fargo account. John now had $25,000 in fraudulent credit card debt, on top of his student loans, and was out a job.[30]

John was lured into a job scam that positioned him as a money mule to transfer fraudulent funds. Bad actors are known to hire individuals through work-at-home job scams, whether they know it or not, to transport fraudulently acquired money to bad actors' bank accounts. Bad actors are even starting to hire "employees" to transfer funds to Bitcoin ATMs, where nonrefundable Bitcoin cryptocurrency gets directly deposited into anonymous Bitcoin wallets of bad actors. Even if a victim thought they were hired for a legitimate job, they can be arrested just like bad actors for the part they played as a money mule. And money mules may be asked to pay back funds that were illegally transferred into their account by bad actors.[31]

To avoid job scammers, remember that it is rare for a company to reach out to you and offer a job or schedule an interview right away—especially without even applying. Always research the company on the Internet, and be aware that scammers copy actual business names and point you to legitimate websites to lure you in. When all else fails, trust your gut. If things feel "off" to you, they probably are.

Charity Scams

Numerous organizations accept charitable donations to help specific causes, but not all of them are legitimate. Mainly when a high-profile event occurs, like a devastating hurricane, bad actors set up fake charity websites and fake disaster relief efforts to profit from people's willingness to help. Bad actors can send out phishing emails or create posts on social media that look like a not-for-profit organization asking for a donation to support a current cause.

To avoid getting tricked into sending your funds to bad actors instead of where you intend to provide relief, research the charitable organization by searching for it on legitimate charity evaluation sites.[32] To avoid getting scammed, always check the phone number, URL address, email address, and more, to ensure it's the genuine contact information for the charity before you donate funds.

Robocalling Scams

WHITELISTING PHONE NUMBERS TO AVOID THE ROBOS

Jane was in the process of applying for a new job. She eagerly checked her phone to make sure she didn't miss any phone calls from potential employers. Unfortunately, Jane kept receiving calls from phone numbers with her area code that ended up being spam. She wanted to make sure she answered a potential employer's call, but after hearing scam after scam, she decided to let all phone calls go to voicemail.

Jane eventually discovered a phone app capable of sending all spam calls directly to her voicemail, so she wouldn't have to hear the phone ring when it was spam and falsely believe it was a potential employer. Now, though, she would have to whitelist known phone numbers to protect herself from the robocalling scams that spoof numbers from her local area code. Since bad actors can pretend they're calling from a legitimate phone number, by making it show up on the caller ID as such, they've made it more difficult for individuals to block their robocalls without blocking every call not known in a person's contact list.

Jane made sure to whitelist potential employer company phone numbers by adding them to the list of allowed calls through the app. There might be a chance a legitimate phone call would get blocked, but she would rather unblock it afterward than continue answering the high volume of robocalls that looked like they were from her area code.

Americans receive more than 4 billion *robocalls* a month.[33] Robocalls can arrive with a ringing sound, or they can land in your voicemail without any ringing sound, otherwise known as *ringless voicemail*, which is less intrusive than receiving a ringing robocall. Bad actors also use call-spoofing tools readily available on the Internet, which allow anyone around the world to place a call to you and make it look like it's from your area code. They could even make it look like 911 or the White House's phone number. Bad actors hope you'll answer the robocalls and fall prey to their phone scams. Robocalls can even come from legitimate businesses, even though they are illegal without your written permission to do so.

According to the FTC, companies use autodialing services to send out thousands of robocalls per minute for a low fee. Robocalling tools don't screen for numbers on the national Do Not Call Registry. In response to this, the FTC warned, "If a company doesn't care about obeying the law, you can be sure they're trying to scam you."

Companies can get mixed up with illegal marketing tactics when purchasing lead generating services from marketing firms. These marketing firms, which use robocalling tools, don't usually share how and from where they generated a lead for the client company. Best practice is for marketing firms to append a statement to each customer file declaring the companies they work with to generate leads.[34]

The FTC charged two robocalling operations that were in violation of the Telemarketing Sales Rule (TSR). The defendants produced billions of illegal robocalls to consumers across the United States in attempts to sell debt-relief services, home security systems, auto warranties, and more. The first operation was run by James "Jamie" Christiano, who controls a number of companies (including NetDotSolutions, Inc., and TeraMESH Networks, Inc.) that operate TelWeb, which is a computer-based phone dialing platform to carry out large volumes of robocalls in a short time span.

Christiano worked with business partners, like Aaron Michael Jones, who resold TelWeb services to other telemarketers. Jones used a tactic called *neighbor spoofing* that involved making malicious calls that trick your caller ID into making it appear as if someone in your area code is calling you. Jones partnered with another robocalling operator, Andrew "Andy" Salisbury. Salisbury ran World Connection, a call center that received transferred robocalls from consumers who "pressed 1" during a robocall message carried out by Jones' robocalling operation.

According to the FTC complaint, the robocalling defendants were charged for facilitating the following illegal robocalling activities: making calls with unlawful prerecorded messages, carrying out calls to numbers on the DNC Registry, creating calls designed to only leave a voicemail and would hang up on consumers who answered, and producing calls with spoofed caller IDs. The FTC is seeking a court order to halt the defendants' illegal robocalling activities, along with correlating civil penalties, once reviewed by the federal district court.[35]

FCC rulings allow phone companies to block robocallers from using phone numbers already registered to current subscribers, but phone companies still decide not to offer these services.[35] This could be happening because caller ID is no longer reliable. The technology to authenticate phone subscribers with their phone numbers is broken and needs to be fixed. Organizations like Alliance for Telecommunications Industry Solutions (ATIS) and the Session Initiation Protocol (SIP) Forum have banded together to come up with a solution to authenticate a phone number instead of using caller ID. The proposed standard to verify phone numbers as legitimate is known as Secure Telephony Identity Revisited (STIR). The technology that will implement STIR is called Signature-based Handling of Asserted information using toKENs (SHAKEN).

Together, STIR and SHAKEN will allegedly provide verified information about the person calling, as well as the origin of the call. This will be the first time this has ever been carried out on a network and would potentially remedy the growing problem of seemingly local robocalls, which spoof the caller ID to lead you to believe it's someone in the area calling you.[36] STIR and SHAKEN will ensure a caller has the right to use the phone number and would then create a "digital fingerprint" for the call. Jim McEachern, a technologist with

ATIS, compared today's robocalling problem to when we didn't have any email spam filters. Now, ATIS is working to create the robocall filter by authenticating the person and their allotted phone number.[37]

To protect yourself from robocall scams, consider these options:

- Check to see whether your phone carrier has robocall protection.
- Obtain a well-known robocall blocking phone app such as Nomorobo.
- Don't answer unknown calls. If you pick up a robocall, bad actors can verify your number works and sell it, and you may receive a higher volume of robocalls.
- Search the unknown phone number on the Web to see whether it has commentary on being a known robocall scammer.
- Locate the genuine phone numbers for highly spoofed agencies, such as the IRS and other federal entities.

Now that you have a grasp on the adversary's common attack methods, you'll learn more specifically about the *attack chain*, which is the chain of events performed by a bad actor to carry out an attack. When you become aware of the attack chain or path, you can better protect yourself and your family by practicing core cyberhygiene habits to stop the attack before it fully executes.

Notes

1. https://www.social-engineer.org/social-engineering/social-engineering-infographic/
2. http://www.ideas42.org/wp-content/uploads/2016/08/Deep-Thought-A-Cybersecurity-Story.pdf
3. http://www.businessinsider.com/apple-statement-on-icloud-hack-2014-9
4. http://www.dailymail.co.uk/news/article-1243634/A-mysterious-email-split-second-mistake-Thats-took-Internet-gangsters-hijack-life-.html
5. https://www.bbb.org/detroit/news-events/bbb-scam-alerts/2017/01/bbb-warning-can-you-hear-me-scam-alert/
6. https://www.thesun.co.uk/news/3314811/this-morning-smishing-scam-santander-bank/
7. https://www.bbb.org/scamtracker/us (Clear out 'Keyword' search field, type "JS Urban Engineering", and press 'Search')
8. https://www.crowdstrike.com/blog/cryptomining-harmless-nuisance-disruptive-threat/

9. http://www.thejakartapost.com/life/2018/02/13/thousands-of-websites-infected-by-crypto-mining-malware.html

10. https://www.wivb.com/news/world/how-your-smart-fridge-might-be-mining-bitcoin-for-criminals/1273383699

11. https://thehackernews.com/2017/11/cryptocurrency-mining-javascript.html

12. https://blog.barkly.com/new-ransomware-trends-2017

13. https://blog.barkly.com/ransomware-statistics-2017

14. https://www.forbes.com/sites/haroldstark/2017/02/28/when-attacked-by-ransomware-the-fbi-says-you-shouldnt-pay-up/#6c5042df5e61

15. https://www.ic3.gov/media/2016/160915.aspx

16. https://www.nbcnews.com/news/us-news/ransomware-hackers-blackmail-u-s-police-departments-n561746

17. https://www.forbes.com/sites/thomasbrewster/2018/01/10/man-charged-over-super-creepy-apple-mac-fruitfly-malware/#744ae74d273b

18. https://en.wikipedia.org/wiki/Connecticut_v._Amero

19. https://www.telegraph.co.uk/technology/2017/08/03/fbi-arrests-wannacry-hero-marcus-hutchins-las-vegas-reports/

20. https://www.helpnetsecurity.com/2018/02/27/mobile-banking-trojans-spread-confusion-worldwide/

21. https://www.theguardian.com/technology/2017/oct/16/wpa2-wifi-security-vulnerable-hacking-us-government-warns

22. http://blog.privatewifi.com/true-story-i-was-hacked-on-home-wifi/

23. https://www.bbb.org/scamtracker/us (Clear out 'Keyword' search field, type "joseph apple", and press 'Search')

24. https://www.nytimes.com/2018/02/23/your-money/income-tax-scam-tips.html

25. https://www.justice.gov/usao-sdtx/victim-witness-program/us-v-hglobal

26. https://www.fbi.gov/news/stories/virtual-kidnapping

27. https://www.aarp.org/money/scams-fraud/info-2015/online-dating-scam.html

28. https://www.ftc.gov/news-events/press-releases/2018/02/ftc-warns-consumers-about-online-dating-scams

29. https://www.consumer.ftc.gov/articles/0004-online-dating-scams#what%20you%20can%20do%20about%20it

30. https://www.bbb.org/scamtracker/us (Clear out 'Keyword' search field, type "Genesis Venture Capital", and press 'Search')

31. https://krebsonsecurity.com/2016/09/money-mule-gangs-turn-to-bitcoin-atms/
32. https://krebsonsecurity.com/2017/08/beware-of-hurricane-harvey-relief-scams/
33. https://www.abcactionnews.com/news/science-and-technology/americans-received-41-billion-robocalls-in-june-1
34. https://krebsonsecurity.com/2017/06/got-robocalled-dont-get-mad-get-busy/
35. https://www.ftc.gov/news-events/press-releases/2018/06/ftc-sues-stop-two-operations-responsible-making-billions-illegal
36. https://sites.atis.org/insights/new-specification-atis-sip-forum-advances-network-capabilities-mitigate-unwanted-robocalling-caller-id-fraud/?mod=article_inline
37. https://www.wsj.com/articles/why-there-are-so-many-robocalls-heres-what-you-can-do-about-them-1530610203

5   Attack Chain

Nolan worked in the information security department at a well-known credit bureau. His primary job responsibilities were to manage the company's firewall, antivirus program, and software updates. Nolan was good at his job, and he always received positive feedback during his quarterly performance reviews. Sure, applying software updates to all systems within the company seemed like quite a feat, but Nolan discovered how he could use compensating security controls on a system when he thought he couldn't apply the software update easily.

This was the case with the credit bureau's primary web server, which hosted their main website and critical business processes. Nolan decided not to patch this web server just yet. He knew if he applied the patch and something went wrong—taking the core site down— he would be in huge trouble with the C-suite. He knew the patch needed to be applied, so he told himself he would test it and apply it after-hours. But then he thought, "What if the software update takes the site down and no one is there to help—it will become a huge disaster that's blamed on me!"

Nolan decided he couldn't risk business processes being interrupted, let alone his reputation. So, until he could figure out a plan of action, Nolan decided he would review the daily web server logs in more detail. Nolan was comforted by the fact that the credit bureau had a good firewall and antivirus program. He told his boss, Nevada, that he put compensating security controls in place to monitor the unpatched web server until there was a better, less "risky" time to apply the patch.

Nolan then went on his annual two-week vacation to Miami and had the intern on his team monitor the logs and told her to not hesitate to call him while on vacation if she noticed anything strange. Finally, out of the office, Nolan excitedly updated his LinkedIn, Facebook, and Instagram accounts with his awesome vacation plans and enabled an automated "out-of-the-office" email reply for anyone who emailed him.

While on the sandy beaches of Miami, soaking up the scorching sun, Nolan received a call from his boss. "This can't be good," Nolan thought. "Hi Nevada, is everything okay?" Nevada's voice was shaking, "We've got a problem Nolan. While you've been away, we've been attacked. You know that web server you waited to patch? Apparently, bad actors used the security hole in it to execute a malicious payload and stole hundreds of millions of Social Security numbers from our database."

Nolan couldn't speak; he couldn't believe what he was hearing. "I am so sorry, Nevada. I can't believe this happened. Next time, I will make it top priority to apply the patches to systems, even if there is a risk to the business." Nevada quickly replied, "Leaving this web server unpatched was a big risk, Nolan. We will talk more about the situation when you get back." Nevada ended the call. He felt completely helpless, "Am I at fault for this? Will I lose my job?"

Nolan's story was inspired by the real-life unraveling of the Equifax breach. Because of an unpatched Apache Struts web server application, bad actors were able to compromise Equifax's network and steal the personal data of 143 million people. Equifax had two months after Apache published the vulnerability and patch to install the security update to protect consumers.[1] If Equifax patched the server, it would've halted the bad actor's "attack chain" from progressing. An *attack chain* is the chain of events performed by a bad actor to carry out an attack.

In Nolan's case, his failure to follow basic cyberhygiene habits, such as applying a software update to a web server, cost the company unspeakable amounts of money in class-action lawsuits and cleanup. Nolan's first mistake was thinking the biggest risk to the business was if something went wrong when applying the system patch and it halted business processes, while the real danger was not patching the system, which resulted in a way bigger mess than he ever considered.

Nolan's second mistake was posting his vacation details on social media. Bad actors monitor employees working in information security departments at high-profile businesses, waiting for an opportunity to strike. When Nolan announced he would be out of town, that was their "go ahead." Not to mention, Nolan's "out-of-the-office" reply message—showing how long he would be gone and who to contact for any questions—served as a green light for bad actors as well. Nolan should have made his automated "out-of-the-office" reply visible only to other employees.

The list of Nolan's mistakes cited earlier allowed bad actors to progress along their malicious attack chain—the events, when all combined, led to the intended outcome of a targeted attack. Each stage of the attack chain presented an opportunity for Nolan to stop the cyberattack forming against him and, ultimately, the company.

When you are aware of the phases of the attack chain, you can better protect yourself and your family by practicing core cyberhygiene habits to stop an attack before it fully executes. Here are just some of the steps you should take:

1. Keep your system and software up-to-date.
2. Enable two-factor authentication.
3. Use a password manager to create and store unique and complex passwords for each online account.
4. Avoid the use of administrative access on a computer.
5. Install and keep your antivirus updated.

By following core cyberhygiene habits, you can thwart most attacks even if you fall victim to social engineering tactics, like phishing.

Check out the following attack chain phases to get a peek at how a bad actor plans, creates, and deploys a targeted cyberattack. You will see how your cyberhygiene habits can stop an attack right in its tracks.

Attack Chain Phases

Each phase, or stage, of the attack chain is a step that bad actors take to carry out an attack. With each "link in the chain," there's an opportunity for you to prevent the attack from unfolding against you and your family.

It's a widely held belief that you must focus on foiling the attack in the beginning stages, but there's just one problem—bad actors aren't following the attack stage in numerical order. They skip steps, add additional actions, and can start an attack from a later phase. Bad actors hide evidence of their cyberattacks within other misleading tactics, such as a distributed denial-of-service (DDoS) attack, which can be used to create significant network "noise" to drown out the evidence. They can also disseminate false data and set up "back doors" on a target computer, which allows for a secret entrance to the victim's system for future exploits.

This unpredictability means it's critical for you to practice the essential cyberhygiene habits laid out in this book regularly to protect your family's devices, information, and identities. There isn't one bulletproof method to ward off bad actors. The combination of applying software updates, enabling two-factor authentication, managing unique and complex passwords per account, backing up your information to the cloud regularly, using effective antivirus, and not using an administrative account with power that a bad actor can use against you will provide multiple defense techniques that can halt an attempted cyberattack.

WARNING   Personal cybersecurity is a multilayered approach. You wouldn't keep your car doors unlocked in the city just because you see a security camera. So, it also makes sense that you wouldn't just rely on antivirus to carry out the core cyberhygiene practices you need to perform yourself to remain safe against cyberattacks.

The following sections highlight the primary cyberattack stages in a bad actor's attack chain, and the cyberhygiene habits to defend against them.[2]

Links in the Attack Chain

1. **Reconnaissance**   Bad actors gather intel on individuals, such as exposed credentials, and information found on social media to use in a social engineering attack.
   Cyber Hygiene   Limit the amount of personal information you share and make applicable social media profiles private. Ask yourself before posting, "How could a bad actor use my posts against me?"

Enable two-factor authentication for all of your sites and create unique and complex passwords for each online account and store them in a password manager. If a bad actor gets ahold of a compromised password—and you used it for all of your sites—they can compromise everything automatically.

2. **Weaponization** Bad actors create or purchase malicious code that can exploit a security vulnerability found on the target's system. It takes a bad actor less than six days to exploit a vulnerability.[3]

    Cyber Hygiene Keep all of your devices up-to-date, as soon as security updates are released, to prevent bad actors from succeeding in cyberattacks against vulnerabilities in your system and software.

3. **Delivery** Bad actors send malicious code to the victim by sending a malicious email link, directing them to an infected web page, or a malware-ridden USB stick is inserted into a victim's computer.

    Cyber Hygiene Use an email provider that has robust spam and phishing filters, like Microsoft's Outlook.com or Google's Gmail. Remain cautious about clicking any links or file attachments in emails. Before downloading files from the Internet, make sure they're from a legitimate page. And never pick up and insert a USB stick you find.

4. **Exploit** This is the phase when the malicious code takes advantage of a security hole, known as a *vulnerability*, on a system.

    Cyber Hygiene Make sure your system is up-to-date to protect it against known vulnerability exploits. Obtain modern antivirus with a robust computer firewall. Automate updates when possible.

5. **Installation** After the vulnerability is exploited, the malicious program installs on the target computer.

    Cyber Hygiene Enable protection against unauthorized program installation when available. Read more about the steps to enable this protection in Chapter 14, "Protecting Your Files."

6. **Command and Control (C&C)** Installed malware creates a communication tunnel from the victim's computer to the bad actor's undisclosed location to receive instructions.

    Cyber Hygiene Make sure your network and system's firewall is capable of detecting C&C callback attempts.

7. **Actions** The bad actor remotely carries out the intended attack goal, such as obtaining sensitive information and PII to sell on the Dark Web, spying on financial transactions to wire out money, using the computer to attack another victim's device, and more.

Cyber Hygiene   At this point, the information is probably out there. Make sure to use all these mechanisms to identify, prevent, detect, contain, and eradicate any malware or suspicious activity. It is important that you use unique and strong password for each of your online accounts to prevent a bad actor from jumping from account to account. Sign up for alerts on the "Have I Been Pwned" website (`https://haveIbeenpwned.com`) to be notified when your credentials have been found to be leaked online.

The attack chain phases repeat until your cyberhygiene habits prevent bad actors' cyberattacks. As you can see by the extent of the attack chain steps, it is vital to implement numerous, essential cybersecurity habits regularly. Antivirus can only do so much. We'll dive deeper into the core cyberhygiene habits of applying software updates, enabling two-factor authentication, managing unique and complex passwords per account, backing up your information to the cloud regularly, and using effective and updated antivirus in Chapter 7, "Brilliance in the Basics."

Now that you've gained an understanding of the attack chain of bad actors and how a handful of cyberhygiene habits can prevent them, you'll learn next about the attack vectors they use in their attack plans, that is, the technology used to carry out attacks.

Notes

1. https://www.wired.com/story/equifax-breach-no-excuse/
2. https://www.csoonline.com/article/2134037/cyber-attacks-espionage/stra-tegic-planning-erm-the-practicality-of-the-cyber-kill-chain-approach-to-security.html
3. https://media.scmagazine.com/documents/343/quantifying_the_attackers_firs_85512.pdf

6 Attack Vectors

Linda was out shopping with her daughter when she tripped on something on the mall floor. "Oh, it's a USB drive. I wonder who it belongs to? It says Family Photos on it." "We should find the owner," said Nora, Linda's daughter.

Linda brought the USB drive home with her. She was eager to get the drive and the photos back to the rightful family, so she immediately plugged it into her home computer. She opened the drive's folder and couldn't find any photos. She gave up, unplugged the drive, brought it back to the mall, and gave it to Mall Security who placed it into the "Lost and Found."

Over the next week, Linda noticed her computer was running slow, websites weren't loading, and Nora wasn't able to stream Netflix as she could before. Something was slowing down their Internet speed. Taking a look at her computer, she noticed a lot of her files were missing from the directory. She started to panic and realized the signs might indicate a malware infection. Linda thought to herself, "Why didn't my antivirus catch this?"

Linda next took her computer to a computer repair technician, and after investigating, the technician found she had hundreds of malware infections, including cryptocurrency mining software, which was depleting all of her computing resources. The technician also found evidence of file exportation, including her previous tax return records. The attacker also disabled her antivirus, which explained the lack of virus detection. Linda tried to think back around when *this all started, "What did I do?" Her heart started racing when she realized, "I picked up the USB stick and plugged it into my computer."*

So, the moral of the story is never eat USB candy from strangers!

We all benefit from the luxuries of technology. We need the ability to email, call, text, and access the Internet to communicate with others. Businesses rely on email to reach their customers, travelers require public Wi-Fi to access their information, and we use our mobile devices to make phone calls and send text messages to reach our friends and family. We all rely on software programs and apps, which allow us to use our computers and smartphones quickly and connect to the Internet. Technology gives us access to desired information and communication—and bad actors use technology as vectors, or steps, in their attack plans against us.

Email

We love email—we need it to communicate, perform our jobs, and run our businesses. Bad actors love it too—email allows for the sending of malicious messages, links, and attachments. As you learned in Chapter 1, "Overview of Cyber Risks," 66 percent of malware infections occur via malicious email attachments, and 1 in 14 people get tricked into clicking a bad link or file attachment within an email.[1]

Email is the most effective attack vector—it costs little to nothing to send, it can transport an abundance of malware, and the adversary can send out millions of malicious emails using automated tools and botnets under their control. *Ransomware*, a form of malware, is primarily spread through wide-scale email phishing campaigns, which use *botnets*—swarms of compromised devices—to do the automated work.[2]

As you have learned, the adversary's goal in sending malicious email is to take your money, capture your personal information, infect your devices, and abuse your computing resources, and email is a valuable starting point in most of the adversary's attack routes.

Bad actors commonly forge, or spoof, the From fields in an email. To verify the sender of an email, check the "headers," which lists vital information about the sender. Most email services show only a handful of fields, such as

To, From, and Subject. There are additional fields that aren't usually shown and can tell you whether an email is from a bad actor. Similar to tracking information for a physically mailed package, headers display a Received field, which shows the source IP address. Bad actors attempt to spoof destination IP addresses, but they can't spoof the first Received field line, which will show you exactly who sent the email and if it's from a valid source or not.[3] For more information on how to read email headers, search *how to read email headers* for the email service you use.

Texting

Texting is another lucrative attack vector for bad actors; it's similar to email, but it comes across as a more intimate form of communication. We receive sensitive text messages with two-factor authentication codes, security notices, and payment confirmations from our banks and online accounts. Bad actors know all of this and use texting as an attack vector to gain access to your personal information and online accounts. We are used to receiving unwanted emails, but with text messages, we expect them to be for us.

Remember the woman in Chapter 4 who lost $90,000 to bad actors spoofing her bank's phone number to lure her in with a fake security warning? The attacker's messages—directing her to investigate "suspicious activity"—displayed in the same authentic text thread as the actual bank.[4]

BEWARE THE "HELPFUL" BANK REPRESENTATIVE

Jessica received an alarming text message from her bank, "Suspicious activity found on your account. Call 800-111-1234 to verify your identity." She dialed the number immediately and reached James, a bank representative who requested her username and password to confirm her identity and access her bank account to evaluate the fraudulent activity. Jessica gave James her credentials, relieved there was someone to help. "Please tell me the passcode, in the form of six digits, which we sent to your mobile device ending in 4567," said James. Once Jessica received the text with the passcode from her bank, she told it to James, "It's 134588." "Thank you, Jessica, after taking an initial look, it is clear I need to have a meeting with one of our identity theft investigators; this looks pretty serious. Don't worry; you're in good hands, I will call you back within 48 hours with updates on your case."

Jessica hung up and breathed a sigh of relief, "At least they are looking into it," she thought. Jessica received another text from her bank, "Secondary user added to your account. Call the number on the back of your debit card if you did not approve this change." "That's strange," she thought. Jessica called the bank's actual phone number and reached Anita, a genuine bank representative who stated, "A secondary user was added to your bank account with the rights to withdraw and transfer funds. They transferred $9,000 to a bank in China. Were you aware of this?" Jessica dropped to the floor, distraught. She recounted the story of what happened earlier. After hearing what happened to Jessica, Anita said, "You approved the additional user by handing over your passcode to fraudsters, therefore allowing them to withdraw the funds. We will see what we can do, but it is tricky since you gave them consent. The bank will never ask you for your account credentials and two-factor authentication passcode over email or the phone; only on the actual website." Jessica was heartbroken. She thought she was doing the right thing by responding quickly to the initial text warning of suspicious activity. Now she knows to slow down before clicking, dialing, or downloading anything.

To obtain your passcode, bad actors use pretexting techniques to impersonate your bank, or another company with which you do business, sending you smishing texts stating "suspicious activity was detected on your account." By obtaining passwords from publicly posted databases via data breaches, the attacker will attempt to log in, but they might need you to give them your two-factor authentication passcode to complete the compromise. After you receive the initial fake security notice, they will prompt you to call the number listed in the text, or they will send you another text requesting the passcode you received to "prevent your account from being locked out." Once the victim texts back their one-time passcode, the bad actor compromises the victim's account and withdraws their life savings.

If you don't have two-factor authentication enabled (which you should activate immediately), the attacker just needs two things—your username and password. Most of us are victims of a breach, like from the LinkedIn breach in 2012, which means our usernames and old passwords are out there. If you haven't changed your LinkedIn password since 2012, assume your account is compromised, as well as any other account that uses the same email address and password. However, if you do have two-factor authentication enabled, the attacker will have a difficult time getting your passcode, unless you hand it over by falling for their text message—based smishing attacks.

Rest assured, if you follow the "Brilliance in the Basics" methods described in the next chapter, instructing you to create a unique, strong password for each individual account and enable two-factor authentication, you are practicing excellent cybersecurity hygiene and significantly reducing your risk of experiencing a damaging cyberattack.

Phone Calls

ALERT AMY!

"Hello Ma'am, I am calling to notify you of a malware infection on your computer." Amy thought this was weird, since the caller didn't identify themselves. She would expect to receive this notification from her antivirus program and not through a phone call. "What happened?" Amy asked. The unidentified caller responded, "Severe malware, known as Koobface, took over the security program on your computer and is continuing to download spyware onto your system. You need to upgrade your antivirus program, as well as hire a security investigator to clean this up. It looks really nasty." Amy asked, "What company are you with?" The unknown representative responded, "Verizon Internet Services," which wasn't Amy's Internet provider.

Amy eventually hung up and didn't provide any information to the fraudster. Some people aren't so lucky, as you learned in the "Technical Support Scam" section in Chapter 4, and have lost thousands of dollars to fraudsters. When we hear a human voice on the other end of the line, speaking with urgency, we can get sucked into their social engineering trap if we don't slow down and rationalize the legitimacy of the call.

The ability to make a simple phone call has existed since 1876, and cybercriminals love exploiting this age-old technology. Every single one of us has received an attack through a phone call or voicemail, whether it's an automated robot saying you've won a free stay at the Marriott or a "tech support representative" claiming you have some nasty viruses on your computer. Phone calls are a more personal attack vector compared to text-based messages, especially when there's a live human on the other end.

As mentioned previously, it is incredibly easy to spoof a legitimate phone number, such as 911, the White House, and so on, using online services that allow users to choose what phone number shows up on the recipient's caller ID. Once the adversary has garnered your trust by impersonating an individual or company, they rely on social engineering skills to phish for your personal information. It is always wise to avoid answering phone calls you don't recognize or are not expecting. If someone wants to reach you, they'll leave a voicemail. If you do receive a voicemail, slow down while listening to it and evaluate its legitimacy. Is the voicemail about a time-sensitive, nondescript matter? Does the person sound disappointed or angry, stating they've been waiting for you to call back about a "previously discussed matter"? Is it the "IRS"—who would never call you? Is it "Microsoft" or "Apple" warning of a virus on your computer, even though they would never call you to say that?" Take a step back, slow down, and listen for red flags signaling common attacks that might use phone calls and voicemails to their malicious advantage.

Websites

The adversary uses websites as an attack vector to target victims who type in an incorrectly spelled URL (known as *typosquatting*)—or click malicious links in emails, social media posts, and websites. Bad actors are known to register websites ending in .cm instead of .com in the hopes someone will accidentally type the wrong extension. This act of typosquatting downloads malicious scareware that overloads a victim's computer with false security alert pop-ups when they visit copycat websites like www.espn.cm and www.itunes.cm. In fact, these typosquatting websites land almost 50 million hits per year. It's good practice to bookmark frequently visited websites or type them into a search engine to navigate to the correct URL address. Directly typing in web addresses can lead to unintended consequences, especially if you miss a letter or two.[5]

Bad actors like to infect web pages with malicious advertising too. Even with widely recognized web pages, company can't always control its advertisers and their potentially malware-injected ads. Malicious advertising, *malvertising*, puts billions of people at risk of malware infections, like ransomware. Just by visiting a web page, your system can become infected with malware that's woven into content delivery networks, web page coding, in-text link advertising, banner ads, and pop-ups that redirect you to an imposter web page. You don't even need to click an ad to get infected—by hovering over an ad on the page, malicious code can run and instantly corrupt your computer.[6]

GandCrab, a newer strain of ransomware discovered in January 2017, infects victims through malicious advertising, leading victims to compromised web pages with exploit kits on them. Exploit kits automatically detect if you have vulnerable software running on your computer. Once the vulnerability is found, malware will automatically download. Then, when it's installed, Gand-Crab demands a ransom ranging from $400 to $700,000.[7]

In the upcoming chapter, you will learn the core cybersecurity habits that'll protect you from becoming a victim of attacks utilizing the Web as an attack vector. In Chapter 16, "Protecting Your Website Access and Passwords," you will gain specific knowledge on how to protect your website browsing. In Chapter 17, "Protecting Your Computer," you will acquire the insight to safeguard your computer from cyberattacks effectively.

Myth   "I can trust any website with a lock symbol in the URL bar. They are secure."

Fact   A lock symbol in the URL bar does not mean a website is secure. Bad actors create secure, fraudulent websites to trick you into thinking you're safe. What the lock symbol actually means, on a malicious website, is that a bad actor obtained an encryption certificate and provided (fake) registration details to receive a secure lock symbol, hoping you'll trust the site and give them your information.

If you get duped into sending your credentials or money through a phishing website, the padlock symbol means your information securely transmits to the attacker. A malicious website without a lock in the URL bar implies anyone can intercept and read the information you send over the Internet and to the attacker.

Lock or no lock, be cautious of the website you are visiting and be wary of typing any sensitive information or clicking any buttons. Bad actors create websites that look similar to ones you intend to visit, so verify the URL for the organization's page you want to visit. Use a search engine to locate a URL, instead of typing it in manually, for even more security. When inspecting a link that you receive in an email or spot in an article you're reading, hover over it and look for the full URL address in the bottom portion of your browser. If it doesn't show up, copy and paste the URL into a search engine and check the "root" domain portion of the address (for example, in `www.google.com/images`—`google` is the root domain) to make sure the URL matches the website you want to visit.[8]

Software

Freeware might seem sweet and innocent, but free software programs could be harboring malicious components behind the scenes. Google declared that unwanted bundled software is more aggressive than malware. In a study performed with the NYU Tandon School of Engineering, Google found that bad actors set up "pay-per-install" incentive websites, enabling software makers to inject their applications with malware and gain a commission on each victim download. So, when you download a "PDF viewer" on a popular freeware downloading site, you might miss where you agreed to the additional malicious programs bundled alongside the PDF viewer. Google analyzed 446,000 offers relating to 843 unique software packages and found most download bundles include ad injectors, browser-setting hijackers, and scareware.[9]

Be vigilant when downloading software from the Internet. Only download authentic software from trusted websites or app stores. Then, always check the user agreement. You may think you agreed to download a "PC cleanup" toolkit when in fact you signed off on accepting nine other unwanted, malicious programs. By keeping your antivirus program updated, which is an essential "Brilliance in the Basics" defense practice, you will prevent malicious software from executing on your computer.

USB Key

While most people use the cloud to store, retrieve, and share their files, USB keys are still prevalent. And the adversary likes to exploit portable storage devices to carry out cyberattacks. As we learned earlier in the story about Linda, bad actors will perform what's called a *candy drop*; attackers buy a bunch of USB keys, install malware, and drop the thumb drives in parking lots, office buildings, shopping malls, and other places where people congregate.

A University of Michigan study performed a "candy drop" of 300 USB sticks around its campus. Of the 300, researchers concluded 98 percent of the drives were picked up, and students opened files on 45 percent of them.[10] The study shows how effective USB sticks can be as an attack vector.

The majority of us are good people, and we want to do what we think is right. That includes finding the owner of a lost USB key. But think of that USB stick in the same way you'd think about food left out somewhere—you can't trust it, and you wouldn't eat it.

Avoid becoming a victim of a cyberattack that uses a USB key as its vector. Don't ever plug unrecognized USB sticks into your computer. If you find one out in public, turn it in at the nearest lost and found or to the IT department of a business to investigate. If you're given one as a gift at a convention, make sure to scan it with your antivirus if you decide to use it.

Wi-Fi

Wi-Fi is a glorious thing, isn't it? It's usually free in public places we visit, and it means we don't need to use up our cellular data. While the advantages are clear, there are some serious risks to using Wi-Fi, especially in public. Cyberattackers like using Wi-Fi as an attack vector; they can easily impersonate nearby Wi-Fi networks to attract victims. Once you connect, bad actors can snoop on your web browsing activity through man-in-the-middle (MITM) attacks, redirecting your Internet traffic to their computer for review and/or manipulation before sendoff. Attackers can also download malware to your system on an insecure network.

Let's say you arrive at Starbucks. You're excited to order a hot coffee and do some online shopping. You check the nearby Wi-Fi network names: "Starbucks" and "Starbucks Wi-Fi" pop up. The former requires a password, and the latter doesn't. You assume "Starbucks" is for their employees and "Starbucks Wi-Fi" is for customers since it's easily accessible. Once you connect to "Starbucks Wi-Fi," you're now on an attacker's network. It's simple to rename a Wi-Fi network, and attackers use this technique to impersonate genuine-looking networks.

Myth "The coffee shop's Wi-Fi network is password protected. Why worry?"

Fact Even when you connect to a company's real public Wi-Fi network, hackers can snoop on your activity or, even worse, collect login information and compromise your accounts. When using public Wi-Fi, assume everything you're doing is viewable by all users connected to the network. Using public Wi-Fi means someone can watch your every move through "sniffing" tools, which allow the viewing and logging of Wi-Fi network activity. If the websites you visit don't have a lock symbol (meaning encryption), attackers can steal the information you send and receive, such as your account credentials, credit card numbers, emails, and more.

ADAM'S COSTLY COMPROMISE

A few years ago, Adam was selling his house and was using Starbucks' Wi-Fi to email his financial manager. Adam noticed his financial manager wasn't responding to his emails, so he called and found out the manager was indeed replying. Why didn't Adam see the financial manager's email replies? Shortly afterward, Adam's two banks started calling him urgently, claiming they were receiving emails from Adam's account requesting wire transfers. Because both banks require verbal and written confirmations to authorize wire transfers, "Adam" stated he was on his way to an out-of-town funeral, attempting to bypass the wire transfer security protocol. Adam talked with his bank's security department, who said, "Look at your email filters." Adam noticed someone set up email filters using the web addresses of both of his banks to capture his sensitive communications. Because of Adam's email account compromise, the attacker knew Adam was selling his house and his bank accounts would be full of cash. The attacker waited until the sale took place and began masquerading as Adam, requesting wire transfers. The hack happened because Adam did his work using Starbucks' Wi-Fi, which can be viewable by anyone. By using various attack methods, the bad actor gained access to Adam's email account. Adam still uses public Wi-Fi today, but only with the added privacy and security of a virtual private network (VPN) connection.

Protect yourself from ending up as a victim of a Wi-Fi cyberattack. Use a trusted VPN service when on public Wi-Fi, and turn off the Auto Connect to Available Wi-Fi Networks option on all of your devices. To read more about safeguarding yourself while using public Wi-Fi, check out Chapter 21, "Protecting Your Information When Traveling."

Next up—the "Brilliance in the Basics" tips. You will learn to implement five essential cybersecurity hygiene habits, which, when regularly performed, will keep you and your family protected.

Notes

1. www.verizonenterprise.com/resources/reports/rp_DBIR_2017_Report_execsummary_en_xg.pdf
2. https://www.symantec.com/content/dam/symantec/docs/security-center/white-papers/istr-ransomware-2017-en.pdf
3. https://www.lifewire.com/email-headers-spam-1166360
4. https://www.thesun.co.uk/news/3314811/this-morning-smishing-scam-santander-bank/
5. https://krebsonsecurity.com/2018/04/dot-cm-typosquatting-sites-visited-12m-times-so-far-in-2018/
6. https://www.cnbc.com/2014/05/20/beware-of-malicious-ads-that-can-harm-computers-without-a-click.html
7. https://labs.bitdefender.com/2018/02/bitdefender-europol-romanian-police-diicot-team-up-for-gandcrab-removal-tool/
8. https://krebsonsecurity.com/2017/12/phishers-are-upping-their-game-so-should-you/
9. https://security.googleblog.com/2016/08/new-research-zeroing-in-on-deceptive.html
10. https://zakird.com/papers/usb.pdf

7 Brilliance in the Basics

Bad actors look for the path of least resistance. Dangerous habits, such as using the same email address and weak passwords for all of your accounts, render you defenseless against the adversary.

Bad actors accessed millions of Twitter accounts in 2016 without ever hacking into the social media site. How did they do it? Simple. The adversary used username and password combinations from previous breaches, like the LinkedIn breach, and tried them on Twitter. They successfully gained access to accounts simply using reused credentials.[1]

Bad actors retrieve databases from breaches and use automated tools to search for usernames and passwords. Once they build a list of potential credentials, bad actors automatically test them on websites all over the Web. By reusing any email address, username, password, or all three, you subject yourself to being hacked in a matter of seconds, especially if you're a past data breach victim, which most of us are.

Then, even if you have a strong password, you are still subject to account compromise if you've reused the same password and do not have two-factor authentication enabled. An attacker can attempt to guess your security questions—based on what they find about you on the Internet—and reset your password to gain access to your account. To keep your accounts protected, follow the "Brilliance in the Basics" techniques in this chapter. Enable two-factor authentication, and use a password manager to create and maintain strong and unique passwords for all of your accounts. Credential reuse and weak passwords are just a couple examples of hazardous habits that make the attack path easier for bad actors. The adversary attempts an array of attack methods, hoping risky behaviors will leave you vulnerable. When you practice the "Brilliance in the Basics" techniques, your consistent cybersecurity habits will prompt the bad actor to move on to easier targets.

"Brilliance in the Basics" consists of five simple cyberhygiene essentials. The most secure people utilize these core concepts. When you put the "Brilliance in the Basics" into consistent practice, you greatly increase the level of protection for yourself and your family and defend against bad actors and their malicious cyberattacks.

Brilliance 1: Update Your Devices

Click Install Now instead of later when prompted to install system updates. The longer you wait to patch your devices, the greater the possibility that a bad actor will compromise your system. It is crucial to update your device software when new versions get released and replace hardware when it is no longer supported by the manufacturer. Because of constant development and the release of more advanced versions, vendors support hardware and software for only a limited amount of time. For example, you should replace Wi-Fi routers and cable modems every four years at a minimum. In doing so, you protect your home network, and you get the best streaming for Netflix!

Outdated equipment means outdated operating systems and software—and a ton of security holes for bad actors to sneak through. Because manufacturers won't support old devices with security and functional updates, end-of-life devices are left wide open for hackers to exploit festering vulnerabilities. Like driving an old car, built prior to today's emissions standards, a legacy device doesn't uphold current cybersecurity standards. Companies that develop software won't create updates and supported versions for unsupported device operating systems. Using outdated hardware and software is like hanging a "Hack Me, Please!" flashing neon sign in cyberspace.

When vulnerabilities in software and devices become known, manufacturers work quickly to create and release security updates to mitigate the risk of malicious exploitation. Once manufacturers release security patches, it is essential to apply them immediately. Software and firmware updates provide critical security fixes as well as functional improvements. Some manufacturers will alert you when an update is available, but others will leave it up to you to check.

Some software, like Adobe Flash and Reader and Oracle Java, are frequently exploited by attackers. It's best not to use them at all; programmers are moving away from dependencies that rely on such highly vulnerable plugins.

Earlier, you learned how clicking malicious ads or links could lead you to exploit-kit landing pages. These harmful web pages search your device for security vulnerabilities, and once those vulnerabilities are found, they infect your computer using the exploits available for your outdated software. WannaCry, the 2017 global ransomware epidemic, relied on a zero-day Microsoft operating system vulnerability. WannaCry festered until the release and installation of the security update that mitigated the risk. Only those who applied the update were safe from harm.

To keep your devices protected, enable automatic updates for your operating system and software programs. Then perform a weekly check to update the software without automatic update capabilities.

Even with the potential hassles of acclimating to new technology and the cost of purchasing vendor-supported devices and software, the effort and expense are well worth it. Ensuring your and your family's identity, money, and personal information remain secure is priceless.

Brilliance 2: Enable Two-Factor Authentication

Two-factor authentication is a secondary method of verifying your identity. In addition to your password, the first factor of verification, the second factor involves a passcode retrieved via a secondary device, such as your phone. Most websites offer convenient, two-factor authentication options. You can have a text message sent to your phone, retrieve a passcode from an authentication app, or receive a notification sent to the website's mobile app (if installed on your phone). For example, when you enable two-factor authentication for Gmail, you can choose to receive a push notification sent to a Google mobile application, which then prompts you to verify your identity when logging into your account. More commonly, you can choose to receive a passcode in a text message. Because of the adversary's ability to spoof phone numbers, as well as intercept SMS messages, it is best to use an authentication app, such as Google Authenticator, when available.

Enabling two-factor authentication is critical to protecting your online account access. You learned how bad actors collect username and password combinations from data breaches, such as LinkedIn, and automatically try them on thousands of websites. If a bad actor tries your actual username and password, they can't get in if you have two-factor authentication turned on. If you use two-factor authentication only on one site or service, enable it on the email account where your password reset emails go, which is often your personal email address (Gmail, Microsoft, Apple, and so forth). If you don't enable two-factor authentication for this primary account, bad actors can access hundreds of your online accounts by compromising only one set of account credentials. Once bad actors are in your main email account, they'll reset additional online account passwords by following the links in email messages.

Some websites don't have two-factor authentication capabilities yet, but they most likely ask security-related questions. Some security questions like "What's your mother's maiden name?" have been around since the days of telegrams in 1882.[2] Now, your mother's maiden name can be found on the Internet in seconds. Make sure to create clever answers to frustrate bad actors and get them to move on to easier targets and keep track of your completely bogus security question answers. When a website asks for your mother's maiden name, create a canned answer that is *not* your mother's maiden name, and store the answer in your password manager. A security question might be "What's your eldest sibling's middle name?" Create an answer like "I love quesadillas." The answer doesn't make sense, which is exactly what you want. Just make sure to save your answers in a secure place afterward, such as a password manager, so you don't confuse yourself, too.

Brilliance 3: Use a Password Manager

The average professional manages nearly 200 passwords.[3] It's no wonder why people opt for weak and easy-to-remember passwords, use the same password on multiple sites, and write them all down on a sheet of paper or an unprotected Word document. I have great news for you—creating, remembering, and managing hundreds of unique, complex passwords can be much simpler. A password manager can do all of the work for you—and then some. *Password managers* create strong passwords for each of your individual accounts and automatically enter these passwords when you visit the corresponding account web page. Password managers can also change your passwords incrementally and notify you of any duplicate login credentials if you've manually created your passwords (you won't have duplication with the password manager's automatic password creation).

Password managers are an encrypted vault that requires a master password, or *key*, to open. Make your master password unique, strong, and complex.

Don't store your master password in the password manager it unlocks or in a web browser. Instead, store your master password in a secondary password management tool or, even better, place it on a piece of paper in a locked safe to create a physical airgap solution and protect your master password from bad actors. This password should be your best-kept secret—it's the key to all of your other keys. Enable two-factor authentication as well.

In addition to using a password manager, it is important to practice all of the "Brilliance in the Basics" techniques to protect you and your family from becoming victims of cyberattacks.

Myth "Password managers aren't secure. Why would I trust a single company/database to store all of my passwords?"

Fact Password managers are the best option for securely creating, storing, and managing your unique and complex passwords. Security incidents *can* occur with password manager companies, but they rapidly respond to security incidents, provide security updates, and communicate openly with their customers. The benefits of using a service like LastPass, one of the leading password managers, tremendously outweigh any risks. Attempting to memorize your passwords is a risky game that doesn't work and leads to duplicate username and password combinations. If you don't follow an easy method of password management, you aren't likely to use it at all. A password manager is an easy solution that solves the problem of having to remember hundreds of unique and complex passwords. LastPass also provides the following features in its free version: automatic form filling, one-click login, computer data encryption, password synchronization across multiple browsers, secure note storage, secure sharing of passwords, password backup and restore, global access, screen keyboard to evade keyloggers, one-time passwords for login on untrusted computers or networks (so you don't have to use your master password), multiple identities management (for instance, work versus personal), and password protection on phishing sites.[4]

Brilliance 4: Install and Update Antivirus Software

Antivirus is the armed security guard between your computer and the Internet. Keeping your antivirus program updated ensures that guard is working 24/7 to protect your personal information, website access, money, and computer files. Not having up-to-date antivirus is like coming home to criminals looting your personal items and finding the guard dog asleep. When your antivirus program is set to update automatically, you receive the latest virus definitions to detect new and evolving viruses.

You might be thinking, "I've heard about antivirus and antimalware programs. What's the difference?" Viruses are a type of malware, as you learned in Chapter 4, "Attack Methods," so you would want a program that fends off all forms of malware (including ransomware, spyware, scareware, viruses, and so on). Because the term *antivirus* is much more widely recognized, companies brand their antimalware products as "antivirus" programs for marketing purposes. When you search Google for *antimalware products*, you won't see as many popular results as you would when you type *antivirus products*. To avoid the confusion, search for *top antivirus [current year]*, and choose a reliable, trusted, total security antivirus program. Use only one antivirus program—multiple programs can conflict with each other, leaving security holes for cyber attackers to slip through.

Once you download and install the chosen antivirus program, enable automatic updates. Sometimes, the program may require you to update the antivirus program manually to the newest version. Do a weekly check to ensure your antivirus version is current and confirm automatic definition updates are working.

Myth "Macs don't get viruses or malware, so I don't need antivirus."

Fact Yes, they do, but they occur a lot less frequently than on a Windows computer. While thousands of new Windows malware versions appear daily, Mac OS machines are certainly getting more and more every day as they become more popular and mainstream. Currently, the most prevalent threats to Macs are adware, spyware, and potentially unwanted programs (PUPs)—and those aren't the cute kind of pups!

Adware can be a severe nuisance, redirecting your web pages to malicious advertisements, overlaying your search engine results with devious links, and creating persistent pop-ups. Apple computers include a built-in malware detection program called XProtect, which can detect malicious programs downloaded from the Internet and prompt you to delete them. XProtect does not guard against the ever-growing problem of adware or other threats, such as visiting phishing websites.[5] Therefore, it is essential to install a dependable, trusted, total security, antivirus program for your Mac and keep it up-to-date to ward off unwanted cybercriminals.

Brilliance 5: Back Up Your Data

Performing regular computer backups is the only way you can be sure you will ever see your information again. With a slew of risks, such as computer crashes, hard drive failure, physical damage, computer theft, software malfunctions, and malware infections like ransomware, it is critical to back up your computer's data frequently. Most of the risks mentioned pertain to physical backups, located on your computer, an external hard drive, or both. To avoid the risk of losing your personal information, perform cloud-based computer backups of your data.

Imagine you spill water on your Mac. You can't turn the computer on anymore, and you're not even sure when you performed your last backup. You take it to Apple technical support, which estimates the damage is close to $1,000, and the files are gone. At this point, it's better to purchase a new Mac. At least you'll have the latest hardware and receive active technical support and security updates. But what about your files? If you had performed an iCloud backup and used iDrive to store all your files, you would be golden. Or, if you had performed a backup to an external hard drive, you'd still be at risk of hard drive failure, which—much like a spill on your Mac—you can't predict.

Don't gamble with the unknown—use cloud-based storage and purchase a secondary cloud backup service as a failsafe for your primary cloud storage account.

Myth   "I don't store my information in the cloud because it's not safe."

Fact   The cloud is safe for everyday file storage when you follow the "Brilliance in the Basics" cybersecurity habits. Turn on two-factor authentication and create strong and unique passwords using a password manager. Most breaches of data in the cloud are the result of individuals getting hacked—not the service provider.

Cloud vendors are responsible for applying updates and protecting their services from cyberattacks. This means you can focus on protecting access to your account instead. Major cloud vendors follow a comprehensive set of cloud security standards set by the Cloud Security Alliance (CSA), which makes sure companies have an effective security program in place—ensuring your data stored on Dropbox, Box, Google, iDrive, OneDrive, and so on is safe.

For added security and data protection assurance, sign up for a cloud backup service. Look for a service provided by a trusted company that will perform secondary backups of your primary cloud storage accounts.

In the next chapter, you will learn how simple mistakes can have unintended, harmful consequences. An email to the wrong person, a lost device, and mixing our work and personal lives can all lead to you being the source of a data breach. Learn how to avoid these pitfalls and keep your information—and reputation—intact.

Notes

1. www.techradar.com/news/Internet/how-hackers-are-really-getting-your-information-and-what-you-can-do-to-keep-it-safe-1323706
2. https://mice.cs.columbia.edu/getTechreport.php?techreportID=1460
3. https://blog.lastpass.com/2017/11/lastpass-reveals-8-truths-about-passwords-in-the-new-password-expose.html/
4. https://lastpass.com/features_free.php
5. https://blog.malwarebytes.com/101/2017/03/mac-security-facts-and-fallacies/

8 Mistakes

Jeff was working with one of his colleagues, Paul Thomas, nicknamed PT, on a spreadsheet with more than 30,000 employee records. They had exchanged the spreadsheet via email several times after each had made some changes.

Once Jeff thought the spreadsheet was completed, he composed a new email where he was going to send the spreadsheet to Paul and a few others declaring his analysis was complete.

Jeff launched Outlook and went to send the spreadsheet as an attachment to Paul and the other members of his team. Unknowingly, when Jeff went to type in Paul's email address, Outlook automatically populated the email address for the PTA group where one of Jeff's children attended school. He hit Send and more than 280 parents received this highly sensitive spreadsheet with all of those employee records.

While this was a "simple" mistake, this mistake cost Jeff's company more than $8 million in legal fees, consumer credit monitoring, and other fines.

We make mistakes—it's human nature. We can feel secure, even if we are not; and we can be secure, even if we don't feel it. Our animalistic DNA hasn't evolved to evaluate security trade-offs appropriately. For instance, should I click a link that looks suspicious, or is the potential of a Starbucks gift card worth the risk?

We make basic security trade-offs every day—we evaluate whether to lock our car doors, consider what method of payment to use, and weigh how much information we should share. We still carry a primitive "fight-or-flight" response, sourced in the amygdala center of our brain. Our ever faithful amygdala keeps us safe when we are in physical danger by shutting down our ability reason so our bodies can focus on fighting.

This response is impractical when it comes to evaluating cybersecurity risk.[1] When we feel secure—without practicing cybersecurity hygiene—we risk becoming the victim of a cyber predator. It's hard for us to feel cyber threats. We can't feel the exposed information floating around online, and we don't sense when the adversary launches a cyberattack against us. Because of this false sense of security, our judgment is impaired. Evaluating cybersecurity risks based on the way we feel is misleading.

It's important to practice the "Brilliance in the Basics" techniques to remain secure in your everyday life. And remember, the feeling of security is false unless you are consistently performing the essential cyberhygiene steps to pursue security in real life.

Being the Source of a Data Breach

Mistakes can make you the source of a data breach—not the adversary. With a click of the Send button and the wrong recipient listed, we can inadvertently leak sensitive information. It's that easy. According to the 2017 Verizon Data Breach Investigations Report, 14 percent of data breaches happen because of human error. Misdelivery of sensitive information, electronically or paper-based, was the top action that led to mistake-driven data breaches. Publishing and disposal errors were the second and third actions leading to data breaches caused by miscellaneous mistakes.[2] Sending a sensitive email to the wrong person is horrifying, both at work and at home, and it can have some serious consequences.

A DREADFUL MISTAKE-DRIVEN DATA BREACH

Consider this– A London, sexual health clinic employee entered the email addresses of 781 patients who had attended HIV clinics in the To field instead of the Bcc field. Because of this email error, the 781 recipients saw the names of everyone else from their small, local community, who had attended HIV clinics in the past. As a result, the 56 Dean Street clinic was fined $250,000 by London's National Health Service (NHS).[3]

It's vital to slow down and verify the recipient is correct before sending emails. Email services, like Gmail and Outlook, offer options to retract emails. When enabled in Gmail, the Undo Send feature allows you to withdraw an email within a certain number of seconds. In Outlook, the functionality is available to recall unread, sent messages. It is wise to enable these features; they might save you from experiencing some major embarrassment in the future.

If you lose a device or it ends up getting stolen, you could be the source of a data breach. If you bring your laptop out in public or leave it on your back seat and not in the trunk, you are at risk. By encrypting your device and setting a strong login password, you will prevent a thief from gaining access to your personal information if the unfortunate happens. You can't stop a thief from attempting to steal, but you can safeguard your devices and, along with them, your identity and personal information. In Chapter 18, "Protecting Your Mobile Devices," you will learn the specific recommendations on how to protect your smartphones and tablets.

Mixing Work and Personal Information

It's also a dangerous mistake to mix your personal and work accounts. There's no better example than the Sony Pictures data breach. The breach was caused by employees who used the same passwords for work as they did for their personal Apple ID accounts. The alleged North Korean hacking group, Guardians of Peace (GOP), leveraged job information found on Sony Pictures employee LinkedIn accounts, in addition to phished Apple ID passwords. Even though the phishing emails, which warned "Verify Your Apple ID Immediately," gave the adversary the credentials to the victim's personal accounts, it was a lucky break that the employees' personal passwords were the same as their corporate ones. The usernames were simple to find too. By searching Google for *@sonypictures.com email*, they found the name pattern to input the target's name (for example, `jsmith@sonypictures.com`). The nation-state hacking group successfully received access to troves of corporate and personal information as a result of the oversight.[4]

As you learned in Chapter 4, "Attack Methods," bad actors use information pulled from LinkedIn and other social media sites to target victims. You might think listing your detailed job responsibilities is harmless, but if this is publicly viewable, bad actors can use this information to their advantage, sending you targeted phishing attacks. The adversary also likes to search publicly available job ads listed by HR departments. Job listings, just like your LinkedIn job details, offer valuable intel on what products and services you use at work. Job description details, combined with an employee's email address who works in the listed job role, make it easy for the adversary to send targeted phishing emails to acquire your personal information, access your employer's network, install ransomware, and more.

Let's say you list on LinkedIn "Sales Manager at ACME Corporation. Certified in 123SalesPro software. Contact me at `asmith@ACME.com`." With this small amount of information, a bad actor has abundant opportunity to send you a targeted spear phishing attack. Imagine these phishing email headlines as a result: "EXPIRED: Renew Your 123SalesPro Certification Now," "Register for 123SalesPro 'Secrets to 6-Figure Sales' webinar," "Renew Your 123SalesPro Subscription Immediately," "INSTALL NOW: Security Update for 123SalesPro Customers," and "WARNING: We've noticed suspicious activity on your 123SalesPro account." The example list of spear phishing emails could go on and on.

Make sure to stay informed about the publicly available information about you on the Internet and be prepared for the potentiality of bad actors using it against you. The size of your digital footprint on the Internet will determine the frequency and sophistication level of the phishing attacks you'll receive. In Chapter 15, "Protecting Your Social Media," you'll read more about how you can protect your social media presence.

In the upcoming chapter, you'll learn the critical response steps to common cyberattacks, such as falling victim to ransomware, clicking a phishing email, and having your email account compromised.

Notes

1. https://www.schneier.com/blog/archives/2008/04/the_feeling_and_1.html
2. www.verizonenterprise.com/resources/reports/rp_DBIR_2017_Report_execsummary_en_xg.pdf
3. https://www.theguardian.com/technology/2016/may/09/london-hiv-clinic-fined-180000-for-revealing-service-users-names
4. https://www.tripwire.com/state-of-security/latest-security-news/sony-hackers-used-phishing-emails-to-breach-company-networks/

9

Incident Response

Jeff got a notification from the Main Street High School where his son is enrolled that his password had been compromised as a result of a data breach of the school's website. The school emailed and said not to worry because they had changed his password, and he would be receiving a separate email with the instructions on how to create a new password. Jeff thought it was good that this was caught and his account was now secure.

However, the "good news" was short-lived. About a week later, Jeff couldn't log into this banking or his email accounts. He soon was getting text messages from friends asking about very weird emails they were receiving from him and odd social media posts. What Jeff didn't realize was that a group of bad actors had stolen his password from the high school website. Once the bad actors got ahold of that password, they started trying Jeff's email address and password against other websites. Since Jeff had used the same password on many of his websites, only then did he realize what he should have done as a result of the high school notifying him of the data breach.

The cyberattack happens—now what do you do? This chapter contains step-by-step recommendations for the most common cyberattack scenarios. These include falling for a phishing attack and clicking a link or entering your credentials, succumbing to malware infections (including ransomware), and finding your email compromised. Foremost, it is important to remain calm, identify the cyberattack that occurred, and carefully follow the incident response steps to protect your information, money, accounts, and devices.

Falling for a Phishing Attack

How to Detect

If you've clicked a phishing email link, chances are malware was downloaded on your computer (see the incident response steps in "Malware Infection"). Your antivirus software, if running and updated, should detect the malware infection attempt. If you have a total security program, it should prevent you from visiting phishing website links with a warning page. If you do not see a warning, it's possible you visited a malicious web page that prompted you for your credentials, personal information, credit card number, or all three. If you entered any of this information, you might see a "Service Temporarily Down" or similar error message after submitting your information. You might notice differences on the phishing web page or notice the URL you clicked wasn't a legitimate one, such as `bankoamerica`
`.com` instead of the legitimate `bankofamerica.com`. If you opened an email attachment, you might've been prompted to "enable macros" if it was a Microsoft Office document. Seeing the request to enable macros (thereby allowing malicious code to run) is a telltale sign of a phishing attack.

If you feel like something suspicious occurred, collect the evidence (like the contents of the email), and use a search engine on a secondary device to find details about the evidence you've gathered. Most likely, if you feel weird about something you clicked or an attachment you opened, you probably experienced a phishing attack. Follow these incident response steps if you believe you've become a phishing target.

Response Steps

1. **Disconnect the Affected Device from the Internet**: You can do this by disconnecting the Ethernet cable or turning off the Wi-Fi connectivity on your computer. In doing so, you'll help prevent the spread of malware, stop bad actors from furthering the attack, and pause the exfiltration of your information.

2. **Restart Your Computer in Safe Mode**: This way, only the minimum necessary components load, and you will be able to perform the next steps without the malware interfering. To find instructions on how to perform a reboot in Safe Mode, type **Safe Mode** and your operating system version into an online search engine.

3. **Back Up Your Files to a Secure External Hard Drive or Portable USB Thumb Drive**: You will want to perform a backup to a cloud storage location after you follow the rest of the response steps. Remember that hardware failures can occur, and storage devices can be lost or stolen. The cloud protects you from the most common ways people lose valuable files and data.

4. **Check for Malware**: Follow steps 4–10 in "Getting Infected with Malware," and return here once finished to move on to the next action steps in "Falling for a Phishing Attack."

5. **Change Your Account Credentials**: From a known clean device change your account credentials. Even if you didn't enter account credentials as part of a phishing attack, malware might've collected this information. It is better to be safe and take precautions rather than to gamble with your identity, money, and device integrity.

6. **Enable a Fraud Alert on Your Credit Report and Freeze Your Credit**: Contact the four major credit bureaus (Experian, Equifax, TransUnion, and Innovis) and request a free 90-day fraud alert on your credit report. To be safe, also request a security freeze with all three. This will prevent the opening of new credit lines until you remove the freeze. You'll learn more about identity theft and how to protect against it in the next chapter.

7. **Report the Phishing Attack to Authorities**: Depending on the severity of the attack, you should report to the various government agencies designed to help prevent and detect these kinds of attacks. Save the original phishing email, and report the attack to the authorities and organizations listed here:

   a. File a complaint at `https://www.ic3.gov/default.aspx`, the FBI's Internet Fraud Complaint Center. Once submitted, your complaint will be processed and then forwarded to the appropriate authority.

   b. Report the phishing attack to the U.S. Computer Emergency Readiness Team (US-CERT) at `https://www.us-cert.gov/`.

   c. Forward the received phishing email to the FTC at `spam@uce.gov`, as well as to the organization the bad actor impersonated in the email. It is essential to include the full email header, which holds important technical evidence. To include the email header, search for the name of your email service (for example, Gmail) with *full email header* using your favorite search engine to receive instructions.

   d. File a complaint with the Federal Trade Commission at `https://` `www.ftccomplaintassistant.gov/#crnt&panel1-1`.

   e. Report the phishing email to the Anti-Phishing Working Group at `reportphishing@apwg.org`. This group consists of Internet service providers (ISPs), cybersecurity companies, financial institutions, and law enforcement agencies.

   f. Depending on the level of damage caused by the attack, you could file a report with local law enforcement, bringing the following information: government-issued photo ID, proof of address (for instance, a utility bill), and proof of theft (such as a billing statement or IRS statement).

   g. Visit `https://www.identitytheft.gov/` for steps to take to minimize your risk of identity theft as a result of phishing.

Getting Infected with Malware

How to Detect   While malware may be difficult to detect or it may show no warning signs at all, some common symptoms include your computer running slowly, using more CPU or data than usual; emails failing to send, videos buffering and sites taking long to load, your browser home page redirecting, pop-up ads persisting, your antivirus failing, your system keeps crashing, an inability to log in to websites, and so on. Always ensure you have an up-to-date, robust antivirus program capable of preventing, as well as detecting, malware infections.

Response Steps

1. **Disconnect the Affected Device from the Internet**: You can do this by disconnecting the Ethernet cable or turning off the Wi-Fi connectivity on your computer. In doing so, you'll help prevent the spread of malware, stop bad actors from furthering the attack, and pause the exfiltration of your information.

2. **Restart Your Computer in Safe Mode**: This way, only the minimum necessary components load, and you will be able to perform the next steps without the malware interfering. To find instructions on how to perform a reboot in Safe Mode, type **Safe Mode** and your operating system version into a search engine.

3. **Back Up Your Files to a Secure External Hard Drive, or Portable USB Thumb Drive**: Ideally you already have your files backed up before the attack. If your personal files aren't backed up, you will want to perform a backup to a cloud storage location after you follow the rest of the response steps. Remember that hardware failures can occur, and storage devices can be lost or stolen. The cloud protects you from the most common ways people lose valuable files and data.

4. **Delete Temporary Files**: Prior to running a virus scan, clean up your computer's temporary files. Temporary files can clog up disk space, causing a virus scan to run slow, and can hide malicious files. Type **disk cleanup** and your operating system version into a search engine for these steps.

5. **Scan Your Device for Malware**: Use your antivirus program to scan for any malware that might be lurking on your computer. Don't reconnect to the Internet if prompted. You should be able to run a scan without doing so. After you complete this initial scan, you can also run a secondary, one-time scan using Malwarebytes free scanning tools (`https://www.malwarebytes.com/`). Download the latest version on a secondary device, transfer it to a thumb drive, and install it manually on the compromised device without reconnecting to the Internet.

6. **Restart Your Computer**: Make sure you power down and then turn your computer back on in normal mode after performing the initial scan for malware.

7. **Repeat Step 5—Scan Your Device for Malware**: Scanning again for malware helps to confirm all the malware is gone when your computer is no longer running in safe mode.

8. **Install Operating System and Application Updates**: Ensure your computer and all of your software applications are up-to-date. This will help prevent cyberattack exploits targeting outdated software with vulnerabilities.

9. **Fix Web Browser Home Page**: If you experience malware that alters web browser home pages, you will need to go into your web browser's preferences and manually change the home page to a desired web address.

10. **Reinstall the Operating System (If All Else Fails)**: If your computer is still showing signs of infection or you simply want to make sure you are completely protected, reinstall the operating system to wipe out

everything. Ensure you have current backups and follow reinstallation instructions by searching for *reinstall* and your operating system version using a search engine.

11. **Change Your Account Credentials**: From a known clean device change all of your online account credentials. It is better to be safe and take precautions than to gamble with your identity, money, and device integrity.

Getting Infected with Ransomware

How to Detect Ransomware, a type of malware, isn't too difficult to detect. Warning signs can consist of a text file on your desktop that shows a ransom note and file extensions changed to something random, like `file.xyz` instead of `file.docx`. There are different variations of ransomware, and you'll need to collect the evidence to narrow down which strain has infected your computer.

Response Steps

1. **Gather the Evidence**: Is your screen locked up with a ransom note? Do you have a text file on your desktop? What does the extension look like at the end of your filenames? What does the ransom note say? Does it claim to be the IRS or the FBI? Collect all the indicators and perform a search on a secondary device, like your smartphone, to locate the specific response steps for the ransomware strain that's taken hold of your computer.

2. **Disconnect the Affected Device from the Internet**: You can do this by disconnecting the Ethernet cable or turning off the Wi-Fi connectivity on your computer. In doing so, you'll help prevent the spread of malware, stop bad actors from furthering the attack, and pause the exfiltration of your information.

3. **Take a Photo and Screenshot of the Ransom Note**: Capturing visual evidence of the ransom note will help you when you file a police report later.

4. **Decide Whether You Will Pay the Ransom**: If you believe you can recover your files from current and clean backups, go on to the next step.

WARNING If you do not have proper backups and decide to pay the ransom, skip the following steps and go to step 11 for instructions on how to pay a ransom. If you attempt to erase the ransomware, you will end up with encrypted files without the unlock key.

5. **Restart Your Computer in Safe Mode**: This way, only the minimum necessary components load, and you will be able to perform the next steps without the ransomware intruding. To find instructions on how to perform a reboot in Safe Mode, type **Safe Mode** and your operating system version into a search engine.

6. **Scan Your Computer for Ransomware**: Follow steps 4–9 in "Getting Infected with Malware" and then move on to the next action steps here.

7. **Identify the Ransomware Strain to Check for Solutions**: Go to `https://www.nomoreransom.org/crypto-sheriff.php?lang=en` and use the Crypto Sheriff tool to help identify the type of ransomware you have. You will need to upload two encrypted files from your computer, as well as an email, web address, `.onion`, or Bitcoin address listed in the ransom note. You can also upload the `.txt` or `.html` ransom note file instead of entering the specifics.

8. **Check for Available Decryption Solutions**: After you've typed in the necessary information to identify the ransomware, Crypto Sheriff will inform you whether there is a tool to decrypt your files. Check additional resources as well by typing in **decryption** and the strain of ransomware into a search engine for potential decryption tools. Make sure to check your antivirus provider's website for any available decryption tools as well.

9. **Reinstall the Operating System**: When dealing with ransomware, it's best to reinstall the operating system versus trusting your antivirus to eradicate the ransomware fully. Ensure you have current backups and follow the reinstallation instructions by typing **reinstall** and your operating system version into a search engine.

10. **Report the Ransomware to the Authorities**: Save the ransomware evidence and report the attack. To do so, file a complaint at `https://www.ic3.gov/default.aspx`, the FBI's Internet Fraud Complaint Center. Once submitted, your complaint will be processed and then forwarded to the appropriate authority.

11. **Pay the Ransom (If All Else Fails):** Before paying the ransom, consider negotiating the ransom price with the bad actor, using contact information from the ransom note. If you feel uncomfortable doing so, follow the payment instructions on the ransom note. Remember, it is not a guarantee that you'll get your files back, but most professional cybercriminals will keep their word—it counts as good "customer service" to them.

Email Compromise

How to Detect   Evidence of email compromise might include friends asking about strange emails you've sent them, all of your emails disappearing, or you can't log in to your email account.

Response Steps

1. **Reset Your Password:** From a secondary device, such as your smartphone, click "Forgot my password" on the email login page to reset your password. Follow the instructions and change your password to a unique and complex one, and store it in your secure password manager.

2. **Enable Two-Factor Authentication:** In your email account settings, activate two-factor authentication to prevent any future compromises from occurring.

3. **Verify You Are the Only Person on Your Account:** The bad actor could have added themselves to your email account. In your account settings, make sure you are the only one listed.

4. **Check Your Email Forwarding Settings:** Ensure you are not forwarding emails to the bad actor. During the account compromise, they had the chance to configure email forwarding to their account. Make sure this is not the case.

5. **Check Your "Sent" Email Box:** Do you see any emails sent from "you" that you don't recognize? Investigate the social damage.

6. **Change Your Account Credentials:** Change all of your online account credentials. There's a good chance the bad actor attempted to reset your passwords on other online accounts found in your email stash, hoping you used the same email account for password recovery without two-factor authentication enabled.

Congratulations! You've made it to the end of Part I of this book. You're learning how to identify, prevent, protect, and respond to cyber threats—celebrate your achievement! You've learned about your level of cyber risk, who the attackers are, and all about their targets, goals, and attack methods and tools. You've discovered the "Brilliance in the Basics" tips—the core cyber-hygiene habits to protect you and your family. And you're now aware of the cybersecurity mistakes you can make and how to avoid them.

Next, in Part II, you'll master the specific recommendations for protecting vital aspects of your and your family's digital life. Let's get started!

Specific Recommendations

10 Protecting Your Identity

Leading up to the 2016 U.S. presidential election, 12 Russian nationals plotted an identity theft scheme to influence the country's vote by promoting presidential candidate Donald Trump. Russian identity thieves purchased six stolen U.S. citizens' identities on the Dark Web to carry out their political conspiracy.

With the help of a Californian who sold fraudulent bank account numbers to people on the Web, the Russian nationals obtained verified PayPal accounts using their stolen personas. The thieves used these PayPal accounts to fund their conspiracy to attempt to influence the U.S. election.

According to the 2018 federal indictment made by U.S. Special Counsel Robert Mueller, the identified Russian nationals were charged with attempts ". . . to defraud the United States by impairing, obstructing, and defeating the lawful functions of the government through fraud and deceit for the purpose of interfering with the U.S. political and electoral processes, including the presidential election of 2016." Specifically, the Russian nationals' political interference operations consisted of ". . . supporting the presidential campaign of then-candidate Donald J. Trump ("Trump Campaign") and disparaging Hillary Clinton."[1]

Dubbed the Internet Research Agency (IRA), the Russian "cyber influence" group used social media as a cultural weapon to attract Trump supporters through false propaganda and ads against the opponents. The IRA accepted $25–$50 payments from individuals who wanted to post content on the social media pages they orchestrated.[2]

Masquerading as various U.S.-based grassroots organizations, the IRA used the stolen identities of Americans to reach out to political organizations and obtain support and promotion for Pro-Trump rally organization in "purple" states like Florida.[1] Some of the nationals even obtained false government documents to travel to the United States to gain intel to further their tactics to tamper with the nation's political system.

Starting in 2014, the IRA employed hundreds of people within their Russian headquarters, all with the goal to "spread distrust towards the candidates and the political system in general." With hundreds of Facebook, Twitter, and Instagram accounts—some with more than 100,000 followers—the IRA promoted Trump, opposed Hillary Clinton, and attempted to dissuade minority groups from voting at all.[1]

The situation of the Russian nationals involved in stealing U.S. identities by purchasing them on the Dark Web is just one example of what can happen when Social Security numbers (SSNs) are exposed from a data breach, such as Equifax. Besides a data breach, there are other ways your personal information can end up in the wrong hands.

Methods of Identity Theft

There are several techniques bad actors use to get their hands on the sensitive information that makes up your identity. These techniques vary in complexity and scope, but the goal remains the same. Bad actors want your personally identifiable information (PII) to open bank accounts and credit cards, obtain loans, submit healthcare claims, and even evade the police (which could risk your going to jail for someone else's arrest warrants). Remember, PII includes the information that can be used to identify you (for example, SSNs, driver's license number, billing address, date of birth, and so forth).

The following are some common methods fraudsters utilize to steal your identity.

Ways Identity Thieves Steal Your Identity

Data Breach   Breaches, such as Equifax in 2017, which exposed more than 140 million SSNs, hundreds of thousands of credit card numbers, and other

PII, create a challenge since an individual's identity is already leaked prior to the company and consumers knowing about it.[3] Equifax's breach cost consumers $1.4 billion, with an average cost of $23 per person, after 20 percent of Americans placed a security freeze on their credit files.[4]

KATIE SAYS, "NO, THANK YOU."

One such individual who was affected by the Equifax breach was Katie Van Fleet, of Seattle, who started receiving "thank you" letters for opening credit lines at 15 retail stores, such as Barneys of New York and Home Depot. Katie was perplexed because she never applied for these accounts.

With the theft of her identity attributed to the Equifax breach, Van Fleet filed a class-action lawsuit based on negligence against the major credit bureau. "I didn't think this would ever happen to me . . . it's been very frustrating," Van Fleet told her local news. Even though she placed fraud alerts on her credit report, she kept receiving those "thank you" letters. What ended up saving her from further identity theft was placing a security freeze on her credit report.[5]

Experian, one of the four main credit bureaus, also experienced an undisclosed breach in 2013 where 200 million consumer records were exposed by a Vietnamese man named Hieu Minh Ngo, who ran an identity theft service online posing as a U.S. licensed private investigator. Ngo paid thousands of dollars to Experian each month to gain access to hundreds of millions of credit files. Ngo then resold these records to more than 1,300 bad actors who subscribed to his identity theft service. Bad actors filed more than 13,000 falsified tax returns using the purchased identity info, which allowed them to collect $65 million in fraudulent tax return funds. Ngo was actually caught by the U.S. Secret Service and was sentenced to 13 years in prison.[6]

Dark Web   Like the story of the Russians who purchased identities of Americans to influence the 2016 presidential election, thieves purchase identities on the Dark Web. PII gets on the dark corner of the Internet through data breaches and social engineering tactics, such as phishing. As you learned in Chapter 3, the identity of a person with a perfect credit score of 850 goes for around $150. And medical information goes for ten times the amount of credit card numbers on the Dark Web because credit card numbers can be changed, but your health history never changes.[7]

Social Engineering   This is the most common tactic for obtaining sensitive information by tricking someone into divulging SSNs, bank account numbers, and other personal details. The range of attack methods are diverse and can include scenarios such as a phishing email from your "bank" to update your information to keep your account active or the "FBI" calling you to warn you of an arrest warrant unless you pay "unpaid taxes." Identity thieves are creative. Remember, this is their job, and they want to do their best to make the most money possible.

Dumpster Diving   Yes, your garbage is wanted by thieves. How many times have you thrown out expired credit cards, credit line offers, bills, and other sensitive paperwork instead of shredding them? Bad actors are banking (literally) on getting any tidbits of PII they can to open accounts and rack up debt on your behalf. Austin-based security researcher and professional dumpster diver Matt Malone found $1.8 million in original and copied checks inside a discarded filing cabinet placed in an Austin remodeling company dumpster during the tax season of 2018. In addition to checks, the company also disposed of their employee W-2s, as well as customer driver's license numbers and other sensitive information. By bringing awareness to what he finds in the trash, Malone hopes more individuals and businesses will take care of what they throw away. "People wonder how identity theft happens," Malone told CBS Austin, "It starts in the trash can."[8] The story of Malone's dumpster finds shows how crucial it is to shred sensitive documents prior to discarding them to protect yourself fully from paper-based identity theft.

How to Check Whether Your PII Is Exposed

There is a way you can check if you've been affected by known data breaches. A website, called Have I Been Pwned (https://haveibeenpwned.com/), operated by Microsoft regional director Troy Hunt, shows you if you're affected by a data breach when you supply your email address. Hunt's website includes information on all known data breaches, as well as the types of information exposed in each incident. By visiting the website for Have I Been Pwned, you can check if your PII is connected with a data breach so you can take the necessary steps to protect the information associated with your presumably compromised accounts.

Identity Monitoring Services

By now, you've probably heard of LifeLock (`https://www.lifelock.com/`). You may even remember the TV ads with previous LifeLock CEO Todd Davis, who publicly displayed his SSN for the world to see to bluntly express his confidence in the company's identity protection services. It is no surprise Davis experienced 13 incidents of identity theft after the ads aired.[9] LifeLock also exposed customer email addresses through a third-party marketing website security flaw that allowed bad actors potentially to enumerate through millions of LifeLock user email addresses, as well as unsubscribe them from all LifeLock official email communications. This flaw could also allow bad actors to craft LifeLock-looking spear phishing email attacks to the listed email addresses. The site flaw exhibited a lack of understanding around website security and proper user authentication, which was shocking coming from a company whose sole claimed purpose is to protect the identities of its customers.[10]

LifeLock has subsequently gone through numerous lawsuits, one which ruled LifeLock's Fraud Alert system illegal. LifeLock floods credit reporting agencies with fraud alert requests (since each one lasts only 90 days) by impersonating the owner of the credit file.

Fraud alerts are federally provided as an option to consumers through the 2003 Fair and Accurate Credit Transactions Act (FACTA) and are only meant to be initiated by the consumer, family member, guardian, or attorney.[11] A fraud alert entitles you to 90 days of free credit monitoring and a copy of your credit report. Federally, you are allowed one free copy annually from each bureau. Fraud alerts only last 90 days, and they don't prevent identity theft. Fraud alerts still keep your credit file open to monitor for changes. It is a reactionary step, similar to any credit monitoring service.

Third-party services, like Credit Karma, provide you with free credit monitoring and accessibility to your credit reports. These services can be beneficial, but they do not prevent identity theft. Most identity monitoring services don't monitor financial identity theft, such as suspicious activity involving your bank account, credit cards, retirement funds, loyalty rewards, and more.

They also don't alert you when a bad actor uses your identity to obtain a new driver's license, passport, or other government documents. Identity monitoring services also don't prevent fraud against tax returns, Social Security, Medicare and Medicaid, welfare, and other government programs. You also won't find out about utility accounts taken out in your name. Identity monitoring services provide minimal benefits to individuals, and most of those benefits are available for free through the government or affected parties in a data breach. Some identity theft protection services offer $1 million in identity theft insurance. Most of the time, this amount of coverage is already put forth under existing laws and zero liability rules with major credit card companies.[12]

The most effective way you can protect your credit, and your identity, is by placing a security freeze on your credit file with the four major credit reporting agencies—Equifax, Experian, TransUnion, and Innovis—in addition to other agencies of importance, such as the National Consumer Telecommunications and Utilities Exchange (NCTUE) for new phone account verification and ChexSystems for new bank account validation.[13] When you place a security freeze on your file, you will receive a PIN that is used to unfreeze your file when needed in the future. Save the PIN associated with the credit reporting agency in your secure password manager.

Because security freezes lock down your credit file and prevent you, and bad actors, from opening credit lines in your name, you will need to remove the freeze temporarily a few times a year when applying for credit. But the simple fact remains—*you* are the only one who can protect your identity. By placing security freezes on your credit file, you pay less than identity monitoring services charge, and your credit file will be protected, preventing any new credit lines from opening.

Recommendations: Protecting Your Credit Identity

Here are essential recommendations to protect your identity and your credit score and to prevent the opening of fraudulent accounts:

1. **Request a Security Freeze**: Security freezes ensure your credit file is secure by preventing any new credit lines from opening in your name. Security freezes are a small price to pay for priceless identity protection

assurance. Place a security freeze with the four major credit reporting agencies—Equifax, Experian, TransUnion, and Innovis.

2. **Place a Security Freeze with NCTUE and ChexSystems**: When purchasing a new mobile phone plan, phone providers use the National Consumer Telecommunications and Utilities Exchange (NCTUE) to check consumer credit. NCTUE allows you to place security freezes on your report by calling 1-866-349-5355. This helps prevent bad actors from opening mobile phone accounts in your name. Also, to prevent bad actors from using your reputability to open bank accounts, place a security freeze with ChexSystems, which verifies customer requests to open new checking and savings accounts.[13] You can do so by visiting the following link: `https://www.chexsystems.com/web/chexsystems/consumerdebit/page/securityfreeze/placefreeze/`

3. **Opt Out of Pre-approved Credit Offers**: To avoid the risk of a bad actor getting ahold of pre-approved credit offers in your mailbox or your trash, remove yourself from the mailing list by visiting `https://www.optoutprescreen.com/` or by calling 1-888-5-OPT-OUT (1-888-567-8688).

4. **Shred Sensitive Documents**: Buy a paper shredder and destroy unnecessary confidential papers. Store necessary sensitive documents in a locked, tamper- and fireproof safe.

5. **Manage Your Mail**: Remove mail from your mailbox as soon as you can, and directly drop-off outgoing mail at the post office instead of letting it sit out for pick-up. If you receive an unsuspected "Change of Address Verification" letter, report the fraudulent change immediately. Bad actors like to maliciously change your address when applying for credit cards in your name, using your stolen SSN.

   Now that USPS offers Informed Deliver, which scans incoming mail and sends it to the email address associated with your address, bad actors have found a way to spy on the mail you receive. All it takes is for bad actors to answer a few knowledge-based questions about your identity (such as your middle name, a previous employer, a road you lived on, and so on), and they can snoop on and disrupt incoming mail.[14]

6. **Beware of Phishing Emails**: Avoid clicking email links and opening file attachments. Don't reply to email users you don't know, and look for phishing email red flags, such as misspellings, unusual domain addresses, and demanding, time-sensitive requests.

Other Types of Identity Theft

The following are some additional types of identity theft. The first—medical identity theft—is a growing concern. As you read earlier, stolen medical information goes for 10 times the amount of financial information. Thieves primarily want the SSN listed on medical documents, which allows them to open up accounts in your name.

The second dominant form of identity theft is the targeting of military personnel. Identity thieves go after active duty individuals since they are most likely not monitoring their credit while overseas. This leaves them vulnerable to attackers unless they take proper precautions to protect their credit file while on duty.

The third area of concern is identity theft against senior citizens. Bad actors target senior citizens because they prefer checks instead of credit or debit cards, which means cold, hard cash for identity thieves. The reason seniors may be more susceptible to identity theft could be generational: seniors tend to trust others and have independent personalities, which could result in not asking family members for help when they receive a suspicious phone call or piece of mail.[15] Read on for more details within each category of identity theft.

Medical Identity Theft

MEDICAL IDENTITY THEFT WITH A HAPPY ENDING

Eric Drew was battling a rare type of cancer and was told he didn't have long to live. While receiving treatment at the Seattle Cancer Care Alliance, he started receiving numerous phone calls thanking him for his credit application. Not sure what the calls meant, Drew disregarded them until collection agents started hounding him for the $10,000 in accrued charges. Drew, incredibly weak from the chemotherapy, pulled a copy of his credit report and found the address the identity thief was using to send his bills. Drew went to the home, knocked on the door, expecting to find the thief, but was disappointed when no one answered. By getting the bills rerouted to his actual address, he began to search through the transaction history. With the help of a local news station, Drew broadcasted his story and pleaded for help in locating the thief. With all of the alleged informants coming up as dead ends, Drew was ready to give up. Meanwhile, the local news station contacted a home improvement store where Drew claimed the identity thief had made fraudulent purchases and requested to review their surveillance footage. Sure enough, based on matching up the date and time of the transaction history with the video recording, the identity thief was found. The assailant was a lab technician at the Seattle Cancer Care Alliance hospital where Drew was receiving treatment. Four days after his identification in 2004, Richard Gibson turned himself in and became the first person in the United States to be convicted under the Health Insurance Portability and Accountability Act (HIPAA), enacted in 1996 to protect patient privacy and accessibility. Gibson was sentenced to jail for 16 months for the theft of Drew's identity. Amazingly, through his battle with cancer and the identity thief, Drew went into remission—keeping his health and restoring his identity.[16]

Drew's story of identity theft isn't uncommon. Not only are patients who are labeled with little chance to live targets for identity thieves, but anyone with a medical history can become a victim of medical identity theft—and medical fraud is growing substantially. According to the National Health Care Anti-Fraud Association (NHCAA), tens of billions in healthcare fraud financial losses occur every year. And criminals are migrating from illegal drug trafficking to healthcare fraud against Medicare, Medicaid, and private healthcare companies. In South Florida, for instance, government and private healthcare insurers are defrauded out of hundreds of millions of dollars by organized crime groups in Central and South America who use stolen patient insurance and provider billing information to submit false claims from fictional clinics. When the claims get paid, medical identity thieves use a freight shipping address to get their payments delivered offshore anonymously.

Billing healthcare insurers for services that never occurred is just one method of medical identity theft. Other methods carried out by dishonest healthcare providers include the following: billing patients for higher-priced treatment than what they received (so-called *upcoding*), falsifying a patient's diagnosis to validate unnecessary medical services performed on patients, misrepresenting noncovered treatments as medically necessary for the purpose of obtaining fraudulent payments, offering incentives for taking part in medical procedures, and more. The impact of medical identity theft on the genuine patients can range from a nuisance to life-threatening situations.[17]

THE DIFFICULTY OF CLEARING ONE'S GOOD NAME

Anndorie Sachs, a Salt Lake City mother of four children, received a call from a Utah social worker who notified Sachs that her newborn baby tested positive for methamphetamines and would be taken away by the state. Sachs was confused for two reasons—she didn't recently give birth, and she wasn't on meth. After Sachs hired a lawyer to investigate, they found the identity thief, a woman named Dorothy Bell Moran, who stole Sachs' driver's license and assumed her identity to give birth.

Even with the thief unmasked, Sachs still faced challenges when she went to the hospital for a kidney infection a few months after the whole debacle. Sachs' found her medical records altered with Moran's information and had to convince the hospital of her serious blood-clotting disorder, which could become life-threatening if she was received the wrong medication. Even after the situation was resolved, Sachs stated, "I have a hard time believing that everything is back the way it was before. It's terrifying to think about."

Medical identity theft victims cope with permanently altered records, insurance coverage limits used up, and years of fighting for one's actual identity after the fact. Medical professionals are wary of people asking to make changes to their medical history and will often "flag" disputed information, rather than removing it.[18] The nonremoval of fraudulent information can lead to continuing battles of clearing information up every time an identity theft victim goes to seek medical care. Some unlucky victims can receive the wrong treatments, fail a physical exam for a potential job, cease to be eligible for healthcare coverage in the future, get arrested for someone else's trail of fraud, and more.

Fortunately, federal law addresses the penalties of healthcare fraud, which carries up to 10 years in prison for defrauding a healthcare benefit program to obtain delivery of, or payment for, billed services. If the identity thief's fraudulent actions result in bodily injury of a victim, they can go to jail for up to 20 years—and if the effects of identity theft include a patient's death, the thief can receive lifetime in prison.[19]

Because of the number of people involved in processing your information when you become ill, it takes only one "bad egg" out of the group to exploit your information along the way. Make sure to follow the steps in this chapter to protect your identity and health history.

Recommendations: Protecting Your Medical Identity

The following are essential recommendations, provided by the NHCAA, to protect your medical identity and prevent fraudsters from tampering with your and your family's valuable patient health information:[20]

1. **Protect Your Health Insurance Card Like a Credit Card**: A medical ID card can be used to purchase services, as well as fraudulently bill your health insurance company. If you lose your ID card, report it to your health insurance company immediately. Only share policy information with clinics that need it, and question anyone else who asks for it.

2. **Guard Your Social Security Number**: Give out your SSN only to those who genuinely need it. Most health insurers *don't* need your SSN—only Medicare—so ask your healthcare provider why they need your SSN. If your doctor's office claims they need it to fill in a computer field, ask them to use all zeroes instead (that is, 000-000-0000). If they need it for "tracking you down for billing," ask if you can provide your last four digits of your number.[21] If it's necessary for them to have your SSN, ask them how it's securely stored.

3. **Read Your Explanation of Benefits Statements**: After receiving or being billed for a service, you will receive an Explanation of Benefits (EOB) form in the mail. Make sure to read them, in addition to your insurance policy, to check for procedures billed that don't match up with what you received. Verify the dates of procedures as well.

4. **Report Suspected Medical Identity Theft**: Notify your health insurance company as soon as you suspect you might be a victim of medical identity theft.

5. **Monitor Health Records**: Stay informed of your health history by requesting copies of your medical records, verify your contact information with the medical facilities you visit, and review all of the medical bills received.

6. **Avoid Free Medical Service Offers**: Clinics involved in healthcare fraud like to offer "free" healthcare services, tests, and treatments so they can bill your health insurance company for treatments you never received.

Military Personnel Identity Theft

MONITOR YOUR CREDIT REPORT

Retired Army Major John Smith (victim's name kept anonymous in the news) just got back home after serving three years overseas in Europe. Smith and his family were excited to be back in the United States and applied for a home loan. To their dismay, they were given an immediate denial—Smith was told he had an insufficient credit score. Smith, puzzled, ordered a copy of his credit report and found his answer. An identity thief racked up thousands of dollars in fraudulent debt—all in Smith's name.

With his credit shot, Smith needed to prove he was not a "bad risk" to creditors. Ten years later, Smith was still feeling the after-effects: his interest rates were higher, and he still needed to defend his good name. Smith, as a warning to others, said, "I made the mistake of not checking my credit annually, especially while I was overseas. If I had, I may have been able to catch the problem sooner and nip it in the bud before it got as far as it did."[22]

Thieves target military personnel because of the slim chance they are checking their credit report while abroad. If you are in the military or know someone who is, follow the recommendations in the next section for identity protection assurance.

Recommendations: Protecting Your Identity While in the Military

The following are essential recommendations for military personnel to protect their identity while they are on active duty, according to the Identity Theft Resource Center:[23]

1. **Enable an "Active Duty Alert"**: Similar to a fraud alert, an active duty alert requires inquiring creditors to confirm the identity of the person who is looking to open a credit line. This alert lasts one year, which is significantly longer than the 90 days of a fraud alert. However, this doesn't prevent identity theft and the opening of credit lines, but it does

make it easier for the military personnel's family to manage their credit while they are away. If there is no need for the family to open credit lines, activating a security freeze with all four credit bureaus is the best defense against identity theft.

2. **Grant "Military Power of Attorney" to a Loved One**: Before members of the military depart on duty, they might consider naming a highly trusted individual to be their "military power of attorney" (military POA). In doing so, a designated individual is trusted with the military member's money, identity, and credit. Naming someone military POA is a good option when the service member wants someone else to take care of the following[24]: accepting delivery of personal property, managing housing and real estate transactions, operating vehicles in the service member's name, performing banking transactions, filing the service member's taxes, paying bills, and more.

Senior Citizen Identity Theft

HOW CARLOS PUT A PHONE SCAM ON LIFE ALERT

Carlos received an automated call informing him "You qualify for a free Life Alert system" and $3,000 worth of grocery coupons. All he was required to pay was $34.95 a month for the medical monitoring service. He pressed the #1 button, as prompted, to talk with a representative for more details. Sarah, the senior emergency care representative, gave Carlos a plethora of information about the system and requested Carlos's credit card number to store as a billing method to be charged once he received the system in the mail. Carlos told the representative he wouldn't give such sensitive information over the phone, or his bank account number, which she requested next. Carlos requested to receive a bill in the mail instead. In reply, Sarah assured him they work closely with all the major credit card companies and listed off the Consumer Credit Protection Act, which the representative stated, "protects consumers from being responsible for any charges to their credit cards if they buy something over the phone." Carlos then got suspicious with the insistence in her voice, almost aggressively demanding his payment information and not responding to his requests for a paper invoice. Carlos then asked where she was calling from, and Sarah replied, "Why are you asking me that, sir?" Her suspicious response was the final red flag he needed to hang up, realizing it was a scam to steal his identity. If Carlos fell for the scam, he would have lost his money, identity, and risked his life by trusting in the delivery of a nonexistent Life Alert system.[25]

Phone scams targeting seniors, like the free offers of Life Alert systems, attempt to steal credit card numbers, bank account numbers, and Medicare numbers (which are also the person's SSN). The phone representative will often sound very professional until they are questioned about their location and inquire about other options, such as mailing invoices and informational booklets.

The legitimate Life Alert issued a "Fraud Alert" statement clarifying that they do not perform cold calls or employ telemarketers, confirming the scams and their intent to steal the identities of senior citizens.[26]

Recommendations: Protecting the Identities of Senior Citizens

The following are essential recommendations for senior citizens to protect their identities:

1. **Verify the Identity of the Caller**: Be cautious of unknown callers. Bad actors can pretend to be your bank, the IRS, law enforcement, car warranty services, utility companies, and family members who need help. Don't ever provide sensitive information over the phone. Hang up a call if you suspect the caller is trying to get your money and personal information. Verify the identity of the caller (for instance, a company or family member) by locating the genuine phone number from a trusted source.

2. **Beware of Free Offers**: Most things in life are not free. If you receive a phone call that declares you eligible for a free service—prompting you to press #1 to learn more—don't do it. By pressing the button, it confirms you are interested and gives bad actors permission to continue spamming your phone. Hang up the call immediately.

3. **Don't Give Personal Information Over the Phone**: Today, most companies don't perform cold calls requesting personal information. Even

if the call is about a legitimate service, tell them you'll visit their web address for more information, or request to receive a brochure in the mail.

4. **Place a Security Freeze on Your Credit File**: This will prevent the opening of credit lines in your name. If you know a senior citizen who receives home healthcare or lives in a nursing home, it is crucial to implement a security freeze. Bad actors will look through paperwork, mail, and Social Security checks while a victim is asleep or not paying attention. Ask the healthcare provider to confirm they've performed background checks on their employees as well.

5. **Register and Lock Down Your SSA Account**: Bad actors are known to register Social Security Administration (SSA) accounts in individuals' names even before they are eligible to receive benefits. Create an online account with the SSA at `https://secure.ssa.gov`, secure it with a strong and unique password, and enable two-factor authentication protection.

   If you are receiving payments and notice a missed one, call the SSA at 1-800-772-1213 or visit your local field office. You can also block electronic access to your Social Security record. This blocks anyone, including you, from viewing or modifying your personal information online or through an automated telephone service. It is unclear if this also prevents a bad actor from succeeding at impersonating you while chatting with a SSA representative, but it does prevent a decent number of attack paths.[27] To enable this protection, visit the previously mentioned SSA site and click the "block electronic access" link at the bottom of the page.

6. **Don't Cash Unknown Checks You Receive in the Mail**: Bad actors can send checks in the mail to seniors that, once cashed, enrolls the victim in a bogus monthly payment program. When dubious checks are cashed, bad actors have enough information provided by the bank (for example, a photo of the check) to enroll them into an electronic transfer program.[28]

You've learned the methods in which identity thieves steal individuals' PII, how to check whether your sensitive information is leaked, and how to protect your identity as well as loved ones' from bad actors. In the next chapter, you will learn how to protect your children and their identities, privacy, and security, too!

Notes

1. http://thehill.com/policy/finance/374258-russians-indicted-for-stealing-identities-to-finance-election-interference
2. https://www.scribd.com/document/371673084/Internet-Research-Agency-Indictment#from_embed
3. https://www.csoonline.com/article/3223229/security/equifae-says-website-vulnerability-exposed-143-million-us-consumers.html
4. https://krebsonsecurity.com/2018/03/survey-americans-spent-1-4b-on-credit-freeze-fees-in-wake-of-equifax-breach/
5. http://komonews.com/news/local/seattle-woman-victimized-15-times-in-two-months-by-identity-thieves
6. https://krebsonsecurity.com/2018/03/san-diego-sues-experian-over-id-theft-service/
7. https://krebsonsecurity.com/2017/12/the-market-for-stolen-account-credentials/
8. http://cbsaustin.com/news/local/austin-man-found-dozens-of-peoples-personal-financial-documents-in-dumpster
9. https://www.wired.com/2010/05/lifelock-identity-theft/
10. https://krebsonsecurity.com/2018/07/LifeLock-bug-exposed-millions-of-customer-email-addresses/
11. https://www.wired.com/2009/05/lifelock/
12. https://krebsonsecurity.com/2014/03/are-credit-monitoring-services-worth-it/
13. https://krebsonsecurity.com/2017/10/usps-informed-delivery-is-stalkers-dream/
14. https://krebsonsecurity.com/2018/05/another-credit-freeze-target-nctue-com/
15. http://commhealthcare.com/protect-seniors-from-identity-theft/
16. http://discovermagazine.com/2008/apr/09-the-man-who-lost-his-name-and-his-genetic-identity
17. https://www.nhcaa.org/resources/health-care-anti-fraud-resources/the-challenge-of-health-care-fraud.aspx
18. www.nbcnews.com/id/23392229/ns/health-health_care/t/impostor-er/#.WsTkdS_Mx-U

19. https://www.law.cornell.edu/uscode/text/18/1347
20. https://www.nhcaa.org/resources/health-care-anti-fraud-resources/the-challenge-of-health-care-fraud.aspx
21. https://www.consumerreports.org/cro/news/2015/03/what-to-do-if-your-doctor-asks-for-your-social-security-number/index.htm
22. http://archive.defense.gov/news/newsarticle.aspx?id=211
23. https://www.idtheftcenter.org/Fact-Sheets/fs-133.html
24. https://www.rocketlawyer.com/document/military-power-of-attorney.rl#/
25. https://www.youtube.com/watch?v=oaQQBAAJlXI
26. www.lifealert.com/fraudalert.aspx
27. https://krebsonsecurity.com/2018/01/registered-at-ssa-gov-good-for-you-but-keep-your-guard-up/
28. www.jacksonville.com/article/20130903/NEWS/801801247

11

Protecting Your Children

When Jeri Marks, mother of 11-year-old Gabriel Jimeniz, went to file her child model son's first tax return, she discovered an unexpected surprise—a return was already filed in his name. Marks notified the police, IRS, and the Social Security Administration, but the identity theft continued.

Many frustrating years later, Marks was reviewing Jimeniz's IRS file and found the identity thief's information. An illegal immigrant was masquerading as Jimeniz to evade deportation. Marks tracked down the identity thief herself and confronted him. Marks recalled to the New York Times, "He said he would give me his refund if I let him continue to use the number." Marks then asked the illegal immigrant to stop using it.

The after-effects of the multiple years of Jimeniz's stolen identity were devastating: Jimeniz couldn't set up bank accounts, get approved for car insurance, or obtain utility accounts in his name. Jimeniz continually had to prove his identity to get anywhere, and his credit was ruined. When looking for a place to live, Jimeniz could only rent apartments that included utilities, because he was told he already had utility accounts opened in his name. It took years for Jimeniz to clear up the false information in his credit history.[1]

Myth "There's a small chance my child's identity will get stolen. They have little to no credit history."

Fact   Actually, bad actors are 35 times more likely to steal a child's identity rather than an adult's. Why? Because children usually don't have a credit history. And unless you are actively monitoring for the opening of a credit file in your child's name, their illegal tactics go unnoticed—sometimes up to 15 years or more.

Parents usually don't check the credit report, or kids don't need to use their credit report until they apply for employment, student loans, or their first car or credit card. This gap in monitoring credit allows thieves to run rampant for many years without setting off any alarm bells. Besides the act of obtaining the Social Security number, the thief also needs to reroute any mailings to a different address to remain undetected. And once an identity thief captures your child's SSN, they can combine it with any person's name and birthdate. Bad actors can find your child's SSN on medical records, as well as on school records, on medical paperwork, in information found on the Internet, and in emails. All it takes is one "bad egg" at a doctor's office, a data breach, or an email compromise to get your child's sensitive information.

Identity thieves can also take more morbid routes to obtaining SSNs, such as perusing a cemetery for deceased children to search for old or latent SSNs potentially to use. Thieves collect bits of information from multiple places, such as school rosters, social media, and Yellow Page–like sites to create a false identity.

MY MOTHER, MY IDENTITY THIEF

Unfortunately, identity theft can also occur inside the family. When an adult wants to apply for a credit line and gets denied, they can go after their child's untouched credit. Axton Betz-Hamilton went to apply for a utility account for the electricity in her off-campus apartment in college. She was denied. Years later, she would discover her identity was stolen when she was in fifth grade—by her mother. Even when Betz-Hamilton won a national award for research on identity theft with her mother standing next to her in honor, she never admitted what she did to her daughter.[2]

The Growing Problem of Child Identity Theft

Each year 1.3 million children have their identities stolen, and 50 percent of those victims are younger than 6 years old.[2] Because of the ease and low detection rate of child identity theft, kids' SSNs are exploited 51 percent more than adults, according to a Carnegie Mellon CyLab study.[3] And unless parents are checking their child's credit report (if there is one active) or receive credit promotions in the mail—or even receive calls from debt collectors—identity thieves can run their credit into the ground, long before the actual child has had a chance to use it.

> **YOUR CHILDREN'S CREDIT RECORDS ARE VULNERABLE—LONG BEFORE YOU THINK**
>
> Shon Shurter started getting worried about his children's identities when his 25-year-old adopted son received a letter about owing money to an online payday loan company. He then thought about his other two children: his 16-year-old daughter and 8-year-old son. Shurter called one of the major credit bureaus to check the children's credit reports. When he got to his daughter's credit file, the woman on the phone had a grim tone; his daughter's credit was ruined. Shurter decided he wasn't going to tell his daughter of his unfortunate discovery, "It's my job as a father to protect my children, and I'm angry, too, and I want to fix it and I can't fix it. I'm in limbo. I'm unable to do anything. This will affect my daughter's ability to get a student loan for college or to get a car after high school or to get her own cell phone. It will affect her for the rest of her life." Shurter also declared a clear warning for parents, "The world is full of predators. It could be your neighbor. You don't know . . . It's a world of information out there, and everyone's getting it, and if you choose not to do anything, you're going to become a victim easily. I never thought it would happen to my kids."[2]

When children are born, the hospital provides information for applying for a SSN—but it's not required.[3] An average child won't enter the credit world until they turn 18 years old. It might be possible to wait on applying for a SSN until they get closer to 18 years of age, but delaying the application could cause complications with doctor's offices, schools, and other organizations that verify identities through a SSN. Read the following for more detailed recommendations on protecting your child's identity.

Recommendations: Protecting Your Child's Identity

The following are the fundamental recommendations to protect the identities of your children from youth into adulthood:

1. **Check Whether Your Child Has a Credit Report**: You may not think to check if your children have credit reports until they reach a certain age, but by not doing so, you don't know whether bad actors have already opened one, racked up debt, and destroyed your child's credit score. Contact all four credit bureaus (Equifax, Experian, TransUnion, and Innovis) to check whether your child has an active report. If there is one, review it to ensure no fraudulent activity has occurred, and place a security freeze on it (see the next recommendation). If there is not a report, you may consider opening one and placing a security freeze on it to keep it locked down vs. being unknown.

2. **Request a Security Freeze**: Security, or credit, freezes significantly reduce the chances of bad actors opening credit accounts in the names of your children. A security freeze prevents new credit lines from opening. In the rare occasions when your child needs to open a credit line, you can unfreeze the credit file temporarily. Security freezes are by far the best method of identity protection, and it's easy to request them.

3. **Guard Your Children's Social Security Number**: Give out your children's SSN only to those who genuinely need it. Most health insurers don't need your child's SSN, only Medicare, so ask your healthcare provider why they need your SSN as well. If an entity does require it, ask them why they need it, how they store it, and how they protect it.

4. **Talk with Your Kids About Keeping Information Private**: Ensure your children ask you, the parent, for permission before giving out sensitive information, such as their SSN, birthdate, mailing address, mother's maiden name, and so forth. Also discuss the implications of sharing information about you, too. Store sensitive documents in a safe with a

strong passcode or, even better, a fingerprint scanner. Avoid using keys, since children can find keys and copy them, resulting in a greater risk of your most valued information getting out.

5. **Be Careful When Opting Out of Preapproved Credit Offers for Your Child**: In doing so, you unknowingly create a credit file for your child. Once this happens, you can either place a credit freeze on the child's credit file to prevent accounts from being opened (highly recommended) or continuously monitor the file, which is less preferable and doesn't prevent credit lines from being opened.[3]

6. **Lock Down Your Child's Federal Student Aid (FAFSA) Account**: Bad actors could gain access to your child's FAFSA account using just their name, SSN, and birthdate. Once in, they can potentially view more than 200 data points, such as a driver's license number, parent's SSN, adjusted gross income (AGI), and more.[4] Ensure your child's FAFSA account has a strong, unique password that is created and stored in your password manager. Save PINs in the password manager as well.

Protecting Your Child on the Computer

THE "SLITHERY" SLOPE OF BEING A CHAMPION GAMER

Danny was becoming a champion at playing the massively popular Slither .io game. He was starting to understand how to create the longest worm to beat players all over the globe. "If I could just figure out how to win more often," Danny thought. Typing "Slither.io win all the time" into YouTube, he watched a video by a popular gamer, called Jelly, on how to beat the game. While watching, he noticed an advertisement in the top right of the YouTube page. It said, "Play Slither.io." Danny clicked it, thinking it would get him to the browser-based game more quickly. It brought him to a landing page that prompted Danny to download a web-based extension. "I didn't have to download a browser extension to play Slither.io before. Maybe this has to do with the secret to winning." When Danny clicked Download, his web browser came back with a pop-up, "Are you sure you want to add this extension? 'Advertisement Offers by GamerSuperstar' can read and change all your data on the websites you visit."[5] Danny noticed the name of the extension was different than the name of the game. Declaring this a red flag, Danny clicked Cancel and found the direct URL to the game. Danny told his parents about the weird run-in with the browser extension so they could run a virus scan to make sure there wasn't any weird malware hanging around after he clicked Download.

Danny's family lived "happily ever after" with no malware, antivirus intact and updated, and clear communication between child and parent about red flags on the Internet. Don't we wish this was true for everyone? Instead, if kids don't have a thorough understanding of staying safe while on the Internet, they will click through as many windows as they need to beat a game or get a high score.

To make sure this doesn't happen, ask your child about the games they are playing and do your research. Make sure they know the risks of bad actors who will do anything to get malware on your PC and steal your information and identity. There are additional risks to privacy when it comes to online gaming, such as the threat of child predators who talk to and stalk children through friend requests and chat features in games.

BE ON THE LOOKOUT FOR ONLINE GAMING PREDATORS

Roblox, an incredibly popular multiplayer, role-playing online gaming site, is known as the "new Minecraft." It caught heat when parents started complaining about predators contacting their children through the chat feature in different game rooms on the website. Ian Morrison, 33, and father of an 8-year-old Roblox player, read an article on potential risks of the game and decided to check out the game for himself. Within 15 minutes of gameplay, he met a potential predator. He went into the first game room and didn't see anything too strange. In the next room, he was propositioned. First, he was asked his gender and age; he said he was an 8-year-old boy. The in-game character asked Morrison to follow him to a house, where they ended up in a bedroom. The anonymous person asked Morrison's character to lay down on top of the other character and started making sexual movements. The anonymous person then said things like, "You look cute/sexy." He stopped playing right there, sickened, and said, "I can imagine if I didn't watch [his children playing the game], and they kept going back to the same rooms and chatting to the same people; it could be so easy for them to take it further."[6]

To mitigate the chances of your child conversing with potential predators, or even bad actors, set the privacy settings appropriately to lessen the chances of conversation with unknown people from occurring. Allegedly, even if the chat settings are turned off in a game like Roblox, gamers can still receive friend requests from strangers.[7] Make sure you supervise your child's gameplay and talk with them about cyber risks, especially when it comes to online chatting.

Myth "To protect my kids on the Internet, all I need to do is to install activity monitoring tools."

Fact Services that implement parental controls and monitor children's web usage can be beneficial, but only when used to supplement an open-door policy of talking about Internet safety and other security measures such as proper password management, device updates, and antivirus technology. It is crucial to communicate the importance of behaving respectfully and cautiously online. By only using monitoring tools without added communication, it can lead to kids finding ways to get past them (they'll try their hardest) and create an environment of distrust and paranoia.[8]

Smart Toy Risks

BEWARE OF TOO SMART TOYS

The "Internet of Toys" is a booming industry, and it is forecasted to exceed $15.5 billion by 2022.[9] Included in the Internet of Toys universe is the My Friend Cayla doll, which allows parents to listen to their children through a Bluetooth microphone and app. In Germany, the Cayla doll is considered a spy and has been ordered to be destroyed. This smart doll, created by Genesis Toys, is forbidden to be sold, purchased, and owned by anyone in Germany. Parents who are caught not destroying the doll could face two years in prison as well as an approximate fine of $26,500. Parents were required to obtain a certificate from a waste management company to confirm it was obliterated to send in to the Federal Network Agency, a telecommunication overseer in Germany.[10] The major concern with the Cayla doll's technology is a bad actor's ability to spy on and converse with a child to obtain sensitive information. A bad actor could hack into the doll's Bluetooth communications using a malicious app up to 50 feet away.

Bad actors aren't the only concern either. Companies that build smart toys for children can sell audio recorded through the toy and hand it over to third parties. Children under 13 have privacy protection through the U.S. Children's Online Privacy Protection Act (COPPA), which mandates companies providing online services to post a privacy policy and obtain consent from parents before collecting and sharing collected data from the smart toy. A complaint was filed against the Cayla doll, as well as similar "spy toys," like the I-Que Intelligent Robot, stating they violate COPPA. The groups that filed the complaint included the Campaign for a Commercial Free Childhood (CCFC), the Center for Digital Democracy (CDD), Consumers Union, and the Electronic Privacy Information Center (EPIC).

CCFC's executive director, Josh Golin, commented on the risks of smart toys by saying, "Children form friendships with dolls and toys with 'personalities,' and confide intimate details about their lives with them. It is critical that the sensitive data collected by these toys be subject to the most stringent protections and not be used for manipulative and sneaky marketing." The filed complaint also exposes Genesis' failure adequately to protect the Cayla doll from unauthorized Bluetooth connection attempts, allowing bad actors to spy on the connection with the right app. EPIC's director of the Consumer Privacy Project, Claire T. Gartland, also warned, "With the growing Internet of Things, American consumers face unprecedented levels of surveillance in their most private spaces, and young children are uniquely vulnerable to these invasive practices. The FTC has an obligation here to step in and safeguard the privacy of young children against toys that spy and companies that exploit their very voices for corporate gain." Included in the complaint are statements that Genesis didn't provide a privacy policy or obtain parental permission before collecting and sharing data from its My Friend Cayla doll.

Genesis also shares its voice recordings with Nuance, an organization that may use the "spy" doll's voice recordings for law enforcement and military intelligence product purposes. Gartland commented on this use of voice recordings, "Genesis and Nuance are completely disregarding their legal and ethical obligations when it comes to kids' privacy. Instead, they have chosen to exploit children's sensitive voice recordings and private conversations for corporate profit. It is extremely alarming that what a child says to her 'trusted' friend could end up in a voice biometrics database sold to law enforcement and intelligence agencies."[11]

Smart toys are known to have embedded technologies like GPS tracking, microphones, cameras, data storage and transmission capabilities, speech recognition, and more. These features are meant to bring a livelier experience but can put your children's and your sensitive information at risk. Not only are bad actors interested in obtaining data from smart toys to perform identity theft, but third-party corporations are collecting and selling toy data too.

On occasion, toy manufacturers experience data breaches, such as Cloud-Pets, where millions of voice messages saved from their smart toys were exposed online. CloudPets stored a database filled with personal information on 821,396 users, which could be used to access more than 2 million voice messages. The parent company of CloudPets, Spiral Toys, moved customer data into a database that wasn't protected behind a firewall or even used a password. Bad actors easily found the database, deleted the data, and held it for a ransom. The breach was far from a "minimal issue," contrary to what the CEO of Spiral Toys stated. Bad actors could use the exposed data to steal the identities of children, and only when the child is old enough to have a credit history will they discover their credit was already tarnished many years prior. Troy Hunt, an investigative cybersecurity researcher and reporter, commented on the negligence, "To suggest that the exposure and ransom of a database containing 821k user records and providing access to millions of voice recordings from and to children represents 'a very minimal issue' is just unfathomable."[12]

The following are the core actions to protect yourself and your children before purchasing smart toys and when using them in your house.

Recommendations: Protecting Smart Toys

The following are the FBI's crucial recommendations to safeguard your children when they play with smart toys connected to the Internet:[13]

1. **Research the Smart Toy's Cybersecurity Practices**: Look into the cybersecurity practices of the toy's manufacturer. Type the toy's name and cybersecurity in a search engine, and you should find tech articles reviewing the toy, its cybersecurity, and whether there are any known risks.
2. **Research the Smart Toy's Privacy Practices**: Find out where the company's data is stored and with whom they share the toy's collected data. Smart Toys used by children ages 13 and younger need to comply with

COPPA regulations. Make sure you can directly contact the company to address any questions or concerns, as well as receive notifications of any known vulnerabilities or security updates available.

3. **Connect Smart Toys to Trusted, Secure Network**: Only connect smart toys to your home network, and if possible, place them on a separate network specifically for smart toys. This will keep the smart toys segregated from your family's core network, preventing any monitoring of your web traffic by the toy, and it will protect the toy from any malware residing on your primary network.

4. **Encrypt and Authenticate Connections to the Smart Toy**: Verify the Internet connection between the toy and the Internet is encrypted, and enable authentication for any Bluetooth connections. Toys that don't have these basic cybersecurity mechanisms are not secure and should not be purchased.

5. **Promptly Apply Updates to the Smart Toy**: Just like your computer can get malware from not having updates installed, smart toys can get compromised too. Apply updates as soon as they are available. Enable automatic updates if possible.

6. **Monitor Your Children's Activity with Smart Toys**: Review and purge recorded conversations and audio recordings through the toy's app, if possible, to ensure there isn't any suspicious activity or sensitive information leaked.

7. **Turn Off the Smart Toy When Not in Use**: To protect your privacy, turn off smart toys when your children are not using them. Toys with microphones and video recording capabilities can still passively record while not in use.

8. **Use Strong and Unique Passwords for User Accounts**: Generate strong and unique passwords for smart toy accounts using your password manager. Enable two-factor authentication if the feature is available.

9. **Input Only Necessary Info for the User Account**: Don't hand over more information than the toy vendor needs. There is a good chance they are sharing this info with other third-party corporations. Also, by reducing the sensitive info you enter, it can limit what bad actors see if the vendor's database is ever breached and exposed online.

10. **File a Complaint If You Suspect the Toy Is Compromised**: Visit the Internet Crime Complaint Center (IC3) at `https://www.ic3.gov/default.aspx` to file a complaint if you suspect anything suspicious is occurring with your child's smart toy.

In addition to these recommendations to protect your children's use of their smart toys, the following are specific steps to protect your children when they use computers and the Internet.

Recommendations: Protecting Your Children Online

The following are core recommendations to protect your child's online presence and device usage, which will resultantly protect your family's identity and device security:

1. **Create Secure Individual Computer Accounts**: Create one account for each individual in your family. Combining everyone, especially adults with children, into one account is a big no-no. In doing so, you increase your risk of infection, loss, and/or manipulation of information you hold dear. When creating an account for your children, remove administrative access, which would allow them to make changes to the computer. Explain to them the reason why you are configuring the settings this way so they can be informed on cybersecurity as they develop their maturity when it comes to computer and Internet use. When it comes to your account, as an administrator, ensure you create a unique username and password and not one your child knows or can easily guess.

2. **Consider Parental Control Software**: In addition to good, clear communication, parental control tools can be helpful when supervising your children's technology and Internet usage. Without a clear understanding of why you are monitoring their activity, children will look for ways around the parental controls by using a virtual private network (VPN) to bypass content filters or trying different browsers until they get through. Parental control tools fall into a gray area when it comes to social media. When your kids log on to their social media accounts, such as Facebook, you'll need to know their login credentials or convince them to install a monitoring app if you want to supervise their activity. Another great feature to look for in parental control tools is remote management, which allows you to respond to time-extension requests, review flagged social media posts, and/or receive notifications when your child attempts to access a blocked site and more. Advanced

tools allow you to track your child's YouTube and Hulu viewing history, track their location, or remotely lock their device. Some well-known, and highly rated, parental control tools include Apple's iOS Software version 12 and above, Qustodio, Net Nanny, Circle, and more.[14]

You've learned some significant ways to protect your child when it comes to their identity, credit file, computer usage, and online gaming and chatting, as well as the best way to mix parental control tools and clear communication.

Next up, you'll learn how to protect your money and keep an eye out for bad actors' financial scams whose aim is to obtain your payment card and bank account information.

Notes

1. https://www.nytimes.com/2007/07/21/business/21idtheft.html
2. https://www.freep.com/story/money/business/2016/08/28/child-id-theft-problem/89352016/
3. https://www.cylab.cmu.edu/_files/pdfs/reports/2011/child-identity-theft.pdf
4. https://krebsonsecurity.com/2017/11/namedobssnfafsa-data-gold-mine/
5. https://blog.malwarebytes.com/cybercrime/2018/04/malicious-gaming-extensions-a-childs-play-to-infection/
6. https://www.thesun.co.uk/news/2872376/horrified-dad-found-sick-messages-from-paedo-predator-in-his-eight-year-old-sons-roblox-ipad-game/
7. https://thecybersafetylady.com.au/2017/06/is-roblox-safe-for-kids/
8. https://www.commonsensemedia.org/blog/5-myths-and-truths-about-kids-internet-safety
9. https://www.juniperresearch.com/press/press-releases/smart-toy-sales-to-grow-threefold
10. https://www.marketplace.org/2017/04/14/world/Cayla-connected-doll-spy-must-be-destroyed
11. https://consumersunion.org/news/internet-connected-toys-are-spying-on-kids-threatening-their-privacy-and-security/
12. https://www.esecurityplanet.com/network-security/cloudpets-breach-exposes-2-million-childrens-and-parents-private-messages.html
13. https://www.ic3.gov/media/2017/170717.aspx
14. https://www.pcmag.com/article2/0,2817,2346997,00.asp

12 Protecting Your Money

Adam Draper had a busy day ahead of him. His entire day was filled with back-to-back interviews to locate startups companies to incubate. By mid-day, Draper's business partner, Brayton Williams, commented on the excessive amount of furniture Draper purchased. Draper did recently purchase a rug, but it wasn't excessive, nor would he classify it as furniture, so he brushed off Williams' comment. Williams brought it up again, "So I don't think you would do this, but I just wanted to check to make sure, I have a bill here for $50,500 worth of furniture." Draper figured this had to be a prank—he was very frugal and would never spend tens of thousands of dollars on furniture. He called his accountant to discuss the furniture invoice. The accountant claimed he received emails from Draper requesting him to pay the $50,500 invoice to the "furniture company." The accountant performed the transfer diligently, even though he thought it was odd, but he wanted to respect Draper's privacy and independence by not questioning the purchase. Draper never sent any emails about paying a furniture invoice. Draper then checked his email account—he didn't see any emails in his inbox from his accountant. Then he checked the Sent box and found emails he never wrote, telling his accountant to complete a transfer to the furniture company.

The bad actor was logged into Draper's email and was even signing fraudulent emails with his actual, unique sign-off. The bad actor hid the conversations by creating a rule to move any emails from the accountant, as well as others associated with wiring money, to the Trash box. Draper immediately changed his email password, as well *as every other account password (since the bad actor could reset all of his accounts if the compromised email account was used as his password recovery email). Draper also turned on two-factor authentication on all accounts, which would prevent the bad actor from getting into his email again. Attempting to recover his funds, Draper called his bank, Wells Fargo, and discovered the wire already went out earlier in the day and now was out of the bank's hands. Because of differing fraud policies between banks, he had to attempt to communicate with a completely different bank—the bad actor's bank—with no sense of assurance or support from his primary bank. After two weeks of not hearing anything from Wells Fargo—except for, "Every day you don't get your money back, the less likely it is you will get your money"—he finally received an email from a Wells Fargo representative to sign a "Hold Harmless and Indemnification Agreement," before they even tried to help him.[1] Draper learned some valuable lessons the hard way.*

I will teach you the essential steps to protect your money, and the money of your company, so you don't lose your valuable assets. In this chapter, you'll learn about the major types of financial fraud to watch out for and how to lock down your money.

Home Buyer Wire Transfer Fraud

Wire transfer fraud is becoming a more significant problem, especially with bad actors posing as real estate brokers and real estate lawyers.

WIRE TRANSFER FRAUD: ALL A BAD ACTOR NEEDS IS INTERNET ACCESS

A bad actor scammed Mike Malone of Upstate New York out of $500,000, meant for his purchase of a vacation condominium in Deerfield Beach, Florida. Malone received an email from someone who he thought was the broker, which included instructions on transferring one-half million dollars to a Bank of America account. Malone's wife went to the bank and performed the wire transfer according to the instructions they received. Malone checked with the broker to confirm receipt of the transmission and learned some shocking news. The broker never sent an email with wire transfer instructions. Upon further inspection, the email address used to send the fraudulent email was similar to the broker's company domain name, except for the letter y. The bad actor registered a similar copycat website and created an email address almost identical to that of the real broker to fool the Malones and other targets. The bad actors also blocked Malone's Internet access and rerouted some of his phone messages to complete the wire transfer fraud scheme. Fortunately for the Malones, and not a common happening, U.S. Secret Service agents helped recover the funds by freezing the bad actor's bank account and making arrests.[2]

Wire transfer fraud, as FBI special agent Michael Nail called it, is like "modern-day bank robbery." All a bad actor needs to steal your life savings is Internet access.

Next up is another scam targeting homeowners, specifically, their home equity lines of credit (HELOCs).

Home Equity Wire Transfer Fraud

Tobechi Onwuhara was a legendary kingpin of home equity fraud, suspected to have brought in $80 to $100 million from "modern-day bank robbing" in less than three years. *Fortune Magazine* described how Onwuhara and his team of bad actors carried out their cyber scams: "He'd set up a boiler room in a fancy hotel (the Waldorf-Astoria was a favorite) to wash information on wealthy victims. Then he'd wash bank accounts. One group in his crew would do online research using databases and websites to harvest names, dates of birth, and mortgage information. They'd build profiles of victims for a second group, who would call banks posing as account holders. The callers cadged security information and passwords, and then Onwuhara would breach the accounts and wire funds from them to a network of money mules he had established in Asia. The money would be laundered and wired back to his accounts in the United States."

Onwuhara specialized in diverting funds from HELOCs at banks, which held sums of money for qualified homeowners. Onwuhara performed the home equity wire transfer fraud by collecting mortgage data on married couples with million-dollar homes since they would be eligible for a HELOC. After locating public real estate documents, Onwuhara would copy the signatures using Photoshop and save them for future signature forging. Onwuhara then built profiles on the targets using publicly available information on background search sites, Ancestry.com, and more. With the profile built, Onwuhara checked the target's credit using AnnualCreditReport.com. He bypassed an identity verification phase that asked personal questions such as "What address did you live at?" by refreshing the page. In doing so, the right answer would reappear, while the wrong ones would randomize. Once he obtained the target's credit report, he identified their HELOC details. At this point, he would call the bank, spoofing his phone number to look like the target's exact phone number, and impersonate the victim to initiate a wire transfer of their HELOC funds out of the country.

Onwuhara's scam grew to where he had multiple employees who took over each phase of the scheme. The FBI began investigating Onwuhara and listened to thousands of recorded calls to obtain his identity. Finally, during one phone call, Onwuhara impersonated a doctor to phone in a prescription to CVS and stated the patient's name—Tobechi Onwuhara.[3] The FBI now had the name of the home equity fraud kingpin, but they just needed to arrest him. Onwuhara stayed on the run for four more years. Onwuhara was finally arrested in Australia and brought back to the United States where he was sentenced to nearly six years in prison, followed by five years of supervised release for his attempts to steal more than $38 million and causing $13 million in victim losses.[4]

IRS Impersonation Fraud

In a new scam, bad actors are breaking into tax preparation firm accounts to submit fraudulent refund requests. Once the money is directly deposited in the client's bank account, the bad actors contact the victim, posing as a collection agency contracted with the IRS and claiming the refund was sent in error. Using fake IRS letterhead, they send an initial email with the subject "Transaction Error Correction Letter." In the email the bad actors claim that the IRS Audit Office investigated the victim and determined the deposited refund was "erroneous" and needs to be returned to them through the outsourced "collection agency." To make the request more believable, they include bits of the client's sensitive information (for example, last four of SSN and bank account, name, address, and so on), which were stolen from the hacked tax preparer's account. The bad actors demand that the full amount be "returned" or else the victim will face criminal charges. The bad actors demand the victim to return the deposit within 24 hours of the receipt of the letter via the wire transfer instructions.

The IRS issued warnings to tax preparers to increase their security because of the elevated fraudulent refund return request attacks. The IRS recommends that taxpayers who received fraudulent tax refunds contact their associated bank, effectively to close the account and open a new one since the bad actors have access to their bank account information. In addition, the taxpayer should also contact their tax preparer to notify them of the fraud. Taxpayers may also discover that bad actors have already filed a return in their name—stealing their hard-earned refund. When any type of tax return fraud occurs, the IRS advises the victim to fill out and mail Form 14039, an *identity theft affidavit*, which attests they were a victim of a tax return scam.[5]

In addition, there a number of steps you can take if you experience an IRS impersonation scam.

1. **Report the IRS Scam to the U.S. Treasury Dept.**: Report IRS impersonation scams at this site: https://www.treasury.gov/tigta/contact_report_scam.shtml.
2. **File a Complaint with the Federal Trade Commission (FTC)**: The FTC investigates consumer fraud. Report an IRS impersonation scam at this site: https://www.ftccomplaintassistant.gov/Information#crnt&panel1-1.
3. **Report Suspicious Phishing Emails to the IRS**: Forward IRS impersonation phishing emails to this IRS email address to report them: phishing@irs.gov.

Credit Card Fraud

When someone catches a suspicious charge on their credit card, panic may ensue, and they want to get to the bottom of the mystery of "How did my credit card get stolen?" This is a losing game. The place where your stolen card was used to make fraudulent purchases is rarely the source of the original breach.

According to Brian Krebs, cybersecurity researcher and investigative reporter, the following are the primary ways credit cards get stolen. All of them, except for one situation, have a low-to-zero chance of discovery. The important thing is to react quickly to halt the fraud and work on recovering your funds.[6]

Hacked Merchant or Restaurant   Occurs mainly from a malware-infected point-of-sale (PoS) device at the location. Bad actors steal credit card numbers and place them on counterfeit makeshift cards to purchase gift cards or high-price items, which are resold for cash.

Bad Actor Employee   Common among restaurant workers who handle your credit card, take it out of your view, and stealthily copy down your information.

Breached Online Store   When an online store's website or customer database becomes compromised, online fraud ensues. Victims may find fraudulent charges on monthly statements and incorrectly assume the company where the fraud took place was where their card number was initially stolen. This is usually never the case. Attempting to find the source of your breached financial information is nearly impossible. And bank customer service representatives are trained specifically not to give out information about a breached online store or certain details about your fraudulent purchase.

Payment Processor Breach   A payment processor, such as Square or PayPal, is the intermediary between the place where you make a purchase and the credit card companies and banks where your funds are located. If a payment processor is breached, a large amount of card numbers can be stolen quickly.

Hacked Point-of-Sale Service Company   A PoS company makes either software, hardware, or both for a merchant's cashier checkout system at a store. When a PoS service company is breached, it results in financial fraud of customer card numbers.

ATM or Gas Pump Card Skimmer Fraud   Bad actors use *skimmers*, which are devices that fit inside a card-swipe mechanism and steal your card information. Skimmers found at ATMs and gas pumps are commonly tied to gangs, and the resulting fraud is hard to detect.

Malware on a PC   When a malicious program downloads in a person's computer, it can record data that has been input into a website, such as a payment card number, bank account information, and more. This data is transmitted back to the bad actors who then commit fraud with your stolen information. You can discover a malware infection if you have a good antivirus program, but discovering the resulting fraud and seeing the correlation between it and the malware can be difficult.

Theft of Physical Paper Records   When an organization loses physical records to theft, such as improperly disposing of sensitive information, your personal information goes into the hands of bad actors. This type of fraud is less common than the others listed.

Lost or Stolen Card   When an individual loses their payment card, they usually know within a short timeframe and alert their bank or credit card company, which can limit the amount of financial fraud that can take place. This is the one case where there is a high chance of a consumer learning about the source of any ensuing fraud.

Gift Card Fraud

Gift cards can sit around for months before they're used, which gives bad actors a running start in their attempts to steal the loaded funds. It is safer to purchase gift cards online, directly from the intended company, than it is to purchase them in a store. Bad actors are known to take nonactivated gift cards and scratch off the back, which reveals the card number and PIN. They purchase rolls of look-a-like scratch-off tape to put back on the card and place it back on the shelf for unsuspecting victims to purchase. The bad actors wait at home and monitor the gift card account and use it immediately after it activates. The victim then gives the already emptied card to someone as a gift, and unbeknownst to them, they won't be able to use it.

To protect yourself from falling victim to a gift card scam, follow these FBI's recommendations:[7]

- Purchase gift cards only from the company's website.
- Verify reputable gift card resellers and read reviews.
- Check the gift card balance immediately upon purchase.
- Be wary of auction listings selling discounted gift cards.
- Use the gift card as soon as you are able; don't let it sit.
- When selling a gift card online, don't publicly list the PIN until someone purchases the card.
- Report any gift card balance fraud to the card seller.

Card Skimmer Fraud

Any time you insert or swipe a payment card at an ATM, gas pump, retail checkout, and more, there is a chance that a bad actor has installed a *card skimmer* —a tiny piece of technology designed to steal your payment information. Card skimmers can be difficult to detect because of their small size or a real-looking overlay of the actual card-swiping mechanism. Bad actors can also install small cameras, hidden from view, that record your PIN as well. Before you know it, a bad actor has your payment information and is off making fraudulent purchases, which can take a while to detect.

To prevent getting foiled by card skimmer fraud, Brian Krebs also recommends following these steps:[8]

Use Credit Cards or Mobile Payment Apps vs. Debit   If you use a credit card and your info gets stolen, it'll be more difficult for bad actors to turn it into cash than if they had your debit card number. Mobile Payment apps are even better because the vendor doesn't know your payment information, and neither does the bad actor. The safest, but less convenient, way to pay for transactions is with cash.

Conceal Typing Your PIN   Bad actors use tiny cameras to record you typing in your PIN at an ATM or gas pump. To avoid detection, use your non-typing hand to cover your typing.

Use ATMs Only on Weekdays   ATMs are inspected by banks consistently during the week and not as much on the weekends. This means bad actors have a greater chance of stealing your payment information through a card skimmer on the weekend. When no one is around, usually on a Friday night or Saturday morning, they install card skimmers and take them out before anyone notices. And they love long, holiday weekends when banks are closed and are not checking the ATMs.

Avoid Using ATMs Not Located at the Bank   ATMs located in third-party locations, such as restaurants, clubs, gas stations, corner stores, bars, and more, are riskier to use. These ATMs are left exposed for bad actors to hack, install card skimmers, monitor, and more.

Pick Your Gas Pump Carefully   Gas pump card skimmers are commonly found at gas stations near highways. This allows for bad actors to escape quickly after installing and retrieving their malicious technology.

When picking a gas pump, choose the one closest to the gas station and the attendant and the one that has security cameras.

Monitor Your Bank and Credit Card Statements   You are responsible for reporting fraudulent charges. Your financial institution will not always catch them for you. If you don't keep a close eye on your accounts and report suspected fraud, you won't be reimbursed. Sign up for text alerts when a new transaction shows up.

Scams Targeting the Unbanked and Underbanked

There are approximately 9 million U.S. households that are unbanked—meaning they don't have a checking or savings account. More than that, nearly 25 million families are "underbanked," meaning they have a bank account but also use alternative financial services (AFS) outside of the banking system, such as money orders, check cashing, payday loans, rent-to-own services, pawn shop loans, and auto title loans.[9]

Bad actors target the unbanked and underbanked through scams such as prepaid card fraud, fake jury duty absence penalties, false lottery winning notifications, offers of nonexistent loans, phishing emails, and more.[10] Some scam scenarios involve bad actors impersonating a utility company or law enforcement claiming the victim needs to pay a fine or else they'll face legal ramifications.

As more Americans rely on prepaid cards, bad actors are shifting their attack methods. They direct underbanked victims to load cash onto a Green Dot MoneyPak card, which has only a 14-digit code on the back. The bad actor requests the 14-digit code and instantly compromises the card and steals their hard-earned funds. Other scams include bad actors claiming to give under-banked individuals a loan, but first they need payments through MoneyPak or a prepaid card. Prepaid and gift cards sometimes don't have the same security features as credit and debit cards provided by major banks and credit card companies. This leaves the underbanked at risk of bad actors using card skimmers more effectively when an EMV chip isn't used on a prepaid card. Green Dot commented on MoneyPak fraud saying, "Consumers should protect their MoneyPak numbers just as they would cash, and Green Dot makes vigorous efforts to remind consumers on the MoneyPak packaging and website never to give their information to a private individual, to someone claiming you have won a prize or lottery, or to pay for items purchased from classified ads."[11]

To protect your family's money from bad actors who are looking to gain access to your payment information any way they possibly can, it's crucial to perform the "Brilliance in the Basics" habits regularly, in addition to the security recommendations described next.

Recommendations: Protecting Your Money

The following are crucial steps to protect your money, bank and credit accounts, and fraud liability, as well as how to use your payment card safely each day.

1. **Enable Two-Factor Authentication**: It is critical to enable two-factor authentication. But the unfortunate truth is most banks haven't adopted two-factor authentication. Banks work to comply with the Federal Financial Institutions Examination Council's (FFIEC) cybersecurity standards, but because of how they're written, banks are left to interpret the need for two-factor authentication implementation.[12] If your bank doesn't have a two-factor authentication option, make sure to create nonpredictable security verification answers.

2. **Use a Password Manager to Create Unique and Complex Passwords per Account**: Since many banks haven't adopted two-factor authentication, it is imperative to create, maintain, and store your passwords using a password manager and ensure your security verification answers cannot be predicted or found in a search engine.

3. **Create a Verbal Password/PIN with Your Bank**: Check with your bank to see whether they will allow you to create a PIN, separate from your debit card PIN, or a verbal passphrase, to lock down your bank account from bad actors who call in and attempt to gain access to your account. Be wary if your bank only accepts an SSN or birthdate as a form of identity verification. This information is found on the Web.

4. **Maintain an Email Account Just for Banking**: Use a unique email address for every category of Web use you perform—banking, shopping, media streaming, and social media. If a bad actor gets ahold of the email account you use for all of your online accounts, the probability of those accounts getting compromised is extremely high, especially if you reuse

passwords (which is a huge no-no). When you use a dedicated email address for banking, you reduce the chance that an adversary will compromise your other accounts.

TIP   Don't put the word *banking* in the email address name; hackers can use this pattern to guess your other email addresses.

5. **Dedicate a Secure Device to Be Used Only for Banking**: Maintain a device, such as a secure iPad, just for accessing your financial accounts through secure banking applications. This can help protect you from downloading malware found in emails and on the Web. When you use a secondary, locked-down device, apart from your primary ones, it works to protect the integrity of your bank account access.

6. **Bookmark Your Bank's Website—Don't Type It In**: By bookmarking your bank's URL, you lessen the chances of incorrectly typing the address in, which could lead you to a copycat, malicious phishing website. Instead, only access your bank account from the bookmarked URL.

7. **Only Use Verified Mobile Banking Apps**: If you perform your banking using a mobile app, ensure you only use verified applications. Bad actors create copycat banking apps, hoping you'll download theirs instead of the real ones. Avast performed a study where it showed participants two different banking app screenshots and asked them which one they thought was authentic and which one was a copycat. Of the 40,000 individuals tested, 36 percent thought the fake banking app was real, and 58 percent of respondents thought the official banking app was fake.[13] In addition to verifying your banking app, verify all other apps on your mobile device and delete any ones that you don't use regularly.

8. **Place a Security Freeze on Your Credit File**: Placing a security freeze on your credit file is the only way to protect your credit. You can unfreeze your credit file when you need to open a credit line, but make sure to reactivate the security freeze afterwards.

9. **Enable Security Alerts on Your Bank and Credit Card Accounts**: Sign up for mobile and email banking alerts to receive notification of suspicious activity. Be sure to watch out for phishing attempts that attempt to impersonate your bank's security alert notifications.

10. **Know Your Fraud Liability**: Ensure your bank has a 0 percent fraud liability policy. As you learned from Claire Pearson's story in Chapter 4, "Attack Methods," if you fall for a phishing scam and provide bad actors

with access to your bank account, you could be liable for accrued charges if you are not covered 100 percent.

11. **Avoid Card-Swipe Skimmers**: Bad actors create tiny electronic devices that fit into the card-swipe machines at ATMs, gas pumps, and more. Unless you know what to look for, you could be entering your credit or debit card into a bad actor's illegal device designed to steal your payment card information. Jiggle all of the parts where the payment card is entered, as well as the PIN keyboard. Crooks create overlays for the card-swiping entry, as well as for the PIN keyboard. When entering your PIN code, cover your typing with your second hand—bad actors can install tiny cameras near the PIN keyboard.[14]

    There are apps available that detect Bluetooth-transmitting card skimmers, which is a more high-tech skimmer.[15] It is best to check the card terminal physically for any red flags. Also, use ATMs and gas pumps in busy areas in clear view of security cameras. Bad actors look for less-traversed ATMs and gas pumps to lessen the chance of getting caught while installing their skimming devices. When in doubt, go to another ATM or card terminal.

12. **Use "the Chip" When Available**: Using chip-based security payment methods, such as dipping your card in the reader or using Apple Pay, is more secure than swiping your card in-person. Most credit and debit cards have Europay, MasterCard, and Visa (EMV) standardized chip technology to secure your transaction by transmitting a one-time use tokenized number instead of your actual payment card number.

    Gas stations are not required to transition to EMV chip card readers until October 1, 2020.[16] Until then, use cash instead of your credit card for the safest transaction possible. If you don't use cash, use a credit card instead of a debit card. Debit transactions are equal to transferring cash, and if you experience debit card fraud, you could be waiting weeks after making a claim to the FDIC. When you use a credit card, your transaction can be retracted more easily.

13. **Dodge Financial Scams**: According to an FTC report released in March 2018, the most reported category of financial scams was fraud—affecting 1.1 million people in 2017. The top categories of fraud included imposter scams, phone services, prize winnings, at-home catalog sales, counterfeit checks, and more.

    Common imposter scams include government agency impersonation (for instance, the IRS), charity organization imitation, pretending to be a family member in trouble, impersonating a real company's technical support, impersonating debt collectors in an attempt to collect fictitious debt, work-from-home scams, and more. In 2017, 350,000 imposter scams occurred with $328 million in total losses.

Seventy percent of financial scammers use the phone to scam victims out of money via wire transfers, which was the most popular choice of payment for bad actors.[17] If you receive a suspicious phone call, slow down and think before responding. When in doubt, hang up and call back the company's genuine phone number. If you feel pressured by bad actors on the phone, reply with one of the following statements: "I need a paper invoice in the mail before paying for anything," "I will look for more information on the company's website and make a decision," or "Sorry, I do not make payments over the phone."

Now you've learned the essential ways to protect your money and payment cards, secure your online bank accounts, spot card skimming devices, and identify and evade financial scams.

Next up, you'll discover how to protect your email account!

Notes

1. https://medium.com/@adamdraper/a-hacker-stole-50k-from-my-bank-account-388822389671
2. https://www.cbsnews.com/news/sophisticated-scammers-now-targeting-homebuyers-by-posing-as-brokers/
3. http://archive.fortune.com/2011/01/24/real_estate/onwuhara_home_equity_fraud_full.fortune/index.htm
4. https://archives.fbi.gov/archives/washingtondc/press-releases/2013/ringleader-of-multi-million-dollar-home-equity-line-of-credit-fraud-scheme-sentenced-to-70-months-in-prison-after-years-as-a-fugitive
5. https://krebsonsecurity.com/2018/02/irs-scam-leverages-hacked-tax-preparers-client-bank-accounts/
6. https://krebsonsecurity.com/2015/01/how-was-your-credit-card-stolen/
7. https://krebsonsecurity.com/2018/05/detecting-cloned-cards-at-the-atm-register/
8. https://www.washingtonpost.com/lifestyle/travel/avoid-atms-on-week-ends-choose-your-gas-pump-wisely-and-other-tips-to-keep-your-finances-safe-when-traveling/2018/04/03/a118a5a2-2ed6-11e8-8ad6-fbc50284fce8_story.html?utm_term=.49261284a7a5

9. https://www.fdic.gov/householdsurvey/2015/2015report.pdf
10. https://cdn2.hubspot.net/hubfs/115290/images/18%20-%20Microbilt-%20 Scams%20that%20target%20the%20underbanked%20SG%20May.pdf
11. https://www.cbsnews.com/news/beware-fraudsters-targeting-the-moneypak-cash-service/
12. https://gizmodo.com/heres-why-your-bank-account-is-less-secure-than-your-gm-1683777281
13. www.businessofapps.com/36-of-people-are-fooled-by-fake-banking-apps/
14. https://www.pcmag.com/article2/0,2817,2469560,00.asp
15. https://www.abcactionnews.com/money/consumer/taking-action-for-you/ free-new-apps-detect-bluetooth-credit-card-skimmers
16. https://usa.visa.com/visa-everywhere/security/emv-at-the-pump.html
17. https://www.forbes.com/sites/zackfriedman/2018/03/09/financial-scam-millennial/#4410e79158e3

13 Protecting Your Email

"You look bored," said Kevin Roose's computer in a monotonic robot voice. Startled, Roose checked his web browser to see whether there were any unclosed videos or ads playing—he couldn't find anything. The string of weird computer events suddenly became clearer—the webcam light turning green intermittently, more error messages than usual, and the creepy voice coming from his Mac—Roose was hacked. And the worst part—he was the one who dared the hackers to destroy his life.

On a quest to investigate how secure he was, as well as to document the experience of being hacked, Roose reached out to two well-known hackers to hack him "as deeply and thoroughly as they could, using all of the tools at their disposal." As the saying goes, "Be careful what you wish for."

Even though he told himself he would be super cautious of what he clicked, Roose fell for a phishing email that granted Dan Tentler, founder of Phobos Group, complete access to Roose's computer. Tentler simply found who hosted Roose's personal website, Square-space, and created a copycat website with "Squarespace" misspelled by one letter. Tentler sent Roose an email from the spoofed Square-space web address claiming there were important security updates available because of "recent security issues," and Roose needed to install an "updated" security certificate on his website to continue to receive the "strongest security." Roose clicked what looked like a genuine link and followed the instructions.

What Roose installed was malware, called a shell, which allowed Tentler to access Roose's computer remotely, record his keystrokes, watch his webcam, and perform any function as if he were Roose himself. Tentler created real-looking macOS pop-up windows requesting Roose's administrator password. Tentler even stole access to his secure password manager, 1Password, because he was logging every button Roose pressed on his keyboard.

Besides spying on Roose through his computer by taking snapshots of his computer screen and of Reese himself through the webcam, Tentler also watched Roose by gaining access to his home security surveillance system. Roose said, "One night, I dozed off while watching Chopped on Netflix, and Dan [Tentler] literally watched me sleep." When Roose met his hired hacker Tentler, he claimed he could've made Roose "homeless and penniless" by draining his bank account, shutting his utilities off, trashing his credit score, deleting troves of data from his devices, and using sensitive information from his email inbox and work chat app to ruin his reputation. With one click of a phishing email link, Roose's life could've been in ruins.[1]

As you have learned, bad actors aren't focusing on you specifically (unless you're a high-profile target—someone very wealthy or who is a celebrity). They're targeting everyone and anyone through large-scale, automated attacks. They're continually delivering concealed cyberattacks to your email inbox, hoping you'll open their malicious email links and attachments to kick off the attack so they can infect your devices and steal your information. Bad actors also steal your email account credentials through the "back door" by looking through exposed data breach databases, such as Yahoo's.

In this chapter, you'll learn more about the damaging effects of data breaches on users and how you can act to protect your email account, even if you are affected by a company's data breach.

Yahoo Data Breach

In 2013 and 2014, Yahoo suffered massive data breaches. A 2013 breach affected 3 billion users; the cause was suspected to be traced back to Russian nationals. The 2014 breach affected 500 million users, and it led to the U.S. Department of Justice indictment of three Russian and one Canadian nationals. Two of the Russian nationals were federal intelligence officers in charge of locating cybercriminals. Instead, they ended up being uncloaked as cybercriminals. The goal of the breach was both political and financial. The hackers searched through the information of those who opposed Vladimir Putin, as well as discovered valuable intel to propel Russia's stance forward. The hacking group invaded the Yahoo accounts of U.S. government and White House officials, military members, and cybersecurity personnel.

The targeted attack against Yahoo didn't just affect high-profile individuals. American citizens felt the aftermath too. Paul Dugas, one Yahoo victim out of the crowd of billions, went to file his taxes after the 2014 breach and was informed that one was already filed in his name. Because of the identity theft, Dugas was unable to apply for financial assistance for his daughter's college tuition. Another Yahoo breach victim, Kimberly Heines, found her Social Security payments were being stolen through an online service called Direct Express, which was connected to her Yahoo email account. Because of the breach and bad actors' exploitation of her email account, Heines was unable to pay her bills and hounded by debt collectors.[2] Even if your email credentials are leaked on the Web, like the billions of unfortunate Yahoo users experienced, you will soon learn the steps to secure your email account from bad actors.

The Value of a Hacked Email Account

There's a good chance you use your primary email address as the username when signing up for an online account. This makes it easy for bad actors to compromise your online accounts once they have access to your email—they already know half of the puzzle to gain entry. In this section, you will learn the importance of creating different email addresses for core purposes, so attackers don't know all the keys to your kingdom. And if you do end up with a compromised email account, you'll make it difficult for them to traverse to your other accounts if they are under a different email address (for example, banking, online shopping, medical information, personal, and so on).

As you know by now, reusing passwords on multiple accounts is comparable to pleading with bad actors to hack you—it's a waiting game before all of your accounts become compromised. And bad actors want access to your email account for countless reasons: to harvest and sell your information and retail accounts, drain your bank accounts, search for job information that could allow them to target your employer, and continue their phishing campaigns by emailing your contacts. Multiple attack pathways can start from bad actors finding your emails with software license keys, cloud storage updates, bank statements, tax filing updates, sent and received files, personal information, invoices for online purchases, work information, access to your email contacts, and more. If a bad actor gains access to your email account, they'll reset your password to delay you from accessing your compromised account, add themselves to your account, forward your emails to specific destinations, add malicious extensions, and/or change your email rules so you can't see their conversations with your email contacts. And if you list a secondary backup email account in your settings, bad actors will attempt to gain access to the secondary account too. The hacking loop continues, but you can avoid becoming a victim by following the fundamental steps to secure your email account in this chapter.

The Challenge of Email Privacy

Email providers offer varying levels of account privacy settings, but most email providers are profiting from your email data. We've all heard the saying "Nothing in life is free," and this applies to free email accounts, too. You may have witnessed an online ad while web browsing that looked eerily similar to what you were talking about with someone through email. This isn't uncommon—email providers use keywords in your emails to send you targeted ads. Google was brought under fire when a U.S. consumer advocacy group discovered the tech giant was allegedly scanning users' emails for keywords to use in targeted advertising. In a 2013 motion to dismiss an individual and class-action complaint, Google stated, "Just as a sender of a letter to a business colleague cannot be surprised that the recipient's assistant opens the letter, people who use Web-based email today cannot be surprised if their emails are processed by the recipient's [email provider] in the course of delivery. Indeed, 'a person has no legitimate expectation of privacy in information he voluntarily turns over to third parties.'" John Simpson, of Consumer Watchdog, responded to Google's analogy in defense of user privacy, "Google's brief uses a wrong-headed analogy; sending an email is like giving a letter to the Post Office. I expect the Post Office to deliver the letter based on the address written on the envelope. I don't expect the mail carrier to open my letter and read it. Similarly, when I send an email, I expect it to be delivered to the intended recipient with a Gmail account based on the email address; why would I expect its content will be intercepted by Google and read?"[3]

Companies need to maximize their profit, and they benefit from providing free accounts. If you have a free Gmail account, configure your privacy settings to reduce the amount of data collection Google performs. Yahoo also got a bad rap in 2016 for creating a custom software program for U.S. intelligence agencies to search all incoming emails to Yahoo users in real-time. Usually, in the case of legal matters, forensic investigators obtain a copy of an individual's emails and search for keyword(s) in a small, defined scope. What Yahoo did for the NSA or FBI was give them access to every single Yahoo user account to search for keywords as emails arrived—with no specific target.[4]

In 2017, the U.S. House of Representatives passed the Email Privacy Act, an amendment to the 1986 Electronic Communications Privacy Act (ECPA), which provides more privacy protections for Americans. The way the ECPA is written, there is no expectation of privacy for email messages. According to Kevin Yoder, a sponsor of the Email Privacy Act, leaving an email on a third-party server "was akin to that person leaving their paper mail in a garbage can at the end of their driveway. Thus, that individual had no reasonable expectation of privacy in regards to that email under the Fourth Amendment." Without the proposed Email Privacy Act, law enforcement can obtain the following without approval of a judge: emails stored longer than 180 days; the email subscriber's name, address, phone records; how long the email account has been active; and IP address. Law enforcement can also acquire the credit card and bank account information of the email subscriber with an administrative subpoena. The Email Privacy Act would require law enforcement to obtain a court-ordered, judge-approved warrant in order to access emails stored longer than 180 days.[5]

Privacy is a balancing act—with more privacy can come less usability. And with more usability may come less privacy. Once you understand your individual needs, you'll be able to choose the right email provider.

Next, you'll learn about locking down your email security, as well as increasing your email privacy.

Recommendations: Protecting Your Email

The following are essential steps to protect your email account—including locking down your email account access, avoiding clicking links in phishing emails, and reviewing what your email provider does with your email data in exchange for signing up for a free email account.

1. **Enable Two-Factor Authentication**: One of the most critical first steps to protect your email account is to enable two-factor authentication, which is sometimes called *two-step verification*. Most email accounts don't enable two-factor authentication by default. Search Google by typing **How to enable two-factor authentication** and the name of your email provider for configuration instructions. Test it by signing out, and back in, to your email. If your email provider gives you a list of one-time passcodes to use when you don't have your mobile device, save it as a secure note in your password manager and not in plaintext.

2. **Use a Password Manager to Create and Manage Unique and Complex Passwords per Account**: It's important to create a complex and unique password for each of your email accounts. To make it more difficult for a bad actor to crack your password, make sure it is complex, it is long, and it doesn't use dictionary words. It is best to use a password manager to create and maintain passwords for all of your accounts.

3. **Create Multiple Email Accounts for Different Purposes**: On a professional résumé, you wouldn't put your personal email `puppy-lover42@email.com`. So, it makes sense then to create a unique email address for each category of your web use—banking, shopping, media streaming, and social media. When creating these different email accounts, don't make it obvious what they are used for. Instead, create an email address that is cleverly disguised. For example, a banking email could be `bluesky@email.com`, with the letter *b* reminding you it's for banking. For online shopping, an email address might be `orangesheep@email.com`, with the *o* reminding you it means "online" and the *sh* translating to "shopping."

4. **Remove Sensitive Information, and Use Secure File Storage**: You have a colossal number of sensitive files and data in your email account. Remove sensitive information from your email account and move it to a secure cloud file storage location. Search for keywords like *default password*, *SSN*, *activation code*, *account details*, and more. Delete unnecessary information or relocate it to a secure location. Soon, you'll learn how to protect your files.

5. **Beware of Phishing Emails**: As you learned in the first story of this chapter, a phishing email can destroy a person's life. Email providers like Google and Microsoft have very good malicious email filtering, and the chance you'll receive one of the simple mass-marketed phishing emails is rare. Still, remain cautious about clicking any email links or

opening any email attachments. Don't reply to email users you don't know, and look for phishing email red flags, such as misspellings, unusual domain addresses (for instance, amazonco.com versus amazon. com), and time-sensitive request demands. Check the sender's email address, and hover over (on the computer) or press down (on a smartphone) on a link to see the actual URL. When in doubt, open a search engine and type in the title of the web page you're looking for versus clicking links in emails.

6. **Access Your Email from Secure Devices**: This may seem pretty straightforward, but it's incredibly important. Ensure the device and the programs you use to access your email are secure and up-to-date. If you access your personal email while at work, on a friend's laptop, or at the library, use a private web browsing page, so your activity doesn't stay on the device's history. And make sure you log out every time (don't enable any "stay signed in" settings).

7. **Check Your Email Account Activity and Settings**: By checking your email account activity, you can remove devices you no longer want connected to your email account, review user access, check for any suspicious login activity, and verify security changes, such as password resets. You can also review the apps or extensions connected to your email account. If you need to use third-party plug-ins, make sure they are trusted, and remove their access once you are done using them. Any third-party who has access to your email account poses a risk to your information. In your email settings, you can manage two-factor authentication, recovery information, and account credentials. Make sure to check settings, such as email forwarding, mailbox rules, plug-ins, and connected devices, too.

8. **Understand Your Email Privacy**: When choosing an email provider, make sure you understand what they're doing with your information, and choose a provider who has experienced the least amount of data breaches and has a robust cybersecurity program (such as Google).

For even more robust email protection, choose an email provider who can't access your emails, provides end-to-end encryption, and doesn't require any personal information to sign-up, such as ProtonMail. ProtonMail is based in Switzerland, home of some of the world's strictest privacy laws, and was founded by MIT and CERN scientists, engineers, and developers who care about protecting online civil liberties. ProtonMail doesn't ask for any personal information to create an email account, it encrypts your messages, your IP address is never tracked, and once you delete your emails, they are gone forever. (There are some downsides to increased privacy.)[5]

In this chapter, you learned about the core ways to protect your email account, what email providers do with your information when you sign up for a free account, and what bad actors want from compromising your email. In the next chapter, you will discover the best methods to protect your files, such as your old tax returns, receipts, travel documents, health records, contracts, real estate documents, and family photos.

Notes

1. https://splinternews.com/i-dared-two-expert-hackers-to-destroy-my-life-heres-wh-1793854995
2. https://torontolife.com/city/crime/kid-made-millions-hacking-emails-fbi-took/
3. www.consumerwatchdog.org/newsrelease/google-tells-court-you-cannot-expect-privacy-when-sending-messages-gmail-people-who-care
4. www.reuters.com/article/us-yahoo-nsa-exclusive-idUSKCN1241YT
5. https://protonmail.com/privacy-policy

14 Protecting Your Files

Sharon, the owner of a small accounting firm, used Google Drive for storing thousands of client files over the years. She knew the benefits of storing files in the cloud and benefited tremendously from her employees' ability to collaborate actively on documents because of Google Drive's features. She took advantage of the live sync feature that allowed everyone at her company to view and modify files on their laptops, which then mirrored all changes in the main Google Drive account.

One day, she went to locate an important client file—it was gone. Sharon started looking in different folders and still couldn't find it. Throughout the day, she started receiving emails from her employees, "Do you know where the files for this month's project went? They might've been moved because I can't seem to find them." Sharon started to panic and checked more file folders and noticed entire folders were missing. Was she the target of bad actors? She then remembered she could check the file activity log in Google Drive.

Sharon reviewed the previous day's activity and found an intern, James, who just started, deleted numerous folders throughout the previous afternoon. "Why would James delete all of these files? This doesn't make sense." Sharon asked James about him deleting folders. James replied, "My laptop was running out of disk space and was running slow, so I deleted folders I wasn't actively using. I don't need to store the entire file archive on my computer, do I?"

Sharon felt embarrassed for not telling James how the file sync feature worked—when anyone deletes a file, it gets deleted from the main cloud account too, not just from the individual's computer. She thought she was doing the right thing by enforcing file sync on everyone's computers without realizing the threat of losing files. She instructed James how to configure his settings properly so he wasn't syncing folders he didn't need to see and store locally. James had no idea his actions on his laptop were impacting everyone else in the cloud.

Next Sharon attempted to recover the hundreds of files, which were all critical to her business, by looking at her Google Drive options. She noticed there was a recycle bin in her account. She went to look and saw some of the files there but didn't see the ones she knew should be there. After performing a partial recovery, she realized she should've purchased a secondary cloud backup program for her Google Drive environment. She would never take such a risk with her precious proprietary files again. Moving forward, Sharon made sure to communicate to new employees about how cloud storage worked when syncing between devices and the main Google Drive account. Sharon realized she couldn't rely on one single storage location to uphold the protection of her files.

Threats to Your Files

Sharon didn't experience an attack from a bad actor, even though she initially thought so. She hadn't anticipated it could be so simple as a misunderstanding of how cloud storage functioned or a simple mistake made by an employee that could cause this terrible file loss.

Sharon could've been attacked by a bad actor if she hadn't secured her cloud storage account, but Sharon knew she enabled two-factor authentication and supplied unique, strong passwords for each of her employee accounts, knowing never to share her administrative account with others. She knew cloud storage provided reliability, accountability, and accessibility for her digital files, but she assumed her files would always be recoverable as they were, which she learned wasn't exactly the reality. Cloud storage provides substantial file protection, storage, and recoverability—but unless you have a secondary backup location, you could find yourself with a *single point of failure*, which occurs when you have your files in only one place, leaving them susceptible to a multitude of risks.

Just as you would perform backups on your computer, it is crucial to perform backups of your cloud storage environment. Sharon never guessed the biggest threat to her files, at that moment, was someone who had access to the cloud storage account but didn't understand how the "file sync" feature worked, which resulted in the erasure of important file folders. Besides accidental data loss, there are a number of other threats to your files—caused by end users or bad actors—which underscores the importance of following the "Brilliance in the Basics" techniques to back up your files in multiple, secure locations for verified file protection.

Threats to Your Files *Not* Caused by Bad Actors

Threats to your files, not sourced from bad actors, can include device hardware/software failure, device loss, electrical surges, waters spills, accidental file deletion, not performing proper backups, not saving your file changes, not performing hardware and software updates, and not storing your files in the best manner possible for accessibility and recoverability.

Threats to Your Files Caused by Bad Actors

Threats to your files, triggered by bad actors, can involve file deletion, modification, corruption, and/or exfiltration of your files. Malware, like ransomware, is one of the biggest threats to the accessibility and integrity of your files. Ransomware comes from malicious links and attachments from emails and web pages and encrypts your files, preventing you from accessing them, until you pay a monetary ransom. There is no guarantee you'll get your files back, and unless you have "clean" backups, without ransomware, usually the only choice of recoverability is to pay the bad actors. Other threats can include lost, damaged, or stolen devices, such as laptops, USB sticks, and external hard drives.

Don't forget to protect physical documents, too. Sensitive paper documents can be vulnerable to damage, loss, and/or theft. Your confidential papers should be stored in a secure, locked safe. Ensure you use a shredder to destroy sensitive information before disposal. And remember, bad actors also like to go dumpster diving for your discarded paperwork, such as credit offers, tax forms, and more!

Cloud Storage vs. Local Storage

Cloud storage is when your files are stored in a cloud provider's data center, allowing you simply to visit a website, or use their application, to access them versus storing them on your computer. Today, we access and share most of your digital media from the cloud, like streaming movies and TV shows instead of buying DVDs, streaming music instead of purchasing CDs, and sharing digital files through email and cloud storage sites versus handing someone a USB stick with your file. The cloud, as compared to storing files locally on your computer, provides immense protection, accessibility, and productivity benefits. Most cloud providers automatically encrypt and protect your files with their security defenses in place in their cloud environment. You can retrieve your data from any device, anywhere, and you can rapidly collaborate and share files with others. To use cloud file storage, you need an Internet connection and to sign up for an account. There are free cloud storage accounts available with specific storage limits. If you know you'll go beyond the file storage limit or you need additional assistance and features, a paid account may provide a better fit.

Additionally, in this section, you will find the core responsibilities you need to carry out when either using cloud or local file storage. You will notice the responsibilities when using cloud storage are less than using local file storage. Cloud providers take care of the security updates, protection mechanisms, encryption, and more, for you. You still need to practice the "Brilliance in the Basics" techniques to protect your devices and information, but cloud providers can make security less of a lift when you want to make sure your files are protected.

Your Cloud File Storage Responsibilities

Using cloud file storage works impeccably as long as you do the following to secure your environment:

- Enable two-factor authentication
- Create a strong and unique password for each account
- Maintain regular cloud backups in a secondary location
- Understand and configure your privacy settings

Your Local File Storage Responsibilities

When storing files locally on your computer, you need to implement the following to secure your environment:

- Encrypt your files on your computer and hard drive(s)
- Use and update your antivirus program
- Enable ransomware protection features (if available through your operating system or antivirus program)

- Keep your hardware and software up-to-date
- Perform regular backups of your files
- Secure access to your computer
- Avoid clicking malicious links and attachments in emails and on web pages

Finding the Right Cloud Provider

There are a variety of cloud storage providers from which to choose. Once you know your specific needs for file storage, sync, and retrieval, you can pinpoint the best one for the job. Well-known, commonly used cloud storage providers include Google Drive, Apple iCloud Drive, Microsoft OneDrive, Dropbox, and Box. Most of these cloud providers encrypt your data for you, but they are in control of the key that unlocks and locks your information.

If you want to be in control of your data encryption, there are cloud providers that have computer programs you can download that encrypt your files locally on your computer prior to being uploaded to their cloud environment. Handling your own encryption has its risks, but it can be a more robust option for those who want to be in control of encrypting their sensitive data. By taking this route, you do so at your own risk. You are responsible for securely storing your private encryption key, as well as keeping your computer's environment secure and up-to-date when accessing the provider's computer application. If you lose your encryption key (aka your password), you cannot retrieve your files because the provider never handles your key.[1]

Cloud Storage Doesn't Equal File Backups

Most cloud storage users choose popular providers—such as Google Drive or Apple iCloud Drive—to store, sync, and retrieve their files. However, there is one caveat—most cloud providers are not backing up your files; they are just syncing them. Commonly used cloud storage providers (for example, Google Drive, Apple iCloud Drive, or Box) are storing your files in a single repository and making them accessible across all of your devices.

Just like backing up the files stored on your computer, you need to perform backups of your cloud storage accounts or else you risk losing all of your information since there is no recovery copy. Remember, a backup is a copy of your data in a secondary location that can be used to recover information if your files have been lost, deleted, damaged, or held hostage by bad actors. It is vital to obtain a cloud account backup service that stores copies of your files in a secondary, cloud location.

Risks of Using Only an External Hard Drive

If you choose not to use a cloud-based backup service and instead decide to use an external hard drive to back up your cloud files, you are susceptible to risks, such as hardware/software failure, loss, theft, and not having up-to-date versions of your files.

It is important to note, because of the risks of ransomware and other forms of malware, you don't want to keep your external storage always connected to your computer. Because of this, you'll need to perform scheduled backups manually to your external hard drive. However, an external hard drive can be good for creating system file backups, as some cloud backup services back up only user-generated files and not the operating system components.

Effective File Management

A good file storage management plan includes primary file storage in the cloud, the use of a cloud-based backup service, and the utilization of local backups as a secondary recovery option.

One of the most popular, and highly rated, cloud-based backup services is Backblaze, which costs around $50/year or $5/month per one PC or Mac. In Toms Guide's testing of multiple cloud-based backup services in April 2018, they made Backblaze Editor's Choice because of the ease of file restoration, the insignificant resource usage, and the low cost for unlimited storage, file size, and backup speed (https://www.tomsguide.com/us/best-cloud-backup,review-2678.html). Backblaze users can also use their own personal encryption key, instead of Backblaze being in control of the encryption. Remember, however, if you lose the key, Backblaze can't get your data back for you. According to Tom's Guide, Backblaze is the least expensive cloud backup solution available. It works on both PC and Mac, and it includes unlimited backups for external hard drives too. Other comparable cloud-based backup services include iDrive, Acronis True Image, and Carbonite.[2]

Next, you will learn the fundamental steps to protect your files, in addition to storing your files in the cloud and choosing a cloud-based backup service.

Recommendations: Protecting Your Files

The following are essential steps to protect your files. Your files are prized digital possessions, and bad actors want to monetize them at every chance they get. Here are key recommendations to ensure your files are secure, private, and recoverable:

1. **Store Files in the Cloud**: Storing files in the cloud provides greater ease of access, protection, and recoverability compared to storing files directly on your computer's hard drive. When you store files in the cloud, using well-known providers, your data is encrypted and stored in guarded data centers that follow strict cloud security standards. When you store files directly on your computer, you risk data loss from hardware/software failure, ransomware infections, and bad actors stealing your unprotected files. You can store an immense amount of data, sometimes for free, in the cloud versus the cost and limitations of physical storage. Instead of choosing which precious photos you will delete to free up disk space on your computer or mobile device, use cloud storage and easily expand the storage capacity when needed.

2. **Back Up Your Files in the Cloud**: Cloud storage services create clones of your files to sync across your devices, sourcing from a central repository, and are not backed up to another location for recovery purposes.[2] If you delete a photo from your device that is synced with your cloud account, it gets deleted from the cloud, too. You may be able to retrieve it for a certain period, but it is riskier than performing regular, automated backups of your files. Choose a verified cloud-based backup service that'll create backups of your files in the cloud. Also, it is a good idea to perform backups of your system and user-created files to an external hard drive for secondary archival purposes.

3. **Enable Two-Factor Authentication for Cloud Storage**: It is crucial to protect your cloud storage accounts by enabling two-factor authentication. Search Google by entering **How to enable two-factor authentication** and the name of your cloud storage provider for configuration instructions. After doing so, test it by signing out of your cloud storage account and

signing back in. If your cloud storage provider gives you a list of one-time passcodes for recovery purposes (used for signing in when you are away from your mobile device), save it in a secure note in your password manager. Never store verification codes in plain text without encryption.

4. **Use a Password Manager to Create and Manage Unique and Complex Passwords per Cloud Storage Account**: It's imperative to use a password manager to create and manage complex and unique passwords for each of your cloud storage accounts. Bad actors are increasingly carrying out "credential stuffing" attacks, where they collect leaked account credentials from data breaches and try to sign in with them, automatically, on popular websites. If you don't use different passwords for each account, you risk experiencing account takeover.

5. **Encrypt Your Files**: When looking for a cloud storage provider, make sure they provide file encryption (most do). Some cloud providers, who focus on strong user privacy, may give you the option of controlling the encryption key—but if you lose the key, they can't access your files, and that means they are unrecoverable. For most users, it is best to use cloud providers who take care of the encryption. If you have a bunch of files on your computer as well, encrypt them using built-in operating system tools (if available) or trusted third-party solutions. The following are the built-in encryption options available per operating system:

   a. **Windows users**: Windows does not provide an encryption service for Windows 10 Home users—only for Windows 10 Pro users. For Windows 10 Home users, it is likely you will need to use a well-known third-party service, such as 7-Zip, which is free to use. If you do have Windows 10 Pro, you can turn on BitLocker, Microsoft's encryption tool, by searching for *encryption* in the Start menu, selecting Manage BitLocker from the results, and clicking Turn On BitLocker.[3]

   b. **Mac users**: Macs come with a built-in encryption tool called FileVault. It is easy to enable FileVault by opening your System Preferences, clicking Security & Privacy, selecting the FileVault tab, and clicking Turn On FileVault. When you turn it on, you'll be prompted to set a password to enable/disable file encryption. Use a password manager to create a strong and unique password.

6. **Protect Your Computer Files from Ransomware**: In addition to backing up your files in a secondary cloud location (which is the best defense

against ransomware), there are ransomware protection tools built in to Windows and Mac computers, which can provide extra piece of mind.

a. **Windows users**: Windows 10 offers ransomware protection that automatically protects Windows system folders (Documents, Pictures, Movies, Desktop) and allows you to add additional apps to the "Controlled folder list," which designates apps that are allowed access to your files and blocks all unapproved apps (for instance, ransomware programs). Windows 10 users can enable this feature by opening Windows Defender Security Center, clicking the shield icon, and toggling on "Controlled folder access." This Windows 10 ransomware protection also provides alerts when an unapproved app attempts to access, or modify, your files.[4]

b. **Mac users**: All current versions of MacOS include a system protection feature called Gatekeeper. By default, Gatekeeper is set to allow apps only from the App Store and identified developers, which protects your Mac from malware, including ransomware, by blocking known malicious applications. Click the Apple icon in the top left of your screen, go to System Preferences, Security & Privacy, and General. Ensure "Allow applications downloaded from:" is set to "Mac App Store and identified developers."[5]

7. **Securely Dispose of Paper Documents**: To protect your physical files sufficiently, consider scanning them into your computer, and perform recommendation step #1 to store them in the cloud with secondary cloud backups. This will create a digital version of your physical documents, which you can locate if your physical version is ever lost, stolen, or damaged. If you don't need sensitive paper documents lying around your house, use a shredder to destroy the files securely before disposing of them. If you need to store sensitive documents, place them in a locked, tamper-, and fire-proof safe—preferably with a fingerprint scanner (especially when storing encryption keys and your master password for your password manager).

You're officially on the way to protecting your files, both digitally and physically. You learned how to store your files securely in the cloud, maintain secure file backups in a secondary location, encrypt your files, and enable file protection features.

In the following chapter, you will learn how to protect your social media accounts—and your reputation along with it.

Notes

1. https://theconversation.com/how-secure-is-your-data-when-its-stored-in-the-cloud-90000
2. https://www.tomsguide.com/us/best-cloud-backup,review-2678.html
3. https://www.tomsguide.com/us/encrypt-files-windows,news-18314.html
4. https://www.zdnet.com/article/windows-10-security-heres-how-to-shield-your-files-from-ransomware-says-microsoft/
5. https://support.apple.com/en-us/HT202491

15 Protecting Your Social Media

Seth, an Egyptian government employee with a well-known travel blog, received a new LinkedIn connection request including a message from a London-based photographer, Mia Ash. Seth filled his head with hypothetical reasonings behind Ash's friend request. He thought, "Maybe my blog is reaching a wider audience, and Mia wants to collaborate with me!" Seth accepted her request, and the two bonded over discussions of travel, photography, and their business professions. Specifically, Mia told Seth about her goal of surveying people from all over the world about their passions. Seth told Mia he was glad to help her with her pursuit any way he could.

Mia emailed Seth an Excel document to fill out for her study, entitled `Copy of Photography Survey.xlsm`. Mia instructed Seth to send the survey to his corporate email account and open the document while at work, claiming it would function properly when doing so. While at work, Seth opened up the Excel document to fill out Mia's survey. After opening the document, a Microsoft Office pop-up appeared, "Security Warning: Macros have been disabled." Seth ignored the warning and clicked Enable Content, remembering Mia declaring the macros were essential to enable him to view her intuitive survey design.

Soon after Seth chose to enable the content, an information security government employee came over and immediately disconnected Seth's computer from the network. "We received an alert that a remote access Trojan, PupyRAT, was downloaded to your PC earlier. Did you notice anything weird?" Seth's stomach grew nauseous, realizing he just put the Egyptian government at serious risk by opening up a malicious Excel document at work. Seth was lucky the malicious Trojan, meant to spy and steal government information, was detected so quickly.

Mia Ash was created as a fake online person by a group of Iranian government-directed bad actors—known as Cobalt Gypsy—to target individuals working for the government, defense agencies, oil companies, and financial services. Cobalt Gypsy's goal was to use the fake persona of Mia Ash to phish targets through social media and convince them to open up infected file attachments while at work. Once they did so, remote access malware would download so the bad actors could steal proprietary secrets.

To create the fake persona on LinkedIn, bad actors copied and pasted job information from someone else's legitimate profile and stole photos from a real individual's Instagram account.[1] Bad actors are creative in their attempts to appear as authentic individuals on social media—they craft an entire persona (which they usually steal from others), create fake "friends" and add them, and orchestrate posts and comments.

Myth "Only legitimate business professionals are on LinkedIn."

Fact Unfortunately, this couldn't be further from the truth. LinkedIn, just like other social media sites, is laden with cybercriminals and scammers. Social media is a hotbed for job scams, financial fraud, and malware-laced links. Most social media accounts are free and only require a bad actor to have the ability to send you a message.

Bad actors send fake job offers from "recruiters" from companies you've probably never heard of and, when researched on a map, don't exist. In addition to made-up job offers, bad actors send malicious links through social media posts and messages—in the hopes you'll click a shocking article or read more about a "job offer"—effectively downloading malware on your device. It is rare to receive a job offer in a private message, especially without ever applying for one. If something sounds too good to be true, it probably is. If you don't recognize someone as a legitimate connection on LinkedIn, don't accept their request—you'll thank yourself later. And make sure it's *actually* them, too.

Creating fake social media personas is just one method bad actors use to obtain your personal information, infect your devices, and propagate through your connected networks. Next, I'll dive deeper into why bad actors love to attack you through social media; how the information you share affects your privacy; and how to protect your social media presence.

Why Bad Actors Love Social Media

A new social media user is created every 15 seconds—adding to the growing bucket of 3 billion social media users. Here are the statistics showing just how much bad actors love popular social media platforms as an attack vector:[2]

Facebook
- 2.2 billion user accounts.[3]
- 270 million are fake user accounts.

Twitter
- 1.3 billion user accounts on Twitter.
- Of the 328 million active accounts, there are 23 million fake bots.

Instagram
- 800 million monthly active users on Instagram.
- 64 million accounts are fake bots.

LinkedIn
- 500 million members in 200 countries.
- There has yet to be a study done, but if we apply the same percentage as Facebook, there could be more than 40 million fake accounts.

Bad actors love social media platforms because they can create tons of fake profiles and posts to trick you into divulging your personal information, handing over your money, and infecting your devices. Social media is prime hunting grounds for bad actors because of the continuously growing user base, heavy consumption, and significant incentive for users to disclose their personal data.

As data science progresses—and people can rapidly collect massive amounts of data from social media—bad actors look for ways to weaponize data science to perform social engineering and send out personalized attacks. Bad actors develop tools to collect large amounts of data from social media users and then exploit the harvested information to send out personalized malicious posts and messages on a large scale. And it works—66 percent of spear phishing messages sent through social media are opened. This is more than double the amount of opened phishing emails by victims, which is around 30 percent.[4]

Next, you'll learn more about the favorite social media platform among bad actors—Twitter—and how Russian-based cyberattackers targeted U.S. Defense Department employees, through their family members on social media, using Twitter.

Twitter: A Bad Actor's Paradise

Twitter is a favorite among attackers because of the abundance of available personal data, bot-friendly web design, and the popularity of shortened links, which hide destination URL addresses. These factors unintentionally support the automated spreading of machine-generated malicious content. Twitter, and other social media platforms, have antispamming policies, which are designed to prevent bad actors from making too many duplicate posts and messages. But bad actors find ways to evade the policy by targeting individuals—who are likely to be phished or seem to be of value—with personalized posts based on their profile, activity, and timeline history.

Bad actors are learning to do this using automated bots. Artificial intelligence bots detect social media users' text patterns to identify topics of interest and generate sentences that appeal to the target. These bots analyze victims' emotions, behavioral patterns, and location data from geo-tagged photos and videos, and if they went to, or plan to go to, a large event. Bad actors' bots use this information to craft personalized tweets automatically. If a victim posts "I need a vacation. Thinking about Hawaii. Any travel recommendations?" then bad actors collect this information and send phishing tweets about travel deals, which include malicious links embedded with malware.

Bad actors' bots don't need to perfect their grammar and language usage either. Twitter accepts broken English as the norm, so language nuances in bad actor's tweets can slip under the radar.[5]

The sending of personalized, malicious phishing tweets is now more than 10,000 U.S. Defense Department employees were targeted by Russian bad actors. One anonymous Pentagon official's computer was compromised because bad actors targeted his wife's Twitter account with travel packages after she publicly discussed travel ideas with her friends. Other Defense Department employees received tweets about recent sports and entertainment events. If a target clicked the malicious link in the phishing tweet, it would take them to a Russian-controlled server that downloaded a remote access control (RAT) malware program to control the victim's device, in addition to their Twitter account.[6]

Twitter experienced a data breach in 2018 of more than 300 million user account passwords, which was sourced from an internal bug that stored passwords in plain text. Because the passwords weren't protected with encryption, bad actors wouldn't have to unscramble the passwords to read them. Twitter advised all users to change their passwords and, if they used the password elsewhere, to change it on all other accounts.[7] Password reuse makes it easy for bad actors to compromise all of the accounts that use the same password. You are also advised to follow the "Brilliance in the Basics" tips and enable two-factor authentication and create strong and unique passwords per account.

> ### ALEXA: DO NOT POST YOUR LOCATION ON SOCIAL MEDIA
>
> Alexa Dell, the heiress to the Dell tech company fortune, documented her every move on Twitter and Instagram, including her exact GPS coordinates. Dell had no idea she was putting herself, and her family, in danger by doing so. Bad actors could've sent her targeted phishing messages, or even worse, potentially kidnapped her for ransom while traveling internationally. After some of her photos tagged with her exact location went viral, Dell had a major wake-up call to watch what she posted and to not tag her location.[8]

Dell's story of sharing too much information on social media is a reminder to evaluate what you share with your friends on social media and with the public. In the next section, you will learn how researchers also use the information you post on social media to analyze your emotions, behaviors, and interests to influence your decision-making, political opinions, and purchasing habits.

How Third Parties Mine Your Social Media Data

Bad actors aren't the only ones profiting from the massive amounts of personal information on social media. Research companies, like Cambridge Analytica, team up with politicians to harvest troves of data elements from social media (such as your gender, life satisfaction, political views, religious views, agreeableness, "sensational interests," belief in star signs, and more). Once this information is collected, research companies provide services to clients, such as targeted ads and fundraising pleas, to specific demographics.

As *Time* magazine stated, "As they tweet and like and upvote their way through social media, Americans generate a vast trove of data on what they think and how they respond to ideas and arguments—literally thousands of expressions of belief every second on Twitter, Facebook, Reddit, and Google. All of those digitized convictions are collected and stored, and much of that data is available commercially to anyone with sufficient computing power to take advantage of it. American researchers have found they can use mathematical formulas to segment huge populations into thousands of subgroups according to defining characteristics like religion and political beliefs or taste in TV shows and music. Other algorithms can determine those groups' hot-button issues and identify "followers" among them, pinpointing those most susceptible to suggestion. Propagandists can then manually craft messages to influence them, deploying covert provocateurs, either humans or automated computer programs known as bots, in hopes of altering their behavior."

This is exactly what voter-profiling company Cambridge Analytica did prior to the 2016 U.S. presidential election. With their data harvesting, they assisted political campaigns, such as the Trump campaign in the primary elections (the Trump campaign later used RNC voter data instead of Cambridge Analytica's, stating it was more accurate).[9] Cambridge Analytica obtained the personal information of more than 50 million Facebook users without their permission by paying Cambridge University psychology professor Dr. Aleksandr Kogan for the data he collected through his personality prediction Facebook app called thisisyourdigitallife. Dr. Kogan claimed in the user agreement that the app was for academic research purposes only.[10] This was not the case, as Dr. Kogan provided the harvested user data to third parties, such as Cambridge Analytica. Facebook's lawyers sent a letter to Cambridge Analytica, after discovering the data leak, stating the user information was obtained and used without permission. Therefore, it couldn't be used legitimately in the future and must be deleted immediately.[10]

This wasn't the first incident where Facebook user data was harvested to further a political cause. In 2012, the Obama campaign promoted their Obama 2012 Facebook app, which collected individuals' personal data, as well as their friends' birthdates, locations, and "likes." The Obama campaign's ability to gather information on the friends of the app's users meant the campaign could reach out to nonsupporters by sending out targeted campaign messages "disguised as messages from friends to millions of Facebook users." Compared to Cambridge Analytica's usage, where most app users did not agree to third-party data sharing, the Obama campaign app users did agree to have their data—and the data of their friends—harvested. Looking at both situations, Facebook allowed massive amounts of data to be collected on its users, caused social unrest, and eventually created stricter privacy policies.[11]

Facebook collects an immense amount of detail about us—our posts (even the ones we type and delete), likes, photos, and both online and offline activity. Going beyond what it collects directly, Facebook purchases data from third parties that can expose our sexual orientation, gender identity, political beliefs, relationship status, drug use, and additional personality elements.

Facebook isn't the only mammoth collecting data about us. According to Harvard Business School professor Shoshana Zuboff, we live in a world of "surveillance capitalism." With Facebook in the spotlight after its connection to exposing user data, other organizations that also collect troves of personal data risk being exposed as well. As more data analytic companies come to the surface, there is a greater chance for a larger discussion around the ethics of surveillance capitalism data collection.

There are around 4,000 data brokers in the United States that are in the business of purchasing and selling personal information—things we would normally not share with others, let alone give knowing permission to corporations to store and resell it. Companies use the information our devices and services collect to learn everything about us—when we wake up, when go to sleep, what we search online, where we travel, and so much more. Uber even used data it collected to detect people having one-night stands. As Bruce Schneier, a widely known security technologist and author states, "Surveillance capitalism drives much of the Internet. It's behind most of the "free" services and many of the paid ones as well. Its goal is psychological manipulation, in the form of personalized advertising to persuade you to buy something or do something, like vote for a candidate. And while the individualized profile-driven manipulation exposed by Cambridge Analytica feels abhorrent, it's really no different from what every company wants in the end. This is why all your personal information is collected, and this is why it is so valuable. Companies that can understand it can use it against you."[12]

In 2018, the European Union (EU) General Data Protection Regulation (GDPR) came into effect, which regulates any organization across the globe that collects, stores, and shares personal data of EU citizens, as well as people traveling through the European Union. With heavy fines, the EU GDPR is not taken lightly by organizations that need to comply. The new GDPR regulation exposed how much U.S. companies expose our personal information too. As an example, PayPal published a list of 600 companies with which it shares your personal information—exposing the gravity of how far surveillance capitalism has gone without regulatory limitations.[12]

Another firm, Deep Root Analytics, stored spreadsheets of highly sensitive data on around 200 million U.S. citizens within a publicly available Amazon cloud server. Anyone who had the URL address could view the trove of voter information stored by the marketing firm, which was contracted by the Republican National Committee (RNC). Data collected included individuals' entire voting history, religious affiliations, ethnicities, and political biases on controversial topics such as abortion rights, gun control, and stem cell research. Names, addresses, and phone numbers of individuals were also included. The data seems to have been collected from social media sites, such as controversial discussion threads on Reddit. "This is deeply troubling. This is not just sensitive, it's intimate information, predictions about people's behavior, opinions and beliefs that people have never decided to disclose to anyone," Frederike Kaltheuner, policy officer at Privacy International, said in response to the Deep Root Analytics breach, "You should be in charge of what is happening to your data, who can use it and for what purposes." Bad actors can use this data not only to perform identity theft but also to blackmail and harass individuals who hold opposing political standpoints.[13]

This story of how your data on social media is shared, bought, and sold should be an eye-opener to look at the third-party apps you use and to read their user agreements thoroughly. Investigate what data they're collecting and how they're using that data. As Tim Cook, CEO of Apple, warned, "When an online service is free, you're not the customer—you're the product."[14]

You've gained a more in-depth understanding of how your data on social media is valuable to both bad actors and data mining researchers. Next, I will share essential recommendations to protect your social media profile, your data privacy, and how to avoid social media-based cyberattacks.

Recommendations: Protecting Your Social Media

The following are the fundamental steps to protect your social media presence, ensure you remain conscious of your data privacy, and ultimately strengthen your cybersecurity.

1. **Enable Two-Factor Authentication**: Protect your social media accounts by turning on two-factor authentication. Type **How to enable two-factor**

authentication along with the name of your social media platform into a search engine for configuration instructions. After activation, test it by signing out of your social media account and signing back in. If the social media platform gives you a list of one-time passcodes for recovery purposes (used for signing in when you are away from your mobile device), save it in a secure note in your password manager. Never store verification codes in plain text without encryption.

2. **Use a Password Manager to Create and Manage Unique and Complex Passwords per Cloud Storage Account**: Use a password manager to create and manage complex and unique passwords for each of your social media accounts. Bad actors launch "credential stuffing" attacks by collecting leaked account credentials from data breaches and attempting to sign into your accounts with them.

3. **Enable Security and Activity Notifications**: In doing so, you can monitor your social media accounts for logins from new locations, changes in your security settings, and more. Without notifications, you may be unaware of attempted, or successful, logins to your account by bad actors.

4. **Review Your Privacy Settings**: In your privacy settings, check the apps connected to your social media account. If you need to use third-party plug-ins, make sure they are trusted. Review the user agreement to see how they're using your data, and remove their access once you are done using them. Any third-party who has access to your social media poses a risk to your information. Go through each of your privacy settings, per social media account, and ensure you configure them to your desired level of privacy. (Do you want to share your posts with the public or only your friends?)

5. **Beware of Clicking Links (Especially Shortened URLs)**: Bad actors target social media users using malicious links that appear innocent or are obfuscated by a shortened URL (popular on Twitter because of the character limit). Search the desired article title in a search engine instead of clicking links to avoid downloading malware to your device.

6. **Validate an Individual's Identity Before Accepting Friend Requests**: Don't assume everyone who sends you a friend request has positive intentions. Even if it's someone you know, double-check their profile to make sure it's *actually* them. For individuals you are unsure of, you can do a reverse image search with their profile photo, or even copy and paste the person's profile information in a search engine, to see whether this information shows up elsewhere (which could be a sign a bad actor is using a fictitious online persona).

7. **Think Like a Bad Actor When Posting Information:** Before you share anything on social media, take a minute to think like a bad actor. Could anything you're posting be used against you in a cyberattack? Are you sharing personal information, such as your location, birthdate, or address? Perform an investigation into what others can see on your profile and change your privacy settings accordingly.

In this chapter, you learned why bad actors love social media, how to protect your social media accounts, and why it's essential to do so. Next up, you'll discover how to safeguard your website access and how to securely, and easily, manage your passwords.

Notes

1. https://www.secureworks.com/research/the-curious-case-of-mia-ash
2. https://blog.statusbrew.com/social-media-statistics-2018-for-business/
3. https://www.statista.com/statistics/264810/number-of-monthly-active-facebook-users-worldwide/
4. https://www.nytimes.com/2017/05/28/technology/hackers-hide-cyberattacks-in-social-media-posts.html
5. https://www.blackhat.com/docs/us-16/materials/us-16-Seymour-Tully-Weaponizing-Data-Science-For-Social-Engineering-Automated-E2E-Spear-Phishing-On-Twitter-wp.pdf
6. http://time.com/4783932/inside-russia-social-media-war-america/
7. https://krebsonsecurity.com/2018/05/twitter-to-all-users-change-your-password-now/
8. https://www.yahoo.com/lifestyle/24-old-billionaire-heiress-dell-150000002.html
9. https://www.nytimes.com/2018/03/17/us/politics/cambridge-analytica-trump-campaign.html
10. https://newsroom.fb.com/news/2018/03/suspending-cambridge-analytica/
11. https://www.investors.com/politics/editorials/facebook-data-scandal-trump-election-obama-2012/
12. https://www.schneier.com/blog/archives/2018/03/facebook_and_ca.html
13. https://www.bbc.com/news/technology-40331215
14. www.businessinsider.com/tim-cook-privacy-letter-2014-9

16 Protecting Your Website Access and Passwords

Sarah was an employee at an online file storage company. She had to remember hundreds of passwords for work and was desperate for a solution. So, she thought of a clever idea—she decided to reuse the super-strong password she created for her personal accounts for her work account too. Sarah thought to herself, "I created such a good password, if I use it everywhere, I am more secure than creating unique ones for each account. Besides, no one at work is going to try to break into my personal accounts."

Months went by when Sarah heard about a data breach occurring on one of the social media platforms she used at home. She dreaded the thought of having to change all of her passwords, so she let it slide and hoped and prayed she wouldn't become a target. Ignorance is bliss, after all, and Sarah didn't want to think about how her duplicate password method may have depleted more of her energy and time than if she created a unique password for each website.

A few more months went by, and Sarah was called into her manager's office. "We've been alerted by our cybersecurity team that your corporate account has been accessed by bad actors," Mark, her manager, said. Sarah was petrified, "How did they get in?" Mark explained how bad actors used the leaked passwords from the previous social media breach and tried them on their company website. "Did you use the same password at work as you did for your social media account?" Mark asked. "Yes, I didn't think it would be a risk because it was a strong password. I had no idea by doing that I caused a problem at work," Sarah pleaded. Mark replied, "And a big problem it is. The bad actors used your employee account to access a large number of our customer accounts. We need you to explain what happened to law enforcement when they come in to investigate. And do us a favor and change all of your passwords for your work and personal accounts, and don't use the same password—ever."

Sarah's distressing experience with password reuse is analogous to the 68 million leaked Dropbox online file storage accounts, which occurred because an employee used their LinkedIn password as their corporate Dropbox account password. After the 2012 LinkedIn data breach, bad actors attempted the 6.4 million breached passwords on thousands of popular web pages at once. In doing so, they obtained access to a Dropbox employee's account, which allowed them to access to 68 million additional Dropbox accounts.[1] When a company performs solid cybersecurity practices and experiences a password data breach, the data is usually in the form of random characters that require bad actors to use password-decoding tools to obtain the plaintext passwords.

Coming up, I will explain how this technique called *password hashing* works and how it serves an important purpose in slowing down hackers to allow companies to perform incident response and notify users to change their passwords. It is then up to website users to change their passwords promptly to remain secure.

Password Hashing Slows Down Bad Actors

When a company experiences a data breach and passwords are exposed, they are usually in a form that cannot be read by humans. Instead, they are jumbled using cryptographic *hashes* (not the tasty breakfast food), which are mathematical algorithms that disguise individuals' actual passwords.[2] When a password database is leaked, proper cryptographic hashing makes it more challenging for bad actors to decipher—the stronger the hash, the longer it takes for bad actors to decode them using password-cracking tools. This provides a short window of time for the affected company to identify, respond to, and communicate the data breach to its users. Meanwhile, once bad actors crack the leaked passwords, they take the decoded password list and then perform credential stuffing on thousands of websites using automated tools in an attempt to access your accounts. In the case of LinkedIn's second data breach in 2016, which exposed 177.5 million password hashes, bad actors took advantage of the social media platform's outdated, weak hashing protections to exploit a large password list to break into victims' LinkedIn and other personal accounts. Because LinkedIn failed to use robust standards of password hashing, bad actors cracked the majority of the leaked password hashes in one day.[3]

The cyberattack technique of credential stuffing relies on password reuse to gain access to online accounts. In this section, I will unveil just how dangerous password reuse can be and why bad actors are so successful with their credential stuffing cyberattacks.

Password Reuse Fuels Credential Stuffing

Password reuse is a widespread problem. It is human nature to think the solution to remembering hundreds of passwords equates to using the same password or making slight variations to a single password. This bad habit allows attackers to compromise all of your accounts that share the same password quickly. The good news is, in this chapter, you'll learn how to protect your passwords and website access and how to become more aware of bad actors' attempts to take advantage of weak, reused, and/or leaked passwords to compromise numerous online accounts at once. *Credential stuffing* is a cyberattack that takes exposed passwords and tries them on thousands of websites at once, using automated hacking tools.

Troy Hunt, security researcher and founder of the website Have I Been Pwned, which checks if your online accounts have been affected by a data breach, describes why credential stuffing is a serious threat by stating it is[4]

- Wildly successful when users reuse the same password across multiple websites
- Difficult for websites to detect because bad actors sign in with legitimate (stolen) credentials
- Simple for bad actors to automate using software that replicates the login process against target websites
- Easy for anyone to perform using publicly available leaked credential lists from data breaches and commonly available exploit tools

On his website Have I Been Pwned, Hunt obtains publicly available leaked databases sourced from data breaches, verifies their authenticity, and loads them onto his website where users can input their email address to check whether their accounts have been affected. Hunt was researching a large number of user credentials for sale on a Russian website—nearly 458 million unique email addresses with correlating passwords—and wanted to find the source of the data to check whether it was an undisclosed data breach or recycled from a previously known incident. Hunt decided to ask a random number of website subscribers who were part of the 458 million affected users to identify which website correlated with their leaked password. Hunt was hoping the users' answers would point to a specific website to identify further the source of the enormous number of exposed credentials. Instead, Hunt discovered the affected users couldn't identify on which site they used the password—they were reusing them or making slight variations between one standard password.[4]

If these affected users created unique and strong passwords per website and managed them with a password manager, they would've lowered their risk of account compromise. Instead of changing hundreds of accounts with the same password, they would change only one account and create a completely unique password. In the next section, I examine another looming danger when it comes to securing your website access—weak password creation.

The Great Password Problem

In addition to the significant risk of password reuse, there are several other threats to your security, which are preventable through proper cyberhygiene habits. The following are some of the top reasons why bad actors target individuals with poor password habits:[5]

Poorly Creating Passwords   Weak passwords allow bad actors to brute-force their way into your online accounts. Mind-blowingly, 10,000 of the most common passwords can access 98 percent of all accounts.[6] Humans have memory limits that present a challenge when attempting to remember several different passwords at once. Because of these limits, individuals often opt for easy-to-remember yet weak passwords (causing password reuse) or secure passwords that are difficult to remember (causing insecure storage habits).[6]

Reusing Passwords   Password reuse allows for bad actors to compromise multiple accounts at once, using leaked passwords from data breaches. Fifty-nine percent of people choose to reuse the same or similar passwords for multiple accounts.[5] Creating slight variations of one primary password isn't much better. Bad actors use automated tools to check for minor differences, as well as common password elements (words found in the dictionary, replacing letters with similar-looking numbers or symbols, and more).

Never Changing Passwords   Humans are susceptible to status quo bias when it comes to the thought of changing their password. Status quo bias is an "emotional overweighting" of the situation at hand.[6] And 39 percent of users would never change their password if it weren't required.[5] When individuals are required to change their password, they tend to modify the original password, creating security vulnerabilities slightly.

Not Changing Passwords *After a Data Breach*   After hearing about a data breach, 53 percent of individuals choose not to change their password—even 12 months after the breach occurred.[5] Status quo bias can also help explain why individuals don't change their passwords, even after a known data breach occurs. Individuals prefer sticking with the status quo (keeping the same password) versus diverting from the status quo (changing the password).[6]

Not Changing Passwords *Even After Being Attacked*   Shocking as it may seem, individuals prefer to stick with an unchanging password they are comfortable with, even experiencing account compromization.[6] And it shows—only 55 percent of individuals would change their password after discovering a hacked account.[5]

Treating Work and Personal Accounts the Same   You learned about the Dropbox employee who used the same password for her LinkedIn account as she did for their work account, which led to 68 million exposed accounts. Even though 47 percent of individuals don't see a difference between passwords for work and passwords at home, combining them creates serious security risks.[5]

Storing and Managing Passwords Improperly   Fifty-seven percent of individuals attempt to memorize all of their passwords, which could explain why "I forgot my password," is the number-one reason why 51 percent of users change their password.[7] Besides memorization as a widespread attempt at password management, 42 percent of individuals store their passwords in an insecure file on a mobile device, in a Word document, or in an Excel spreadsheet.[5] If you don't use a password manager, write your passwords down on a piece of paper and leave it in a locked safe.

Not Believing Passwords Can Be Guessed from Social Media Fifty-one percent of individuals don't believe a bad actor could guess their passwords from information found on their social media.[5] Bad actors collect bulk amounts of data from social media to guess users' passwords and security verification questions automatically.

Denial of Being a Target Thirty-eight percent of users believe their accounts are not valuable enough to make them a significant target for bad actors.[5] As you learned previously, bad actors aren't targeting you specifically, but they aren't leaving you out of the broader picture. Cyberattacks are automated, using mass-collected information, which leaves everyone who has an online account vulnerable.

Now that you've immersed yourself in the key reasons why bad actors are successful in their attacks against users with poor cyberhygiene habits when it comes to passwords, I will discuss practical and powerful password design. You'll learn what makes up a good versus a bad password, as well as how to create strong and unique passwords while storing and managing them securely.

Effective Password Management

I recommend a password management approach that primarily relies on a password manager (such as LastPass) to create, store, and fill in automatically generated strong, complex, and unique passwords for all of your websites and apps. However, there may be times where you encounter devices that don't support your password manager app (streaming devices, and so forth). In these situations, it is best to follow the password creation guidance given here to make more easy-to-input passwords for these specific scenarios and save them securely in your password manager.

Popular sites are starting to support USB security keys, a form of multifactor authentication, known as a *universal second factor* (U2F). USB security keys are inexpensive devices that provide physical authentication for account login. After you initially type in your username and password on a site that supports a security key, you plug the USB key into your computer and press a button to finish the login process. Once your U2F security key is activated on your account, you don't need to type in your password again unless you use a different device to access the account. Because U2F is a growing open source authentication standard, only a number of high-profile sites support it (for example, Facebook, Dropbox, LastPass, and so on). More sites are sure to adopt

U2F as time goes by. USB security keys make it difficult for bad actors to steal since they would need to be in close proximity to you, and security keys lessen the amount of password typing, which lessens the risk of bad actors recording the passwords you type in.

Google, with more than 85,000 employees, hasn't experienced a successful phishing attack since it rolled out the implementation of U2F using physical security keys. The Google Chrome, Mozilla Firefox, and Opera web browsers support U2F technology. It is uncertain whether Apple will hop on board and provide support for security keys on its Safari browser. One of the well-known makers of security keys is Yubico. Their security keys are low in price, and they have options available for mobile devices too.[8]

When it comes to the concept of changing passwords, as long as you have strong, complex, randomized, and unique passwords, you don't need to change them as frequently (depending on the website). The National Institute of Standards and Technology (NIST), the go-to government agency for today's cybersecurity standards, released a new password standard draft for companies. The document contained a shocker—NIST advised not to periodically change secure passwords unless there's been a breach or a user requests to do so.[9] And a study performed by Carleton University discovered that password changes had a minimal effect on preventing bad actors from accessing accounts through brute-force attacks.[9] This means that changing your password periodically doesn't provide much benefit to maintaining strong cyberhygiene habits, as long as the other security elements are met (strong, complex, randomized, and unique passwords).

Password Creation Formula

The following are the recommended steps to create a strong, unique, easy-to-remember, and easy-to-type password for situations where your password manager's automatically generated, complex passwords aren't as user-friendly (for example, streaming, gaming devices, and so on):

1. Pick three unrelated words: `ketchupwillowsandstorm`
2. In between two words, place two to three numbers: `ketchupwillow84 sandstorm`
3. After the numbers, place a symbol: `ketchupwillow84!sandstorm`
4. Misspell one of the words: `ketchpwillow84!sandstorm`
5. Capitalize one letters in a random location: `ketchpwillow84!sandstorM`

The password we just created, `ketchpwillow84!sandstorM`, would take an average home computer six octillion years to brute-force, which is an incredibly long time![10] However, it is important to note, because we used a specific formula to create these passwords, bad actors can attempt to re-create and input these patterns into their automated password-cracking tools. It is best to let your password manager build random, complex, and unique passwords. Just make sure the number of characters is set to a minimum of 24 characters. If you can, however, make it even longer if the website allows. (Websites all have different password length limitations.)

As long as you follow these recommendations, you will be doing your absolute best to practice good cyberhygiene habits when it comes to password management. Next, I'll share a couple of mistakes people tend to make when creating passwords.

Password Creation Mistakes

Here are some password creation mistakes people often make:

1. **Switching Out Letters for Numbers and Symbols, or "leetspeak":** *Leetspeak* is the act of switching out letters with similar-looking numbers and symbols (for example, `D0gC@t`). Leetspeak was invented and made popular by hackers in the 1980s as informal Internet slang.[11] Bad actors are well aware of this method, and password cracking tools come preloaded with ways to detect and decode the language. Using leetspeak to create your passwords is a common mistake. If you've used this method to create your passwords, make sure to change them and create new ones using the recommended password creation method.

2. **Using Words Found in the Dictionary:** You might be thinking, "But you used dictionary words in your password creation formula." That's correct, but we made sure to misspell one or more words. Bad actors will always find a way to identify, replicate, and use patterns of password creation to use in their password-cracking tools. By misspelling the words, it will take a bad actor longer to crack, since the word doesn't match their list of dictionary words their tools check against. Again, the best method of password creation is to use your password manager to generate randomized, strong, complex, and lengthy passwords.

Now it's time to share the entire list of recommendations to protect your passwords' online account access. By following these recommendations, you are on your way to maintaining proper cyberhygiene habits—causing bad actors to look elsewhere.

Recommendations: Protecting Your Website Access and Passwords

The following are essential recommendations to keep you secure while accessing your online accounts and managing your passwords:

1. **Enable Two-Factor Authentication for All Accounts**: Protect your online accounts by turning on two-factor authentication. Two-factor authentication uses two forms of authentication to verify your identity—your credentials plus a secondary factor. If the site supports it, use an authenticator app before using a SMS text option; the former is more secure since text messages can be intercepted. By enabling two-factor authentication, you will prevent bad actors from gaining access to your account, even if they have your password. For each of your online accounts, use Google to search for *How to enable two-factor authentication* along with the name of the website. After enabling, test it by signing out of your social media account and signing back in. If the website gives you a list of one-time passcodes for recovery purposes (used for signing in when you are away from your mobile device, which is commonly used to verify your identity), save it in a secure note in your password manager. Never store verification codes in plain text, without encryption.

2. **Use a Password Manager to Create and Manage Unique and Complex Passwords per Online Account**: Use a password manager to create and manage complex and unique passwords for each of your online accounts. Bad actors are increasingly carrying out "credential stuffing" attacks, where they collect leaked account credentials from data breaches and try to sign in with them on popular websites using automated hacking tools. If you don't use a unique password per account, you risk account takeover.

3. **Create Strong, Unique, and Easy-to-Remember Passwords**: I recommend primarily relying on your password manager to generate

randomized, complex, and unique password per account. However, there may be times where this is an inconvenience, such as typing in a complex password on a device that doesn't support your password manager (for instance, a streaming device). When this happens, use my "Password Creation Formula," listed previously in this chapter, to create complex and unique passwords. Make sure to store your passwords in your password manager.

4. **Use a VPN Service to Access Your Online Accounts**: A virtual private network (VPN) service creates a private tunnel for your web traffic. Using a VPN protects both your privacy and your security by shielding your data from your Internet service provider (ISP), who can view and sell your browsing history to third parties, as well as from bad actors, who attempt to view and intercept your web traffic.

5. **Think Before You Click Website URL Links**: Before clicking a website link, make sure it's legit by previewing the destination. This can be done by hovering over the link with your mouse pointer. If you don't see a preview of the link, usually located at the bottom of the browser, make sure the setting is enabled. For example, for Safari users, click View in the menu bar and then click Show Status Bar.

   If the link is shortened, go to (`http://checkshorturl.com`) and input it to expand the link and check the destination. If the link is in plain text and doesn't reveal the destination, don't visit it. Instead, search for the legitimate site you want to visit in a search engine and then click it from there.

6. **Get Alerts When a Website Is Breached**: Good password managers will alert you when a website you use is breached. You can also enable notifications for security news updates in your individual accounts. If the website doesn't have this option, you can subscribe to the Have I Been Pwned website, where you can check if you've been affected by a breach and receive notifications too.

7. **Change Your Password When a Website Is Breached**: After you become aware that a website you use has been breached, it is imperative to change your password. Remember, bad actors gain access to the exposed password lists and automatically attempt them on multiple websites all at once, automatically. The quicker you are at changing your password—and enabling two-factor authentication—the less you risk your account being compromised.

8. **Create Nonsensical Security Verification Answers**: Some websites are behind the times and still don't use two-factor verification. In its place, they use security verification questions to confirm your identity. When this happens, create nonsensical answers to the security verification questions and store them securely in your password manager. For example, a security question might be, "What's your mother's maiden name?" You can create an answer like "Chocolate Bunny." The answer doesn't make any sense, which prevents bad actors from looking for your mother's maiden name online and attempting to gain access to your account. As legendary hacker Kevin Mitnick said, "The more red herrings (misleading information) you provide, the more you become invisible online."[12]

9. **Enable Security and Activity Notifications**: When you enable notifications and alerts for your online accounts, you can monitor for things like logins from new locations, changes in your security settings, and more. Without alerts, you may be unaware of attempted, or successful, logins to your account by bad actors.

10. **Verify Website Encryption Before Entering Information**: After you've verified the website you are on is the legitimate one connected to the organization or person with whom you intend to connect, confirm the website is encrypted as well. When a website is encrypted, it masks the information being sent back and forth, so any prying eyes on the same network can't see what you're sending. For example, if an online store wasn't encrypted—and you were on a public Wi-Fi network making a purchase—anyone with a tiny amount of hacking ability could obtain your login credentials, credit card number, and more. With encryption, information isn't sent in plain text over the network. You can check if a website is encrypted by looking for the padlock symbol (sometimes in green) in the URL bar of your web browser. The word *Secure*, in green, can also appear. If a website isn't encrypted, you may see an *i* in a circle. When you click the *i*, the web browser will provide more details about the lack of security. Always look for the padlock.

11. **Add Ad-Blocking and JavaScript-Blocking Extensions to Your Browser**: Verified, authentic ad-blocking, and JavaScript-blocking browser plug-ins can help to limit the number of malicious ads and dynamic content. Websites use JavaScript, known as *scripts*, to

automate the execution of tasks, which can be used for good or evil. By blocking these elements, you reduce your risk of experiencing drive-by downloads of malicious scripts when you visit a site. A good antivirus program, which provides Internet security, will defend against these dangers. Ad blocking can also protect you from the plethora of malicious ads out there, but it can also detract from a website's business, which relies on advertising income. When using an ad-blocker, websites may block content until it's turned off or ask for a donation. Script-blocking browser plug-ins can require additional maintenance because they can block nonmalicious scripts unless you approve the content to run.

12. **Don't Use Vulnerable Web Plug-ins Like Adobe Flash**: One of the most exploited plug-ins, which is targeted heavily by bad actors, is Adobe Flash. Because of its many security holes, it hasn't been allowed on Apple iOS products since 2010, and it officially hits its end-of-life in 2020.[13] If you must use Flash in the meantime, use it on a separate browser, apart from your primary one, and disable it when not in use.

13. **Avoid Using Your Google or Facebook Account to Log In to Other Websites**: When creating a new profile on a website, such as a music-streaming service, it may ask you if you want to use your Facebook or Google account to log in. This provides a lack of security because you're attaching these websites to your primary account, and if your primary account or the attached accounts becomes compromised, all of the other ones do too. Instead, choose the option to create a manual account using unique login credentials.

14. **Access Your Online Accounts from Secure Devices**: Ensure the devices you use to access your websites are secure and up-to-date. Don't ever use foreign devices, such as a friend's laptop or a library computer, to access your personal information. You don't know who accessed it before you and what they plugged into it. You also can't guarantee they practice good cyber hygiene. These systems could be compromised, and they don't know it and neither will you. Unless it's an emergency, avoid accessing your personal accounts on your work computer. You don't know if your employer is practicing good cyber-security also, and therefore you can't guarantee your information will be kept secure and private. Besides this being a potentially prohibited action at work, by not doing so you'll keep your personal information

secure and private. This also allows for you to keep any written passwords left secured at home.

15. **Review Your Privacy Settings**: In your privacy settings, check the users and devices connected to your online account. If you use third-party plug-ins, make sure they are trusted, review the user agreement to see how the plug-in is using your data, and remove their access once you are done using them. Any third-party who has access to your online accounts poses a risk to your information. Go through each of your privacy settings per online account to configure them to your desired level of privacy. Websites tend to collect as much information as they can on you by default.

Well done! You can start practicing secure and effective password and website access management. You've gained insight into common issues with passwords, the dangers of password reuse, and how to practice good cyber hygiene by primarily using your password manager to create and maintain your passwords—only manually creating passwords when needed. By following my list of recommendations, you'll keep your online accounts—and your access to them—safe, secure, and out of bad actors' reach.

Notes

1. https://www.wired.com/2016/08/hack-brief-four-year-old-dropbox-hack-exposed-68-million-peoples-data/
2. https://www.wired.com/2016/06/hacker-lexicon-password-hashing/
3. https://arstechnica.com/information-technology/2016/06/how-linkedins-password-sloppiness-hurts-us-all/
4. https://www.troyhunt.com/password-reuse-credential-stuffing-and-another-1-billion-records-in-have-i-been-pwned/
5. https://blog.lastpass.com/2018/05/psychology-of-passwords-neglect-is-helping-hackers-win.html/
6. http://www.ideas42.org/wp-content/uploads/2016/08/Deep-Thought-A-Cybersecurity-Story.pdf
7. https://www.valuewalk.com/2018/03/password-security-habits-tips/?utm_content=buffere2dcb&utm_medium=social&utm_source=twitter.com&utm_campaign=buffer

8. https://krebsonsecurity.com/2018/07/google-security-keys-neutralized-employee-phishing/

9. http://www.ibtimes.com/my-password-secure-nist-advises-against-periodically-changing-passwords-2541293

10. https://thycotic.com/resources/password-strength-checker/

11. https://www.pcworld.com/article/248526/web_jargon_origins_revealed.html

12. Mitnick, Kevin. *The Art of Invisibility: The World's Most Famous Hacker Teaches You How to Be Safe in the Age of Big Brother and Big Data* (p. 279). Little, Brown and Company.

13. https://krebsonsecurity.com/2017/08/flash-player-is-dead-long-live-flash-player/

17 Protecting Your Computer

Mario became acclimated to his computer's fan running more frequently. He assumed the system temperature was getting hotter because his computer was getting a bit older, so it took more computing power to do everyday tasks. Another month went by, and Mario noticed the increasing slowness, and sometimes his computer would crash completely. He was becoming accustomed to managing the nuances of his computer's "personality," and he didn't think anything was wrong with it otherwise. After all, he had antivirus software and wasn't alerted about any infection.

One day, Mario's friend Jamie mentioned something alarming she read in the news, "Did you know bad actors are stealing people's computer's unused CPU power to mine cryptocurrency? They're taking advantage of innocent individuals' computers across the world to create a botnet-like supercomputer to earn loads of money." Mario replied, "I did not. How do you know if your computer is being used for mining cryptocurrency?" Jamie explained, "It can be difficult to pinpoint because while some bad actors use cryptomining malware downloaded from malicious links and attachments, other bad actors' cryptomining attempts are hidden in your computer's background processes. The sneakier kind automatically strikes if you visit a website with cryptomining code or malicious ads. The process will continue running in a well-hidden pop-up window long after you've closed a web page."

Mario was shocked, "I wonder if my computer is being used to mine cryptocurrency—it's turning to sludge, and the fan is always going because it's overheating and I'm barely doing anything." Jamie then advised Mario to check his computer's computing power usage by opening up either Activity Monitor for Mac or Task Manager for Windows. Jamie said if any web process goes over 20 percent during casual web browsing, it could be a sign that someone is using his resources to mine cryptocurrency. Jamie advised him to look for hidden pop-ups and recommended that Mario completely quit his browser and see if his CPU drops and the fan stops running.

Mario went home and compared his CPU usage before and after he quit his web browser—it decreased significantly. Unfortunately, the implications of the cryptomining processes running on his computer, without his knowledge, included an exceptionally high electricity bill and wear and tear to his computer, which shortened the life of his hardware. Mario decided it was necessary to find a suitable antivirus program capable of detecting and preventing web-based cryptomining processes, in addition to defending against cryptomining malware.

Early in the story when Mario experienced strange computer behavior, he ignored the notion that malware could be the culprit since he never received any security warnings. In this chapter, I'll address a similar myth and explain why it's vital to incorporate additional essential cyberhygiene habits on top of having a reliable antivirus program.

Myth "I have antivirus running on my computer, so I am protected."

Fact Antivirus is only part of the security equation. There are other elements that you'll need to practice to more fully protect yourself against cyber threats. The reason antivirus isn't a stand-alone solution for your cybersecurity is because it's predominantly a reactive approach. Most antivirus software programs are signature-based, which means they detect threats only when the antivirus company's virus signature database is current. Unless you enable automatic updates for your antivirus software, you won't be protected against the latest cyber threats. Also, if there is an unrecognized threat that is not yet in the antivirus company's database or you didn't enable automatic updates or a malicious process unfolds silently in the background, your antivirus may not adequately protect you. To shield yourself fully from cyber threats, you need to practice other core cyberhygiene habits—the "Brilliance in the Basics" tips and some supplementary recommendations I provide at the end of this chapter.

Next, I'll unravel the mystery of the cyberattack known as *cryptojacking*, where a bad actor hijacks your computing power—and your electricity, causing your bill to skyrocket—to mine cryptocurrency and turn a profit. I'll also discuss how everyday websites are beginning to ask site visitors to opt in to giving them their unused CPU to mine cryptocurrency, which provides income for the website. Websites cryptomining their web visitors, otherwise known as *web mining*, is becoming a popular alternative to ad revenue.

On a positive note, you'll learn how some individuals even choose to donate their unused CPU to scientific pursuits, such as fighting disease, searching for extraterrestrial life, and more. Because cryptojacking is becoming the top cyber threat against computer users, I chose to discuss it in depth in this chapter. Beyond cryptojacking, there are other severe threats to your computers, such as ransomware and other types of malware, data loss, hardware/software failure, and more. At the end of this chapter, I include a list of key recommendations to protect your computer against these threats to your information and devices.

The Rising Threat of Cryptojacking: The Illegal Form of Cryptomining

Without your knowledge, a bad actor could take over your computer (or mobile device) and force it to mine cryptocurrency—damaging your hardware, increasing your electric bill, and slowing your computer down to a halt. In Mario's story of being cryptojacked, his computer was almost irreversibly damaged, and his electricity bill went through the roof—all because he left his web browser active—allowing cryptomining processes from one of the websites he visited to expend all of his idle CPU.

Because the act of web mining visitors doesn't involve the installation of a malware program, it's difficult to detect and remove, unless your antivirus program was developed to do so. In addition to web mining, bad actors spread cryptomining malware through infected email attachments, links, mobile apps, and web pages, as well as compromised Wi-Fi hotspots. Cryptojacking is more lucrative for bad actors than other attacks, such as ransomware, because it doesn't require any interaction with the victim, it can persist for extended periods of time, and it can be performed from anywhere in the world. Because of the anonymity of cryptocurrency, bad actors don't need to hide or launder profits. Cryptojacking is carried out through malicious links, attachments, websites, malicious advertisements, and software downloads. So, if your browser and/or computer isn't up-to-date, cryptojacking attacks can happen even faster and spread to other devices on your network, similar to how the WannaCry ransomware spread so rapidly around the globe.[1]

To provide you with some background on cryptojacking, I will discuss what cryptomining is and why there's a massive incentive for both bad actors and everyday people to mine cryptocurrency. Bitcoin, a popular form of cryptocurrency, rose to a startling value of $20,000 per coin in December 2017.[2] Because miners receive Bitcoin payments as a reward for solving the mathematical algorithms to validate cryptocurrency transactions (that is, *mining*), there is a heated competition between groups of cryptominers to be the first one to "crack the code" and process a Bitcoin transaction. To put things into perspective, mining one single Bitcoin requires around 237 kilowatt-hours, which is more than what a U.S. home consumes in one week. The electrical power used to mine Bitcoins is estimated to be equal to the electricity consumed by the entire nation of Denmark. Cryptomining puts a significant strain on the global electrical grid and is resource-intensive. For these reasons, Bitcoins, as a form of currency, aren't as sustainable as other forms of cryptocurrencies, like Monero. Because mining Bitcoins requires a large amount of electrical power, it also increases the burning of fossil fuels. Because of the growing need for cheap power resources, Bitcoins are primarily mined in countries like China, where coal is widely used and there aren't many emission restrictions.[3] Because of the high demand for more electricity at a cheaper rate, bad actors developed a method to obtain more computing resources while avoiding paying for their electricity—by targeting your computer and your electricity.

In the next section, I'll discuss how bad actors, and nonmalicious websites, mine web visitors without ever downloading a program onto your computer. Toward the end of this chapter, you'll learn must-have methods to protect your computing resources from being used to power cryptomining, as well as other threats.

Cryptomining Using Web Visitors' CPU Resources

Cryptojacking isn't just performed by bad actors; it's an opportunity for any website to earn alternative income as compared to advertising. Some websites even offer visitors a choice to let the website use their available CPU instead of the company losing out on ad income if the person uses an ad-blocking extension. Using the computing resources of online visitors to mine cryptocurrency is technically legal if the visitors opt in to it.[4] This is why some antivirus programs may not automatically block web mining processes.

Cryptojacking services, like the ever-popular Coinhive, allow bad actors (or anyone) to put cryptomining code on their websites and in advertisements on a page. The code's purpose is to exploit the computing power of visitors. Unless the affected visitor closes their browser completely—and makes sure there are no hidden pop-ups still lingering—cryptomining processes can run in the background and cause damage to their computer. To disperse the cost and power needed to mine valuable cryptocurrency, bad actors inject cryptomining code into thousands of websites at once by targeting the primary website from which thousands of sites load content.[5] This allows bad actors to cast a wide net to catch cryptojacking victims to further their chances of receiving momentous rewards for mining cryptocurrency like Bitcoin.

Not all cryptocurrency requires massive amounts of computing power to mine. Digital currencies, like Monero, are faster and more straightforward to mine, but it's less mature than Bitcoin. Most web miners focus on cryptocurrencies like Monero, which is less intensive, which makes it harder for ad blockers and antivirus to detect.[4] Whichever one they choose, both bad actors and everyday people are looking to make a profit from mining cryptocurrencies—using your computing power.

Bad actors also can target Industrial Controls Systems (ICS), which are responsible for automating critical industrial processes, such as packaging food or testing water. Cryptomining malware was discovered in a water utility's Human Machine Interface (HMI), which is a legacy Windows XP system that allows the operator to control the Supervisory Control and Data Acquisition (SCADA) server network. The found cryptomining malware was believed to have originated from a malicious advertising link on a website.[6] It is not uncommon for SCADA environments still to have end-of-life operating systems running, like Windows XP, which makes the systems incredibly vulnerable to malware that mines cryptocurrency or holds the systems for ransom.

In my list of recommendations on how to protect your computer, you will find the steps you can take to protect your computer from cryptojacking as well. Next, I'll briefly discuss how some computer users choose to donate their unused CPU for beneficial causes.

Donating CPU Resources for Good

The concept of individuals taking advantage of the world's computing resources—acting as a pooled supercomputer to mine cryptocurrency—can be seen as both frightening and remarkable. Interestingly enough, pooling computing resources together toward a single aim isn't a new breakthrough. For years, computer users have been able to donate their unused CPU to pursuits of advancing science, searching for alien life, finding the cure for diseases, and more. Every day, humans create 2.5 quintillion bytes of data; that's written as 2,500,000,000,000,000,000,000,000,000,000! This is a colossal amount of information, and researchers struggle to parse through it without the use of quantum computers, which would make the process considerably faster. However, the future of quantum computers for researchers is still on the horizon, so researchers use a tool to allow volunteers to donate their unused CPU resources to help parse through the hefty amounts of data to help further necessary research. The Berkeley Open Infrastructure for Network Computing (BOINC) program allows individuals to download a simple program that allocates their extra CPU toward a list of initiatives, such as controlling the spread of malaria, discovering new particles in space, and detecting earthquakes faster.[7]

Now you can see how a pool of computer resources can be used for good or evil. Cryptojacking, the evil side of exploiting computer resources, is just one of many cyberattacks bad actors use to abuse your computer for a profit. Next, you'll learn how to protect your computer from these cyber threats, as well as others not sourced by bad actors, such as data loss, hardware/software failure, and more.

Recommendations: Protecting Your Computer

The following are the core steps to keep your computer secure—protecting your information, identity, and integrity of your devices. It is important to remember that you can't rely on one defense mechanism, such as antivirus, to protect your computer fully. Cybersecurity is a layered defense approach, and it works efficiently only when the layers are combined regularly.

1. **Encrypt Your Hard Drive**: Encrypt the files stored locally on your computer using built-in operating system tools (if available) or trusted

third-party solutions. These are the built-in encryption options available per operating system:

a. **Windows users**: Windows does not provide an encryption service for Windows 10 Home users—only for Windows 10 Pro users. For Windows 10 Home users, it is likely you will need to use a well-known third-party service, such as 7-Zip, which is free to use.[8] If you do have Windows 10 Pro, you can turn on BitLocker, Microsoft's encryption tool, by searching for *encryption* in the Start menu, selecting Manage BitLocker from the results, and clicking Turn on BitLocker.

b. **Mac users**: Macs comes with a built-in encryption tool called FileVault. It is easy to enable FileVault by opening your System Preferences, clicking Security & Privacy, selecting the FileVault tab, and clicking Turn On FileVault. When you turn it on, you'll be prompted to set a password to enable/disable file encryption. Use a password manager to create a strong and unique password.

2. **Apply the Latest Updates**: Make sure your computer and all of your software applications are up-to-date. Performing frequent updates can help prevent cyberattacks from occurring, such as ones that exploit outdated software with known security holes. Ransomware and cryptojacking malware look for system vulnerabilities so they can spread their malware to other devices on your network.

3. **Enable Antivirus Protection**: Antivirus is the armed guard between your computer and the Internet. Enabling your antivirus program to stay up-to-date automatically protects your computer from infections, malware, and other cyberattacks. To defend against cryptojacking, one of the top threats against computer users, look for an antivirus that detects cryptojacking malware and web mining scripts.

4. **Install Only Verified Software and Uninstall Unneeded Programs**: Bad actors like to hide malicious code in software applications you download on your computer. Always verify what you're downloading is the real thing. What you might think is a desktop wallpaper application might be hiding cryptojacking code to steal your CPU to mine cryptocurrency—wearing down your computer and driving up your electricity bill. Make sure to uninstall any software programs you don't need or use, too.

5. **Perform Regular Backups**: In Chapter 14, "Protecting Your Files," I discussed the best method to protect your files, which is a blend of cloud storage, performing secondary cloud backups of your cloud storage environments and your computer, and physical backups of the local data on your computer periodically. Having real-time file backups in the cloud is one of the greatest protection mechanisms against ransomware, data loss, and other hazards to your computer and files.

6. **Monitor Your CPU Utilization**: Keeping an eye on your CPU utilization can help you see potentially suspicious spikes in your power consumption, which could indicate a cryptojacking attack, the exfiltration of data, and more. Here is how to monitor your CPU by operating system type:

   a. **Windows**: Right-click the taskbar and select Task Manager. Open the Performance tab to view your real-time CPU utilization. If you see processes running strangely high, it could indicate a cryptojacking attack. Quit any open web browsers, run an antivirus scan, and check the CPU again.

   b. **Mac**: Go to Finder, then Applications, and then Utilities, and click Activity Monitor. Once there, select the CPU tab to see your CPU utilization. To keep a close eye on it, put a real-time graph icon in your dock by clicking View in the Activity Monitor menu bar; click Dock Icon and choose Show CPU Usage. If you see any of the bar graphs remaining at the top consistently, check whether any of the current processes are running strangely high, which could indicate a cryptojacking attack. Quit any open web browsers, run an antivirus scan, and recheck the CPU.

7. **Protect Your Computer from cryptojacking**: Cryptojacking web visitors' computers to mine cryptocurrency is one of the largest cyber threats targeting computer users. Coinhive is one of the leading cryptojacking mining script providers. By enabling JavaScript- or script-blocking browser extensions, you can protect yourself from the code activating and stealing your CPU to mine cryptocurrency. If you don't want to use a script-blocking extension, you can install antimining browser extensions, such as the popular No Coin. It is crucial to verify the authenticity of browser extensions before installing them.

8. **Don't Pick Up or Insert Unknown USB Sticks**: Rogue USB sticks can contain malware. Don't ever stick them in your computer. If you find

an unknown USB stick, don't pick it up. As I said before, picking up USB sticks on the ground and sticking them in your computer is like eating a stranger's leftovers. You just shouldn't do it.

9. **Set a Strong, Unique Login Password**: Using the password creation techniques I lay out in Chapter 16, "Protecting Your Website Access and Passwords," create a strong, yet memorable password, and store it in your password manager. Make sure the password is nonpredictable, and if other people, such as your kids, use your computer, create individual accounts for each person.

10. **Wipe Old Devices Before Getting Rid of Them**: When you go to sell, give away, or discard a device, don't leave your information on there for bad actors to find and exploit. Use a verified program to remove your data permanently.

In this chapter, you gained a deeper understanding of one of the fastest growing threats facing computer users—cryptojacking—and how your computer's CPU can be used for good or evil. You also gained an understanding of how to protect your computer better using basic cyberhygiene habits that will safeguard you from a multitude of evolving cyber threats.

Notes

1. https://www.zdnet.com/article/cryptocurrency-mining-malware-why-it-is-such-a-menace-and-where-its-going-next/
2. https://www.pri.org/stories/2018-03-11/hackers-find-processing-power-they-need-mining-cryptocurrencies-through
3. https://www.sciencefriday.com/segments/the-high-energy-cost-of-bit coins-rise/
4. http://www.thejakartapost.com/life/2018/02/13/thousands-of-websites-infected-by-crypto-mining-malware.html
5. https://www.kaspersky.com/blog/web-miners-protection/20556/
6. https://www.cnet.com/how-to/find-out-if-websites-are-mining-bitcoin-cryptocurrency/
7. https://motherboard.vice.com/en_us/article/bmj9jv/7-ways-to-donate-your-computers-unused-processing-power
8. https://www.tomsguide.com/us/encrypt-files-windows,news-18314.html

18 Protecting Your Mobile Devices

It was a Friday evening, and Oliver was binge-watching his favorite show on Netflix. He was thrilled to relax after a long week at work. In the midst of scrolling through Instagram and chatting with friends, Oliver noticed texts weren't sending, and he stopped getting messages from his buddies. Unless his friends were "ghosting" him, he realized something might be wrong with his cellular service. After a call to his friend didn't go through, Oliver concluded his service might be disconnected. Oliver always paid his bill on time, so he was pretty confused about the whole situation. He grabbed his laptop and attempted to log in to his account management console, and to his dismay, his password wouldn't work. Oliver was getting frustrated, and a little anxious, thinking about the potential scenarios that could be unfolding.

Because he couldn't make any calls, Oliver used the online chat feature on the wireless provider's website to reach someone and explain what was going on—that his phone service stopped suddenly, and he couldn't access his online account. Rachel, a customer service representative, asked Oliver to verify the last four digits of his Social Security number to access his account and investigate. Rachel discovered someone with the same name as Oliver called in less than an hour before and requested to "port out" his phone number to another cellular company. Oliver asked Rachel how this could conceivably happen to him. Rachel replied that Oliver didn't have a PIN code set to verify his identity when he called in to make changes on his account, such as porting out his number to another provider. Rachel also mentioned that the person who impersonated Oliver had his Social Security number, so they had no choice but to assume the other Oliver was authentic.

Oliver was now awash in horror thinking about how the bad actor probably used his leaked Social Security number from the Equifax breach to gain access to his cellular account and transfer his number to a different provider. Oliver thought of how the bad actor was probably looking at all of his texts, calls, and phone contacts. He started to fear that the bad actor would try to target his friends and family too. Oliver asked Rachel to change the password on his account immediately and set up a PIN to prevent any additional attempts to take over his account.

Oliver hoped he could soon breathe a sigh of relief and get back to watching his TV show. However, after he got his device's phone number and service reactivated, a flood of notifications came in. The first concerning messages he received were from his bank—someone wired $2,000 out of his bank account to a person with the same last name as Oliver, at a different bank. Oliver was becoming sick to his stomach, afraid of what was to come by reading each incoming notification. After going through his email and text messages one by one, he was beginning to see more and more damage. It was clear that once the bad actor gained access to Oliver's cell number, they were able to reset his password with the phone company, as well as gain entry to a multitude of other accounts.

Because Oliver used the same phone number for his SMS-based two-factor authentication on some of his accounts, the bad actor was able to reset some of Oliver's passwords, pilfer his personal information, and steal his money. Not only that, Oliver received follow-up texts from his friends asking if everything was okay—apparently, the bad actor texted his friends as Oliver and claimed his mother was on life support in the hospital and needed money right away to pay the bills or else the hospital would "pull the plug." Luckily, Oliver's friends knew this kind of thing would never happen at a hospital. Oliver was left with a huge mess, which would take weeks of cleanup, while it took the bad actor less than 20 minutes to wreak havoc on his life.

What Oliver experienced was a mobile "port-out scam," also known as *porting*, where a bad actor steals your phone number to leave you without phone service, money, and access to your online accounts. The primary goal of the port-out scam is to obtain access to your bank accounts and scam your phone contacts while you're unable to send and receive calls and texts. Once a bad actor gathers together your name, address, Social Security number, birthdate, and other personally identifiable information (PII), they can impersonate you to gain access to your phone number. A bad actor will call your phone provider, pretend to be you, and claim "their" phone got stolen and they need to port the phone number to a new device. If they succeed, the bad actor is in control of your two-factor authentication mechanism and can access your online accounts without your password. Once the bad actor has your phone number, they proceed to reset all of your online passwords using their automated tools. Their first stop is usually your bank account. If you have automatic payments set up with your mobile provider, the bad actor can identify your banking information and proceed to gain access to your account and wire money to their accounts. They may even create a fraudulent bank account using your name so they don't raise a red flag when transferring a great deal of money.

BE ON GUARD AGAINST SIM SWAPS

One T-Mobile retail employee was caught making unauthorized changes to a mobile customer's account to hack into their Instagram account and steal their highly coveted three-letter username. Even though the T-Mobile customer, Paul Rosenzweig, took steps with T-Mobile to prevent account takeover, the bad actor retail employee was able to perform a SIM swap, which transferred the victim's information to a new SIM card on a bad actor's mobile device. Once Rosenzweig's information transferred to the bad actor's device, the crooked T-Mobile employee gained access to Rosenzweig's Instagram and Twitter accounts and changed the email addresses to the bad actor's. Rosenzweig never received any notification from T-Mobile about the unauthorized SIM card transfer on his account because T-Mobile's policy was to only send a text message and not an email. By the time the SIM swap occurred, the bad actor was the one who received the notification and not Rosenzweig.[1] Two good methods of defense against SIM swapping attacks include performing a SIM lock freeze on your mobile account and setting a SIM PIN on your phone, which locks the SIM to your mobile device. You'll learn more about the two in the following recommendations.

In the next section, I lay out the specific recommendations to protect yourself from mobile port-out scams. Because this type of scam has been around for quite some time and there has been a significant uptick in occurrences, I highlight it in this chapter.

Protect Against Mobile Port-Out Scams

The following are the steps to take to protect yourself from experiencing mobile port-out scams—keeping your money and online account safe:

1. **Set a Passcode/PIN Code on Your Account**: Each major phone provider has additional security measures you can enable to protect yourself from port-out attacks. This is usually done by setting up a unique PIN, passcode, or verification question and answer to prevent unauthorized individuals from transferring your phone number and making other changes to your account. Once you enable one of the security verification measures, make sure it applies to all account changes and all phone numbers. Treat your mobile phone account like your most valuable bank account—and not just another utility service. To think like a bad actor, ask your phone provider how they identify you if you forget the passcode to see whether there is another pathway you will need to block from bad actors. The following are instructions per provider to enable a passcode.[2] It is important, in all cases, to not make the passcode/PIN predictable (that is, don't use the last four digits of your SSN or your debit card PIN).[2]

   a. **T-Mobile**: Add a 6- to 15-digit port validation passcode to your account by calling 611 from your T-Mobile phone, or 1-800-937-8997 from anywhere.

   b. **Verizon**: Add a password or PIN to your account, if not already enabled, by accessing your online wireless account or by visiting a local store.

   c. **Sprint**: Add a PIN to your account, if not already set up. Sprint requires all customers to create a PIN during their initial account activation.

   d. **AT&T**: Enable the Extra Security feature on your account and create a unique passcode. The default is the last four digits of your SSN, which you do not want to use. Change it to a unique passcode.

2. **Use Authenticator Apps vs. Text-Based Authentication**: Whenever you are provided with the choice, choose third-party authentication apps, such as Google Authenticator, to verify your identity versus relying on text messages. Texts can be intercepted by bad actors through port-out scams.

3. **Enable a Port Freeze and SIM Lock**: Ask your phone provider if they are capable of enabling a "port freeze" to keep your phone number from transferring without your authorization. Also ask if they are able to lock your account to your current SIM inside your phone, which would prevent a SIM swap scam. You can also set a SIM PIN number on your phone, which would lock your SIM to your device. Search for *set SIM PIN* along with your phone manufacturer and carrier to find instructions on how to set the PIN. Store this PIN in your password manager because if you lose it, it will be difficult to recover access to your SIM when needed.

4. **Watch Out for "Emergency Calls Only" Notifications**: If you see "Emergency Calls Only," or similar, on your mobile device's status bar, this could be a sign your phone number has been ported out. Contact your phone company immediately by using a secondary phone, making a call from your computer, or using the chat feature on your phone provider's website to talk with customer service and get your phone number back. Simultaneously, keep an eye out for communications from your bank, and other online accounts, alerting you to any suspicious changes, wire transfers, or password resets.

5. **Use a Different Phone Number for Two-Factor Authentication**: Another option is to create and use a Google Voice number for *two-factor authentication* (2FA) on accounts that don't offer authentication app capabilities. Google Voice numbers link to your Gmail account, so it's essential to use an authenticator app for your Gmail's 2FA. By using a Google Voice number for authentication versus your actual device's phone number, you'll make it difficult for bad actors to gain access to your online accounts during a port-out scam.

6. **Use a Different Email Address for Your Phone Account**: Bad actors look for any piece of information they can find to gain access to an account. By using a one-off email for your phone provider account, you create a dead-end for bad actors who attempt to compromise your email account once they identify it on your online phone provider account.

Now that you've learned how to guard yourself against the growing threat of mobile port-out scams, I will address other significant dangers targeting mobile device users, so you'll know what to look out for and how to shield your device from bad actors.

Mobile Malware

Your mobile device—a productive computing environment overflowing with convenience—holds the keys to your digital identity, your family's identity, and your entire digital life (and sometimes literally the keys to your house). Working alongside the advancement of mobile technology, bad actors design malware and hide it in real-looking apps in Google Play and the Apple App Store. Their primary objective is to steal your hard-earned savings, monetize your identity, and use your data to their advantage.

According to McAfee's 2018 Mobile Threat Report, the top five threat campaigns found hidden in the Google Play store include the following:[3]

Adware/Click Fraud Apps ($40 Billion Market) *Adware* and *click fraud apps* conceal themselves in innocent-looking applications, and once they download, they cause users to force-click implanted advertisements in the background. This allows bad actors to earn advertising income while infecting your mobile device with ads.

Banking Trojans ($1 to 2 Million Market) *Banking trojans* also hide in everyday apps. Once they download, they work to gain access to your bank account and drain your funds.

Cryptojacking Apps (Million-Dollar Market Potential) *Cryptojacking apps* conceal themselves to use your mobile device's computing power to mine cryptocurrency. Since 2017, McAfee reported an 80 percent increase in malware related to Bitcoin mining.[3] Cryptojacking malware destroys phones when the hardware is overworked (article).

Spyware Apps *Spyware*, hidden in apps, lets bad actors snoop on your personal information. They'll look for anything of monetary value, such as your Social Security number, and more.

Botnet/Command and Control Apps Bad actors use *botnets* to take over a device and turn it into a bot controlled by a bad actor. Bad actors usually have thousands of bot devices under their control. To make money, they rent out their botnets to other bad actors so they can carry out cyberattacks using the controlled devices.

One vicious Android trojan, Laopi, is dubbed a "jack-of-all-trades" malware since it incorporates almost every attack method designed for mobile devices. According to a Kaspersky Mobile Threat report, Laopi is so exhaustive that it can bulge out the battery and obliterate a phone in 48 hours. Found hidden in Google Play apps, Laopi exploits the mobile device's CPU to crank out Monero, a Bitcoin alternative. Laopi also forces the phone to visit 28,000 URLs in 24 hours to earn ad revenue. Additionally, Laopi can sign up the user for premium online services without their knowledge and perform actions posing as the user, such as sending texts. The only other attack method not found within Laopi is spyware, but researchers claim bad actors can quickly add it to the mix.[4] The Google Play store is constantly under attack by bad actors. The iPhone App store can also house malicious apps, but because of the secure design of Apple iOS devices, the impact is less severe than downloading a malicious app on an Android device.

Bad actors are increasingly attacking iOS devices, such as iPhones and iPads, with malicious phishing emails that claim to be a "critical alert" from Apple, stating Apple detected a blocked sign-in attempt to the person's iCloud account. When the victim clicks the phishing link in the email, they are brought to an "AppleCare" phishing website, which claims the individual's phone has been "locked due to illegal activity" and to call AppleCare to unlock the phone. Before the person can do anything on the website, a system dialog box pops up to prompt the person further to make the call.[5] Instead of clicking anything, attempt to close the open browsing tab, window, or app. Then, make sure to mark the phishing email as Junk, so it will be flagged and removed from your inbox. Report phishing emails designed to mimic Apple by forwarding the received email to Apple at reportphishing@apple.com.

Next, I will address the longstanding, controversial debate over which mobile device is more secure—an iPhone or Android device—and why it's important to understand when it comes to making the best decision to protect you and your information.

iPhone vs. Android Security

You might notice a common theme among the cyberattacks and security vulnerabilities discussed in this chapter—a greater part of them involve Androids, which is no coincidence. The Android platform is low-hanging fruit for bad actors who want to target more than two billion users through the exploitation of the platform's open application distribution methodology.[3] Also, because the Android mobile operating system can run on a variety of phone manufacturers and carriers, it's difficult for Google to enforce security patches. Android device vendors are guilty of not making security updates available, delaying the release of updates, and telling the user, "Your device is fully up-to-date" when it's not.[6]

Compared to Androids, Apple has a more controlled and secure methodology of app distribution in its store. Apple ensures users remain secure by approving the application's code and reviewing the digital signature, which signifies the authenticity of the app. Apple iOS is designed to sandbox apps, which prevents them from interacting with other apps on your device. Because of these security features, Apple makes it difficult for bad actors to design malware economically for Apple's mobile operating system. Remember, just like a generic car thief, if the doors are locked, they'll pass on by to find a vehicle with unlocked doors. By using an Apple iPhone, you make it more difficult for bad actors to compromise your mobile device through malware found in Apple's app store.

Apple ensures all of its supported devices receive security updates. Apple also sends reminders if the user hasn't installed their update yet. As you learned before about Androids, Google releases monthly security updates, but the problem lies with varying Android manufacturers not making them available to its users.[7] No matter which mobile operating system you use, you'll learn the essential ways to protect your mobile devices from bad actors—protecting your digital identity and integrity of your device.

Next up, I discuss mobile device loss and theft as a significant concern for device users and the importance of locking down your mobile device security to protect you and your family's identity.

Device Loss and Theft

Seventy million smartphones are lost each year, and a laptop is stolen every 53 seconds.[8] If you lose your mobile device and have no way of tracking it down, it would take a miracle to get it back. The cybersecurity company Symantec unveiled what people do when they find a smartphone on the ground. Symantec's experiment, called the Smartphone Honey Stick Project, scattered 50 Android smartphones without passcodes in five U.S. cities. The researchers purposely placed smartphones in locations where they'd be easily found by strangers—in elevators, shopping malls, food courts, and more.[9]

Here's what happened when someone found a phone:

- 89 percent people opened personal apps and looked at data, such as online banking.
- 83 percent clicked business information.
- 72 percent viewed photos.
- 60 percent looked at social networks and email accounts.
- 57 percent tried to open a Saved Passwords file.
- 50 percent attempted to return the device to the owner.

The Symantec study indicates a 50/50 chance the individual would get their phone back. The core lessons of Symantec's research are to put a passcode on your device to prevent bad actors from gaining access to your sensitive information, finances, and more. Make sure to enable Find My Phone features, which provide ways to locate your phone if it's lost or stolen. For both the iPhone and Android devices, you can send a text to your lost device with your contact information, so whoever finds it can call you and coordinate your device's return. If you lose track of your iPhone completely, you could remotely wipe the data from it so bad actors can't access anything. And if by chance you didn't set a passcode, you have the option to lock your device remotely by setting one.[10,11]

Now that you've learned about the massive issue of mobile device loss and theft—as well as how you can protect your device if it's lost—you'll discover the essential recommendations for ultimate mobile device security in the next section.

Recommendations: Protecting Your Mobile Devices

The following are the central recommendations to keep your mobile devices secure—protecting your personal information and identity:

1. **Use a Securely Designed Device**: To stay secure, you should use authorized Apple mobile devices. The Apple operating system has a secure design, the amount of malware targeting Apple users is less, and security updates are managed directly by Apple. If you are not able to purchase an iPhone or have your heart set on Android devices, choose

a Google Pixel device, produced directly from Google (which means regular security updates). Devices that are not managed directly by Google can have malware preloaded on them. In 2018, around 5 million Android devices had a preloaded RottenSys malware program on them, disguised as a System Wi-Fi service app. RottenSys was found on Android devices manufactured by Honor, Huawei, Xiaomi, OPPO, Vivo, Samsung, and GIONEE.[12] Stay secure and use an iPhone instead. If you can't, use a Google Pixel phone.

2. **Don't Use a Jailbroken Device**: Jailbreaking is when someone modifies a device's operating system to add unauthorized apps and capabilities. When a phone is jailbroken, it is no longer secure. If someone modifies their iPhone's operating system, security capabilities like sandboxing no longer function.[13] So, instead of having a secure phone where the apps don't interact with each other and can access only certain parts of the iOS, it becomes a free-for-all for bad actors and a security nightmare for you. Jailbreaking also makes any device warranty invalid.

3. **Enable Lock Screen Code**: Because mobile devices are prone to getting lost or stolen, it's vital to create a passcode. Just like passwords, the longer they are, the longer it'll take bad actors to crack them using hacking tools. Instead of opting for a simple four-digit passcode, create an unpredictable one that is 6 digits or longer. If you have an Android device, create a hard-to-guess passcode instead of a pattern you swipe on the lock screen. Patterns are easy to guess and simple to replicate by bad actors watching you from a distance, compared to a passcode. If you do use a pattern, start at the middle-right point (which is the least used) and choose eight or more points in your pattern. And don't use letter-like designs, which are easy to guess.[14]

4. **Know the Risks of Biometrics**: Biometric sign-in options, such as using your fingerprint, may seem more secure, but they actually carry some risks. Fingerprints are easy to steal; you leave them everywhere. If a bad actor gains access to your phone, either through cracking your passcode or using a copy of your fingerprint, they can change your fingerprint information and update it with their own. Biometric authentication, like fingerprint scanning, makes the sign-in process convenient, but it is not the holy grail.[15] Keep this caution in mind when enabling biometrics on your device. Always make sure to have a secondary sign-in method, such as a strong and secure passcode.

5. **Encrypt Your Mobile Device**: It is important to encrypt your mobile device fully to protect your information if your device becomes lost or stolen. Apple iPhones are automatically encrypted when you set your passcode and are decrypted when you unlock your phone. To enable encryption on an Android, open the Settings app, click Security, and click Encrypt Phone.

6. **Apply Updates**: When you regularly apply security updates as they become available, you are doing your utmost best to protect your device. Bad actors exploit security holes in mobile devices, and manufacturers fix these issues and send out a system update. It is up to you to apply it promptly.

7. **Back Up Your Data**: To protect your information from loss or damage, sync and store your mobile device data in the cloud and perform backups using a secondary cloud storage location. Physical devices are vulnerable to loss, theft, infection, and damage. It is best to store and back up your data in the cloud. As a secondary backup, you can connect your mobile device to your computer and store a backup on your computer and also on an external storage device.

8. **Install Verified Apps from the Official Store**: To avoid downloading malicious apps, use the official app store on your device. For iPhone users, you have security built-in to ensure you use the official app store. For Android users, enable the setting to block downloads from unknown sources. Before downloading any app, make sure it's legit by checking its reviews, checking how long it's been on the app store, and making sure it's not asking for invasive permissions.

9. **Consider Mobile Antivirus for Androids**: If you have an Apple device, mobile antivirus won't provide any benefit to you. Apple iOS devices are secure by design. Through the use of sandboxing, apps are separated from the operating system. The only way apps can access more of your device is if you allow it through the app permissions. If you were to install a mobile antivirus app for iOS, it wouldn't be very effective and could even create security vulnerabilities by exposing locked-down areas of your Apple device. Most of the mobile security apps available for iOS devices offer features already available through Apple (such as remote data wiping and password-protection, protection against malicious websites).[16] Using mobile antivirus is a primary recommendation for Android phones because of the high levels of

malware targeting device users, and it's a more open operating system design. Android does implement app sandboxing techniques but with fewer restrictions than Apple. If you have an Android device, make sure to install a verified, top-rated mobile security app to protect your device from malware infections. One highly rated Android antivirus program is Bitdefender Mobile Security, which you can obtain for a low annual fee.[17]

10. **Safeguard Your Devices from Theft**: When you enable Find My Device features built in to both Apple and Android devices, you increase the chances of retrieving a lost or stolen mobile device. If retrieval is unlikely, however, there are built-in tools to remotely wipe your data. This prevents a bad actor from stealing the information on your device. The following are instructions for each mobile operating system to enable remotely locating your device, as well erasing it, if needed.

   a. **Apple iOS Devices**: Enable Find My iPhone by opening your Settings app, clicking your name at the top, and tapping your device name at the bottom of the screen. Once there, enable both Find My iPhone and Send Last Location. The Send Last Location option will send you the devices most recent location before the battery dies. The Find My iPhone feature allows you to activate Lost Mode, which locks the device with a passcode (if not already done so), tracks the location, and displays a custom message with your phone number on your lock screen. It also disables the use of Apple Pay. If device retrieval is bleak, you can remotely erase the data. When you choose Erase iPhone, it also removes your device from the list of trusted devices for Apple two-factor authentication.[18]

   b. **Android Devices**: Enable Find My Device by opening your Settings app, tapping Security & Location, and then tapping Find My Device. Once there, turn on "Remotely locate this device" and "Allow remote lock and erase."[19] If device retrieval isn't likely, you can erase the data on your device, but it might not erase any inserted external SD cards.[20]

11. **Beware of Unsolicited Texts and Phone Calls**: As you know, bad actors target your mobile device by sending spam texts and phone calls to try to get information from you and infect your device to make money off of you. The best practice is never to answer texts or calls you don't

recognize. Search the phone number in Google, and check for suspicious reviews. If the spam number is persistent, block it.

12. **Think Before You Click Email and Site Links**: Bad actors love to target mobile device users through phishing emails and websites. Before you click a link, make sure you check where it's taking you. For mobile users, hold down on the link to see the full URL address. If the link is shortened, you can paste it in a site like `http://checkshorturl.com` to expand it and check the destination. If it's plain text and doesn't reveal the destination, don't visit it. If it's not easy to see the destination, don't use the link. Instead, search for the website you want to visit in a search engine and then click it from there, if it's a legitimate website.

In this chapter, you learned about how to protect yourself from mobile port-out scams, the current threat landscape of mobile malware, iPhone versus Android security, and how to best protect your mobile devices from loss, theft, and malicious infection. Next, we'll dive into your home network and how to safeguard it from bad actors.

Notes

1. https://krebsonsecurity.com/2018/05/t-mobile-employee-made-unauthorized-sim-swap-to-steal-instagram-account/
2. https://krebsonsecurity.com/2018/02/how-to-fight-mobile-number-port-out-scams/
3. https://www.mcafee.com/us/resources/reports/rp-mobile-threat-report-2018.pdf
4. https://securelist.com/jack-of-all-trades/83470/
5. https://9to5mac.com/2018/07/30/ios-phishing-applecare-attempt/
6. https://www.wired.com/story/android-phones-hide-missed-security-updates-from-you/
7. https://motherboard.vice.com/en_us/article/d3devm/motherboard-guide-to-not-getting-hacked-online-safety-guide
8. https://www.forbes.com/sites/steveolenski/2017/12/08/is-the-data-on-your-business-digital-devices-safe/#561e3a034c6a
9. https://www.symantec.com/content/en/us/about/presskits/b-symantec-smartphone-honey-stick-project.en-us.pdf

10. https://support.apple.com/kb/ph2700?locale=en_US

11. https://support.google.com/android/answer/6160491?hl=en

12. https://thehackernews.com/2018/03/android-botnet-malware.html

13. https://www.tomsguide.com/us/iphone-jailbreak-risks,news-18850.html

14. https://www.kaspersky.com/blog/lock-screen-patterns-predictability/9528/

15. https://www.schneier.com/blog/archives/2009/01/biometrics.html

16. https://www.tomsguide.com/us/iphones-dont-need-antivirus-software,news-23111.html

17. https://www.tomsguide.com/us/best-antivirus,review-2588-7.html

18. https://support.apple.com/en-us/HT201472

19. https://support.google.com/pixelphone/answer/3265955

20. https://support.google.com/accounts/answer/6160491?hl=ee

19

Protecting Your Home Wi-Fi

Linda always prided herself on having a strong password for her home Wi-Fi network, which was protected using the recommended Wi-Fi Protected Access II (WPA2) encryption. She even changed the default password on her Wi-Fi router's online administrative console to a strong and complex one. Anyone looking in would see how conscious Linda was of practicing good cyberhygiene habits.

For this reason, it was a huge surprise when Linda started receiving a number of cease-and-desist letters from her Internet service provider (ISP). The letters threatened potential legal action, as well as the termination of her Internet connection if she continued to "download copyrighted media content." Linda was aghast—she would never download copyrighted content illegally without paying. Panicked, she contacted a friend, Ben, who was knowledgeable in Wi-Fi home security. Linda told Ben how she thought she was doing everything right—she set a strong password for her Wi-Fi network, used WPA2 encryption, as well as set up a strong password for the admin console.

After investigating her Wi-Fi router, Ben found someone in Linda's neighborhood was using her home Wi-Fi network to download copyrighted content through the anonymous web browser, Tor. Ben performed a factory reset on Linda's router, as well as applied firmware updates, created a new SSID Wi-Fi network name, and made her passwords longer and stronger. Ben told Linda she should be all set because that would've kicked anyone out who obtained her Wi-Fi password through brute-force hacking. Linda, slightly relieved and *hopeful, updated her ISP with the information she gained from her friend Ben's investigation of her Wi-Fi router.*

A couple weeks went by, and Linda received more cease-and-desist letters in the mail. This time, her ISP recommended that she obtain legal counsel. Now, she was starting to get frustrated and angry at whichever bad actor of a neighbor was taking advantage of her Wi-Fi network to perform illegal actions. Linda called Ben to investigate further. Ben reviewed the list of devices connected to her network and found the suspicious computer again. This time, Ben checked Linda's security configuration settings and found she had Wi-Fi Pro-tected Setup (WPS) enabled, which would allow anyone who knows, or can crack the eight-digit PIN code, to connect to Linda's network. Even though Linda had a super awesome and strong password set, there was a security loophole the bad actor neighbor was able to exploit. Ben disabled WPS and kicked off the bad actor's device, and the Wi-Fi intrusion, along with the cease-and-desist letters, finally stopped.

Linda was confused how someone could use WPS to connect to her network—didn't they need to press the button on her router and physically look for the PIN on the back of the device? Ben explained how all a bad actor would need was to brute-force guess the eight-digit PIN code. With the immense amount of hacking tools out there, Ben stated the bad actor would need only a few hours to crack it.[1]

Linda experienced a brute-force attack on her home Wi-Fi network through the insecure WPS feature on her router. You have all been taught to use WPA2, and not WPS, for your network's security, but you may not have been told to disable WPS. Some less secure routers keep WPS active, even after it's disabled, too. It's important to obtain a modern, secure router that makes it easy to apply firmware updates and locks down the router's security easily.

In the upcoming sections, I will discuss additional cyber threats to your home Wi-Fi network, as well as how to protect yourself and your family from these attacks and keep your information safe.

Threats Against Your Home Wi-Fi Network

Wi-Fi routers are commonly neglected, as compared to our computer and mobile devices. Not managing our networking devices properly—which operate as the gate to your digital life—is like living in a high-crime area and leaving all of your doors and windows unlocked. And when it comes to the Internet, we all live in a bad cyber neighborhood. When your Wi-Fi network becomes infected with malware, all of your Internet-connected devices are at risk, including your smartphone, computer, smartwatch, streaming device, smart home devices, and more.

In the following list, you will gain insight into some of the primary threats your home network faces:

Malware Infections   In May 2018, the FBI sent out a warning about a rapidly spreading malware infection called *VPNFilter*, which attacked more than 500,000 home and office Wi-Fi routers. The VPNFilter malware, designed by Russian state-sponsored hacking groups—known as APT28, Fancy Bear, and the Sofacy Group—is able to steal web credentials, load spoofed websites, block network traffic, and make the router self-destruct, rendering it useless. VPNFilter can even load spoofed banking websites, which look like the one you actually use, and steal your credentials and empty your life's savings.

VPNFilter can also mimic your email account site to swipe your credentials and surveil your communications. VPNFilter has been found to target Linksys, MikroTik, NETGEAR, and TP-Link Wi-Fi networking devices. The FBI advised home users to perform a factory reset on their routers to help them kick out any potential malware. However, to protect against Wi-Fi router malware, other steps need to be performed, which are noted in my recommendations—setting strong passwords, disabling insecure protocols, updating the firmware, and more.[2]

Encryption Vulnerabilities   Researchers have found a security hole called Key Reinstallation Attack, otherwise known as KRACK, within the WPA2 security standard for Wi-Fi networks. KRACK allows bad actors to inject and manipulate data into websites you visit if they compromise your home network.[3]

We've all been told to set our Wi-Fi networks to WPA2 security while setting our password. This is no mistake. WPA2 is the most secure standard compared to its predecessors, but there are still secondary precautions that are necessary to take. A bad actor does need to be in physical proximity of your home Wi-Fi range, so make sure to place your Wi-Fi router in the middle of your house to limit your range. Besides following the security recommendations to protect your home Wi-Fi network, found in the next section, you should only visit sites with HTTPS encryption (that is ones that start with https://). When you visit legitimate, encrypted sites, you ensure the activity and data you transmit is protected from prying eyes. There are even browser plug-ins, like HTTPS Everywhere, which forces sites to use encrypted connections, if possible. You can also use a virtual private network (VPN) service to protect your privacy while on the Web. I discuss the benefits of using a VPN—whether at home or in public—in the upcoming recommendations.

Bad Actor Neighbors　In the beginning story of this chapter, you learned how bad actors can sometimes be neighbors who want to use your network to download illegal content—and you received their cease-and-desist letters instead. From just wanting to take advantage of "free" Internet to intentionally causing harm to your network and reputation, it's crucial to follow the upcoming guidance to protect your home network from bad actor neighbors. Even if your neighbors are not bad actors and you let them connect to your network, keep in mind they can see everything you do on the Internet by using simple tools.

Improper Router Management　One of the biggest reasons why home Wi-Fi routers, and other networking devices, are insecure is the lack of device management. Most people plug-in their Wi-Fi router and forget about it. Some may not even realize there is an online management console that anyone connected to your network can see—and make changes on. As you read in the earlier story, even though Linda had a strong password set for her management console and was using WPA2, the bad actor was able to get on her network and download tons of illegal content because she had the insecure standard WPS enabled. This allowed a connection loophole to fester, resulting in a multitude of cease-and-desist letters from her ISP to stop downloading copyrighted media. Even though Linda wasn't doing anything of the sort, her Internet almost got disconnected for the actions of the bad actor neighbor.

Now that you've learned about the common threats to your home Wi-Fi network, I'm going to provide you with a list of vital recommendations to protect your network from bad actors.

Recommendations: Protecting Your Home Wi-Fi

The following are the essential recommendations to protect your home Wi-Fi network and keep your and your family's devices and the flow of personal information safe from the eyes of bad actors.

1. **Use a Securely Designed Modern Wi-Fi Router**: Your home Wi-Fi security is as good as the router you have. You can apply all the security configurations possible, but by having an outdated router, you allow a giant security hole in your home network. It's like having an ancient house that's about to fall down, but instead of updating it, you decide to put the money into a gated fence that surrounds your home.

   Make sure to purchase your own Wi-Fi router versus renting one through your ISP. Always be cautious of renting Wi-Fi router/cable modem combined gateways. It's best to purchase your own, secure, up-to-date networking devices. Remember to replace your router every few years or when the device is deemed "end-of-life," which means it will not receive any future security or functional firmware updates.
   Many of the routers affected by the VPNFilter malware were more than five years old.[4] To ensure you have a modern router, check the information available on the manufacturer's website, such as the release date. Also, if you can't find a firmware release within the last year, this can be a tell-tale sign your router isn't supported anymore and is now a threat to your home network.

2. **Lock Down Your Wi-Fi Router's Online Console**: To access your router's administrative console, make sure you're connected to your Wi-Fi network and type the URL address **192.168.1.1**, **192.168.0.1**, or similar into your web browser. If neither address works, search for your Wi-Fi manufacturer and router model in a search engine to find the correct IP address to use. Once you obtain the correct address, you should see a login screen. If you haven't already changed the default credentials

for your Wi-Fi router, they can be found using a search engine. Commonly, it is admin for both the username and password. Some routers won't encrypt the login page unless you enable it, so the first time you enter the default credentials it will be in plain text over your local network. The nonencryption of the login page makes it even more important to change the default credentials immediately by following the "Password Creation Formula" I described in Chapter 16 to create unique, strong, and complex passwords and store them in a password manager. If you don't change the password, anyone who connects to your network can change your configuration settings, as well as view your personal web traffic.

3. **Update Your SSID Network Name and Password**: Most routers come in the box with a default SSID (network name) and password. This password is usually the first part of the router model number with a few random numbers at the end. This lets bad actors easily guess the password to your home Wi-Fi, snoop on your traffic, and access your devices.

   In the Wi-Fi router configuration page (see previous step), change your SSID to something generic that doesn't identify your household) or is even misleading, like Chromecast. Make sure to set a strong, complex, and unique SSID network password using the "Password Creation Formula" in Chapter 16 and store it in a password manager.

4. **Apply Regular Firmware Updates**: In step 1, you learned the importance of using a modern, secure router. In this step, I'll address the importance of updating your router's firmware, or software system, just as you would your computer and smartphone to keep your network safe from evolving threats.

   Some routers are not super security-centric and tend not to release firmware updates as frequently as ones that focus primarily on cybersecurity. Some routers can make it challenging to apply firmware updates, so make sure to find one that is easy to use and places cyber hygiene on the forefront. Just like a computer or your mobile device, it is vital to update your Wi-Fi router regularly with the latest firmware updates. Remember, bad actors take advantage of outdated networking devices to spread malware and exploit your personal information. Enable automatic updates, if available. If not, sign up for email updates so you can be notified when your router manufacturer releases a system update for your device.

To locate instructions for installing the latest firmware, search your router model number and the word *firmware* in a search engine to locate the manufacturer's site page with firmware download options. If you use a router managed by a broadband provider, contact their customer service department to ask if your router has the latest firmware installed.

5. **Apply Strong Network Encryption (WPA2)**: When you set your SSID network password, you'll have a choice of network security standards. The strongest and recommended choice is WPA2, which mandates the support for military-grade AES-based encryption. WPA2 is the accepted choice until its security-improved, more modern successor, WPA3, is released and integrated with networking devices.[5] Anything else—such as WPA, WEP, or WPS—is not secure.

6. **Update Your Router's Security Configuration Settings**: When you are logged into your Wi-Fi console, it is important to make your settings more secure. First, disable any insecure security standards, such as WPS. Instead, enable secure functions to connect, such as WPA2. Disable additional insecure protocols, such as Universal Plug and Play (UPnP), PING, Telnet, SSH, and HNAP.[6] Also, make sure to disable remote management of your router. This protects your router from the public Internet. Check to make sure the router's built-in firewall is active too.

7. **Consider Using a VPN Service**: A VPN is a secure and private tunnel in which your web traffic travels. Everything you do on the Web, no matter if the site uses encryption or not, is hidden from prying eyes when using a secure, reliable VPN service. Services, like Tunnel Bear, are user-friendly and provide a free data allowance per month.[7] A trusted VPN service is helpful for those times where you need to perform a sensitive transaction or you're using public Wi-Fi (which you'll learn more about in Chapter 21, "Protecting Your Information When Traveling").

8. **Set Up a Guest Network for Visitors and IoT Devices**: Look for a Wi-Fi router with the capabilities to set up a guest network. By setting up a separate network for guests and less secure devices, such as IoT devices, you can segregate any infection from affecting your more valued

personal devices. And if your guests want to connect to your Wi-Fi, give them your guest network credentials. This will limit any spread of potential malware infection, as well as keep your personal network information and traffic private from others.

9. **Consider Turning Off Your Wi-Fi When Not Home**: When you turn off your Wi-Fi when you are not home, or even at night when you are asleep, it prevents attacks from unfolding off-hours for you to discover later. This is an extra security precaution that makes it even more difficult for bad actors to compromise your home Wi-Fi network.

Now that you've learned what the current threats are to your home Wi-Fi network, you're able to put into practice the specific recommendations to lock down your Wi-Fi router—protecting your family's networking devices and use of the Internet.

Next, you'll learn how to safeguard your Internet of Things (IoT) devices— such as your streaming devices, fitness trackers, smart toys, and more. By following the recommendations in the next chapter, you'll protect your IoT devices from becoming a bot in a bad actors' botnet army of controlled devices across the globe.

Notes

1. https://www.csoonline.com/article/2925636/security/how-to-stop-wi-fi-hackers-cold.html
2. https://krebsonsecurity.com/2018/05/fbi-kindly-reboot-your-router-now-please/#more-44020
3. https://krebsonsecurity.com/2017/10/what-you-should-know-about-the-krack-wifi-security-weakness/
4. https://www.nytimes.com/2018/06/13/technology/personaltech/wi-fi-router-security.html
5. https://www.wi-fi.org/news-events/newsroom/wi-fi-alliance-introduces-security-enhancements
6. https://www.tomsguide.com/us/home-router-security,news-19245.html
7. https://www.tunnelbear.com

20 Protecting Your IoT Devices

Rajesh was excited to install the two home security cameras he bought for the front and back of his house. They were simple to set up with Wi-Fi built into each of the cameras, and Rajesh was able to connect them to his wireless home network quickly. The cameras, which were the best deal he could find on Amazon, also came with a mobile app and an online dashboard page where he could enable motion-detection notifications, review past footage, and more.

After just a week with the cameras and mobile app installed, his Android phone started to act up. Every time Rajesh opened his phone, ads would increasingly pop up and take over his device. He tried restarting his device, cleared the browsing history, and even performed a factory reset. He couldn't understand where the ads were coming from. He could barely use his device anymore.

In the meantime, Rajesh was using his laptop to research what the problem could be with his phone. Suddenly, a black screen with red writing took over his display. Rajesh knew precisely what this meant—ransomware. He'd seen what the ransom notes looked like from news articles he'd read in the past. "What is going on with my devices?" Rajesh thought to himself, "A ransomware infection and an adware-infected mobile device, what else could go wrong?"

Rajesh decided to go to the grocery store and buy some food to keep him fueled for his attempts to clean up the mess. After his hot, delicious food was all bagged up and Rajesh swiped his card, the cashier said, "Your card was denied." Rajesh tried swiping it two more times *and then realized there was something very wrong. He called his bank from his infected phone, which was barely workable, and his balance was $0. He couldn't believe this was happening.*

Luckily, he had just enough cash to buy some of his groceries. If he hadn't, he wouldn't have known what to do. Rajesh went to a friend's house and told her what was going on. His life was in disarray, and he felt truly hopeless in his efforts to figure out what was happening to his phone. Natasha, Rajesh's closest friend, asked, "When did this all start?" Rajesh replied, "If I had to guess, it would've been around when I installed my new security cameras." It finally clicked. "Wow, what if the cameras I bought are infected with malware or something?" Natasha searched the make and model on Google, and articles came up warning against the device because of malware-laced firmware, as well as an opening in the network connection, which allowed bad actors to remote into his security cameras, access his home network, and download the ransomware to his computer. Natasha read a portion of the article to Rajesh, "These security cameras were found to be packaged and shipped off with the malicious code embedded in the firmware. The cameras, and other malicious Internet of Things (IoT) devices, then show up on Amazon and look reputable. Just because something is cheap and has some good reviews doesn't mean you should buy it. Always research the manufacturer to see whether they've gotten into trouble selling malicious IoT devices."

Rajesh couldn't believe the two security cameras caused so much damage to his devices, his bank account, and his life. Rajesh uninstalled the app from his phone immediately and installed a mobile antivirus for his Android phone to clean up the mess left behind. Luckily, Rajesh had a cloud backup of his PC, so he performed a factory reset, reinstalled the operating system, and restored his files prior to his security camera installation. "What a nightmare," Rajesh sighed.

The story of Rajesh's purchase of malware-infected home security cameras wreaking havoc in his life is not uncommon. As you learned in the previous chapter, even some Android device manufacturers have sold smartphones pre-loaded with malware. These hidden threats, already implanted in IoT devices, urge us to vet the manufacturers, products, and sellers carefully before we purchase them. If you go for the cheapest deal without looking into the product, you could risk hidden dangers taking over your digital and physical lives—leaving you to clean up their mess.

Malware-laden IoT devices is just one threat. In this chapter, I point out other common dangers to IoT devices.

Threats Against IoT Devices

> **MY JEEP IS UNDER ATTACK!**
>
> Andy was driving 70 mph on a highway outside of St. Louis when his Jeep Cherokee started going haywire. His air conditioning turned on full blast, and the radio volume went up to its highest setting. Andy tried to turn the fan and the volume down, but nothing changed. Then Andy's windshield wipers turned on and the fluid continuously sprayed, obstructing Andy's view. "What else can go wrong with this car? It's brand new!" Andy thought. That's when the transmission ground to a halt. Andy was stuck in the middle of traffic, with no shoulder on which he could pull over, and all of his attempts to turn on his vehicle failed. His Jeep was taken over by bad actors.[1]

Luckily, Andy's experience with his remote-controlled Jeep was an agreed upon, monitored IoT cyberattack experiment with two security researchers, Charlie Miller and Chris Valasek. Nowadays, vehicles come equipped with their own cellular connections and Wi-Fi hotspots, transforming our vehicles into smartphones. This can be convenient for those riding in the vehicle, but it's also opportune for bad actors to control a car remotely—cutting the brakes, disabling the transmission, controlling the steering, and more. Miller and Valasek stated, because of a vulnerability in Uconnect, a feature in most Chrysler vehicles, bad actors can locate a vehicle anywhere in the United States just by figuring out its IP address. Once bad actors connect to the vehicle remotely, they rewrite firmware code on a chip in the vehicle's hardware to then take over the car's internal computer network.

At the time of their research, Valasek and Miller estimated there were around 471,000 vulnerable vehicles with Uconnect systems on the road. Chrysler ended up issuing a recall for 1.4 million vehicles after learning of the result of the vulnerability in its Uconnect system.

Vehicle manufacturers, like Chrysler, release firmware updates for IoT smart cars.[1] The problem is, most consumers don't hear about released software updates for their vehicles—some might not even realize their vehicles' computers need to be updated when a patch is released. When a consumer does find out about an available firmware update for their vehicle, it's up to them to schedule an appointment with the dealership to have the update manually applied to the internal computer network. *Our vehicles are now computers we need to protect and update regularly.* If we don't, we risk the exploitation of personal information (such as our Global Positioning System [GPS] location, contacts, phone calls, and so forth), as well as the remote takeover of our vehicle—putting our lives and our family's lives—in danger.

Bad actors taking control of an Internet-connected vehicle is just a single example of an IoT cyberattack. The following are additional dangers to IoT devices:

Botnets   *Botnets* are armies of compromised IoT devices controlled by bad actors. One such botnet, called Mirai, even used a refrigerator—among a sea of 10 million IoT devices—in a DDoS attack to take down a large DNS provider that provided support for popular services like Spotify, Twitter, and more. Bad actors gained ahold of the IoT devices using Mirai malware, which searches the Web for IoT devices that are unpatched or use default or weak login credentials. Mirai turns the device into a bot, which is then under the control of a bad actor or "botmaster."[2] Going beyond just disrupting services, researchers believe bad actors will evolve to begin monetizing their IoT bot attacks.[3]

Ransomware   Bad actors can spread ransomware to IoT devices, such as smart TVs, smartwatches, and more. Because IoT devices are infrequently patched, which leaves security holes, bad actors can use this to their advantage to carry out ransomware attacks. For instance, if a smart TV uses unencrypted data transmissions while a user wants to download an app, a bad actor could use a man-in-the-middle (MitM) attack to take over their legitimate request and instead provide the IoT user with a malicious lookalike app to install, which secretly houses ransomware behind the scenes.[4]

Spyware Some IoT devices, such as smart vacuums, can have security vulnerabilities that allow bad actors to spy on home users without even being on their home Wi-Fi network. One such vulnerability, called HomeHack, takes advantage of the web and mobile app portal SmartThinQ for the LG Hom-Bot smart robot vacuums. Because of a weak login process, bad actors were able to create a MitM attack to manipulate the login process through the app and easily gain access to users' accounts, allowing them to view the live feed from the vacuum's viewpoint. LG has since released a patch to close the HomeHack cyberattack vulnerability.[5]

Besides these harmful threats directed by bad actors, IoT devices can also carry privacy flaws—exposing your data to the public eye. Next, learn about IoT privacy holes and how a fitness app leaked top-secret military base location information.

IoT Privacy Issues

Strava, a social networking app for athletes, unveiled a data visualization map to the public that depicted the details of all physical activity tracked by its users—including users walking around secret military bases and spy outposts. After the map's release, military analysts caught wind of the map's disclosure of incredibly sensitive location information of active duty military personnel. Nathan Ruser, a military analyst for United Conflict Analysts, commented on Strava's map, stating it "looks very pretty," but "U.S. bases are clearly identifiable and mappable."[6] Ruser discovered the fitness routes of military personnel at secret U.S. military bases in Afghanistan, Syria, a potential CIA base in Somalia, as well as Area 51. Researchers also located a secret Russian military base in the Ukraine, a hidden missile base in Taiwan, and an NSA base in Hawaii.[7]

Strava's heat map turns a dark color at night, making it easy to spot foreign U.S. military bases, which light right up and expose their top-secret locations. Analyst Tobias Schneider shared suspected screenshots of military outposts around Mosul, stating sarcastically they could also be ". . . locals who enjoy running in close circles around their houses."[8] Researchers also found ways to deanonymize the Strava heat map, creating a list of individuals and their exercise locations.

In response to the research findings, Strava stated, "Our global heat map represents an aggregated and anonymized view of over a billion activities uploaded to our platform. It excludes activities that have been marked as private and user-defined privacy zones. We are committed to helping people better understand our settings to give them control over what they share."[7]

The primary lesson coming out of the Strava heat map unveiling secret military bases is for users to check and configure their privacy settings to limit their location and data sharing to avoid their fitness paths being shown to the world.

You learned how the Strava fitness app leaked the locations of classified military bases, how a smart home can spy on you, and what your IoT devices are doing behind your back. Here, I will bust a myth that claims fitness trackers can't disclose your ATM code and passwords. Read on to find out the facts.

Myth "I wear a fitness tracker band to track my steps. Bad actors can't guess my ATM code and passwords."

Fact Bad actors can learn your ATM code numbers and your passwords using motion sensor technology in fitness trackers and smartwatches. Yan Wang was a graduate student at the Stevens Institute of Technology and was one of five researchers on a team led by Yingying Chen that developed a technique to combine data from embedded sensors in wearables (such as fitness trackers and other similar devices) with a specific algorithm that could then crack PIN codes and passwords with 80 percent accuracy in just one attempt. After three tries, they achieved a 90 percent accuracy rate. Over an 11-month period, the researchers ran 5,000 key-entry tests on three key-based security systems and concluded there is a "serious security breach of wearable devices in the context of divulging secret information (for example, key entries)."[9] Make sure you only wear your fitness tracker when necessary and review your privacy settings to review collected data.

Now, you'll gain deeper insight into what your smart home IoT devices are doing behind the scenes—the data they are they collecting, where are they sending it, and who's watching.

Smart Homes

Kashmir Hill, a Gizmodo reporter, purchased IoT devices for her family's home to participate in a study to identify how much information was being transmitted from the smart home devices, what type of personal data was sent over the Internet, and who else was viewing it. Kashmir's colleague,

Surya Mattu, set up a Wi-Fi router specifically for the IoT devices to determine how much he could learn about Kashmir's family's habits from merely investigating network packets. What Surya could see on the router is also what a bad actor or an Internet service provider (ISP) could see. Ever since Congress voted to allow ISPs to snoop on and sell customers' Internet activity, any information Surya found is also what third parties would be able to see and profit.

Kashmir purchased smart house lights, a coffee maker, a baby monitor, vacuum, child toys, a toothbrush, photo frames, security cameras, sex toys, and a bed cover—and attempted to integrate them with an Amazon Echo. To do so, she had to download 14 different apps to control everything, as well as hope that Alexa, Amazon's search assistant, would be able to control everything through voice commands. Things didn't go as smoothly as she hoped. Besides the compatibility issues between all of the different manufacturers' IoT devices in her home, she also had some privacy snafus. The day after she set up a motion-detecting security camera with air quality sensors in her living room, she found it had recorded her walking naked through her living room and was sent to the manufacturers' cloud and saved to the device's correlating app on her phone. She was shocked—this would be the first nude video of her on the Internet—the idea of home security turned into a privacy nightmare. Surya found the video data to be encrypted over the Internet (phew!), but the idea of someone hacking into Kashmir's IoT cloud account was still frightening to her.

Surya was able to see what Kashmir and her family were watching on Hulu, since it sends its data unencrypted. Netflix, on the other hand, encrypts all of its data except for photos of recommended shows. Surya was able to collect these photos to view their media watching interests. Surya could also tell when the family woke up because Alexa would start playing Spotify from 6 a.m. to 8 a.m., although Surya couldn't tell which songs were playing. Likewise, at night, he could tell Kashmir was using the Alexa Sounds app between 6 p.m. and 8 p.m., which was when she would put her daughter to sleep. Everything Surya could detect on the network could also be seen by advertisers, intelligence agencies, and corporations.

Kashmir's Vizio smart TV was also sending all of their activity to market research websites—Scorecard Research, a digital behavior tracker. Kashmir wrote, "All of the anxiety you currently feel about being tracked online is going to move into your living room." Unless a user chooses to turn off data sharing, smart TV providers share your activity with advertisers and other third parties.

Even more shocking is the fact that Internet-connected sex toys can track your usage, and one company, We-Vibe, was caught collecting statistics on its users' orgasms for "market research." We-Vibe ended up paying millions of dollars to customers in a class-action lawsuit over the privacy invasion. After the study concluded, Kashmir wrote, "When you buy a smart device, it doesn't just belong to you; you share custody with the company that made it." Before bringing IoT devices into your home, make sure the functionality is worth the data being transmitted, stored, viewed, and potentially sold to third parties.[10]

Researchers at Princeton University also looked into what IoT devices do in the background. IoT Inspector was designed to analyze the security and privacy levels of IoT devices by inspecting the data they transmit over the Internet. The following are their shocking findings from the study, showing the privacy holes in IoT devices:[11]

1. **Many IoT Devices Lack Basic Encryption and Authentication**: A great number of the IoT devices analyzed sent data unencrypted over the Internet. Children's toys were a big culprit—sending data in plain text, as well as making it easy for bad actors to retrieve user profile photos because of the lack of proper authentication. Another IoT device, a smart blood pressure monitor, transmitted the word *blood pressure*, along with the device brand, over the Web. This meant that bad actors could learn someone in the house used a blood pressure monitor and could see how often they used it based on the number of data requests.

2. **User Behavior Can Be Inferred from Encrypted IoT Traffic**: As you read in Kashmir's smart home study experience, Suryu, the researcher who was monitoring her family's IoT-only Wi-Fi router, was able to tell when her family woke up, what they were watching on Hulu, and more. ISPs or anyone who has network packet sniffers nearby can analyze a person's in-home behavior from looking at the traffic spikes and their frequency.

3. **Many IoT Devices Contact a Large and Diverse Set of Third Parties**: It's easy to assume your streaming device or your fitness tracker is only chatting with the manufacturer's home base. Unfortunately, this is not usually the case. In fact, Princeton researchers discovered it to be quite the opposite. IoT device manufacturers tend not to disclose the third parties with whom they share your data, which makes it

difficult to judge the truthfulness of their privacy policies—what they're doing with your data and who's analyzing and profiting from your activity.

IoT devices have benefits in helping with daily tasks, enhancing home security, and monitoring your health. However, as you've learned, there are some innate security and privacy risks with many manufacturers. Luckily, there is a movement to create a standard for IoT devices to uphold high levels of security and privacy. The IoT Cybersecurity Improvement Act was introduced in 2017 by Senator Mark Warner, and its purpose is "to provide minimal cybersecurity operational standards for Internet-connected devices" purchased by the federal government.

The pending legislation warns:[12]

> *"While 'Internet of Things' (IoT) devices and the data they transmit present enormous benefits to consumers, the relative insecurity of many devices presents enormous challenges. Thus far, there has been a significant market failure in the security of these devices. Sometimes shipped with factory-set, hard-coded passwords and oftentimes unable to be updated or patched, IoT devices can represent a weak point in a network's security, leaving the rest of the network vulnerable to attack. Additionally, the sheer number of IoT devices—expected to exceed 20 billion devices by 2020—has enabled bad actors to launch devastating Distributed Denial of Service (DDoS) attacks. This legislation is aimed at addressing the market failure by establishing minimum security requirements for federal procurements of connected devices."*

The important aspect about this legislation is the pressure it would put on IoT manufacturers to comply with the bill. This would have a positive impact for consumers because of the increased security and privacy demands placed on the IoT manufacturers.

Next, you'll learn how you can also protect your privacy when it comes to reviewing IoT devices before making a purchase, checking how much data your IoT devices are tracking about you, and evaluating how the device is publicizing your information on the Internet.

Recommendations: Protecting Your IoT Devices

The following are the essential recommendations to protect your IoT devices, as well as your family's privacy and level of security:

1. **Review IoT Brands Before Purchasing**: Review the company's cyber hygiene habits by reading tech-themed reviews and by checking the vendor's patching history to review their frequency of security updates. As you learned in Chapter 18, "Protecting Your Mobile Devices," some manufacturers have been caught preloading malware into devices they sell to consumers. Always stick with reputable, well-known manufacturers. And be cautious when purchasing used IoT devices—they could potentially harbor malware or may have been tampered with maliciously.

2. **Review IoT Device's Privacy Policy**: Reading the details of the privacy policy is important, or find an article by someone who has analyzed it already. Princeton researchers found many IoT devices sharing collected data with numerous third-party entities. This data is sold and used to analyze consumer behavior. Prior to purchasing, review what personal information the device tracks and shares.

3. **Change Default Passwords and Create Strong Ones**: Most IoT devices come with default login credentials, such as *admin* for both the username and password. Worse yet, some IoT devices have the credentials hard-coded, meaning you can't change them, and they can be easily discovered by bad actors. Make sure to obtain an IoT device that allows you to create your own strong and unique credentials. You can locate the password-changing instructions by searching your IoT device model and manufacturer in a search engine. Refer to the "Password Creation Formula" tips in Chapter 16 to create one-of-a-kind, strong, and memorable passwords for your IoT devices. Make sure to store them in your password manager. Doing so will make it easier to type in your password manually on IoT devices, such as streaming sticks.

4. **Install Firmware Updates Regularly**: Install updates as soon as they are released and enable automatic updates when possible. If they are not automatically available, sign up for email updates so you can be notified when your router manufacturer releases a system update for

your device. Promptly installing updates prevents bad actors from more easily compromising your network-connected devices using malicious exploits that target known system vulnerabilities. Some IoT device manufacturers created products without the ability to update the firmware. If this is the case, the only option to keep it secure is to upgrade to a modern, supported version, if possible. Some IoT makers are considering creating a trade-in program for customers who have insecure IoT devices with default, hard-coded credentials, and non-upgradeable firmware.[13] Use a search engine to determine how you can install firmware updates on your IoT device.

5. **Verify Apps Before Downloading**: Malicious apps can carry malware, spyware, ransomware, and more. Make sure to enable proper security settings for your device model to prohibit the downloading of unverified publisher apps.

6. **Configure Security and Privacy Settings**: Review and configure the settings on your IoT device for maximum security and privacy, depending on your needs. Search your IoT device model online, along with the words *configure security and privacy settings* to find articles with instructions to protect your device and your identity.

7. **Secure Your Home Wi-Fi and Create a Separate Network for IoT Devices**: In the previous chapter, you learned how to secure your home Wi-Fi network. The recommendations listed in Chapter 19 need to be implemented in addition to following the recommendations in this list to protect your IoT devices fully. Consider creating a separate network, protected by a network firewall, for your IoT devices if the feature is built in to your Wi-Fi router. If your Wi-Fi router doesn't have this feature, consider getting a secondary router for a segregated IoT network. Having a separate network for IoT devices means if your IoT devices become infected with malware or are compromised by bad actors, the malicious programs would stay on that isolated network—and not on your primary home network.

8. **Disable Features You Don't Use**: Some IoT devices come with microphones and cameras. If you don't plan to use these, attempt to disable them in the device's settings. You can also cover the device's camera for an assurance of privacy. You can purchase camera covers that slide back and forth, allowing for ease of use when needed and an extra sense of privacy when not in use.

You've learned about IoT devices and how they can pose a threat to your family's privacy and security at home, while driving, or even while jogging. You also gained the intel on how to protect and secure your IoT devices. In the next chapter, you'll learn the skills to provide ample protection for your information when traveling—to the local café or abroad.

Notes

1. https://www.wired.com/2015/07/hackers-remotely-kill-jeep-highway/
2. www.bbc.com/news/technology-37738823
3. https://www.darkreading.com/vulnerabilities---threats/6-cybersecurity-trends-to-watch/a/d-id/1331103?_mc=rss_x_drr_edt_aud_dr_x_x-rss-simple
4. https://www.symantec.com/connect/blogs/how-my-tv-got-infected-ransomware-and-what-you-can-learn-it
5. https://thehackernews.com/2017/10/smart-iot-device-hacking.html
6. https://www.theguardian.com/world/2018/jan/28/fitness-tracking-app-gives-away-location-of-secret-us-army-bases
7. https://thehackernews.com/2018/01/strava-heatmap-location-tracking.html
8. https://twitter.com/tobiaschneider/status/957336807812804608
9. https://www.computerworld.com/article/3092407/security/hackers-can-exploit-smartwatches-fitness-trackers-to-steal-your-atm-pin.html
10. https://gizmodo.com/the-house-that-spied-on-me-1822429852
11. https://freedom-to-tinker.com/2018/04/23/announcing-iot-inspector-a-tool-to-study-smart-home-iot-device-behavior/
12. https://www.warner.senate.gov/public/_cache/files/8/6/861d66b8-93bf-4c93-84d0-6bea67235047/8061BCEEBF4300EC702B4E894247D0E0.iot-cybersecurity-improvement-act---fact-sheet.pdf
13. https://krebsonsecurity.com/2016/10/who-makes-the-iot-things-under-attack/

21

Protecting Your Information When Traveling

Isabella put on her headphones, started playing her self-curated travel mix, and attempted to relax in the airplane seat. While her eyes were closed—close to dozing off to sleep— she felt the plane oddly jerk to one side. She's felt seemingly normal fluctuations in-flight before, but this was one of those movements where you almost feel like you're in a trick plane, almost spinning upside down. Isabella looked around; everyone's faces shone of pure terror. A few minutes later, the oxygen masks all dropped down. "Oh no," Isabella thought, "this can't seriously be happening." Passengers put on their oxygen masks and waited to hear an announcement from the pilot and crew. Finally, a voice came over the speaker, "Attention Flight 7109 passengers, we are experiencing some technical difficulties. The cabin pressure is perfectly normal. You don't need to use the oxygen masks. We are waiting for approval to land at a nearby airport. Please remain calm and stay in your seats."

The pilot's words were not very comforting, "Why would the oxygen masks drop if there wasn't a change in cabin pressure?" Isabella asked herself. In an attempt to distract herself and contact her family members in case something happened to her, she connected to the plane's in-flight Wi-Fi. She sent messages to all of her family members who had Apple iMessage, describing the weird situation on the plane. Afterward, Isabella logged in to her email account and sent messages to her family members who couldn't send texts over Wi-Fi. Finally, they landed and switched planes. Isabella arrived back home safely, although quite shaken.

Within the week after her arrival, she went online to pay her bills. She remembered not to perform any sensitive transactions while traveling abroad. But to her dismay, she was locked out of most of her sites, including her bank account. "This is strange," Isabella pondered, "I better check my bank account balance." Isabella called the bank's hotline and found her entire bank account—her life savings— was depleted. Isabella was frazzled, "How did I get hacked?" After resetting all of her passwords, including her email account, and regaining access to all of the sites she normally visited, she couldn't help but wonder how this all unfolded.

Later that month, Isabella was reading the news and came across a startling headline, "Hacker Takes Over Flight: Snoops on Passengers' In-Flight Wi-Fi Traffic—Programs Plane to Tilt and Deploy Oxygen Masks." Isabella read further and realized the plane they were talking about was the one she was on. She then phoned the FBI, as recommended in the article, and explained she was on the plane, her accounts got compromised, and she lost her money.

Isabella's experience is inspired by the real-life story of a security researcher, Chris Roberts, who spent years researching security vulnerabilities on airplanes. Roberts flew on a number of flights and allegedly tested out potential cyberattacks, like executing commands to cause "one of the airplane engines to climb resulting in lateral or sideways movement of the plane," according to the search warrant written by FBI special agent Mark Hurley. Roberts' goal was to bring public attention to the lack of cybersecurity on flights.

One such vulnerability was the fact that airplane's avionics and in-flight entertainment (IFE) systems were sometimes on the same network, potentially allowing a bad actor to hack into the IFE network and traversing into critical aviation controls. Roberts felt it was his duty to expose these issues so airline companies and airplane manufacturers could address them to keep passengers safe from cyber or terror attacks. In response to the search warrant, Roberts insisted he accessed in-flight networks only about 15 times to observe the data transmissions (for instance, passengers browsing the Web, sending emails, and so forth).

Roberts gained access to the in-flight networks by opening the seat electronic box (SEB) found underneath his (and each) passenger seat, connecting a modified Ethernet cable, and typing in generic default credentials. What got him detained by the FBI when he got off of his flight was this tweet he published midair:

> Find myself on a 737/800, let's see Box-IFE-ICE-SATCOM, ? Shall we start playing with EICAS messages? 'PASS OXYGEN ON' Anyone?

Roberts was referring to potential vulnerabilities found in the engine indicator crew alert system (EICAS), in which he could've enabled the passenger oxygen masks. Roberts' tweet was meant sarcastically, in a way to bring attention to the vulnerability, but the FBI and the United Airlines' Cyber Security Intelligence Department thought differently. They saw Roberts as a threat to the well-being of other passengers. Roberts denies the claim that he caused an airplane's engine to climb, resulting in sideways movement. Roberts stated he performed this testing in a virtual environment and not in-flight.[1]

Just like public Wi-Fi in a café or a restaurant, bad actors can hack the Wi-Fi on a plane, while unlikely, to monitor your web traffic for sensitive information, to access your financial details, and to infect and compromise your device. In this chapter, you'll learn about additional risks that can occur you when you connect to publicly available Wi-Fi networks. Later, you'll learn how to protect your Internet access from bad actors, no matter where you are in the world.

Public Wi-Fi Dangers

PLAYING POLITICS WITH WI-FI

Three British politicians participated in a study to show the risks of public Wi-Fi. Security researchers recorded the username and password of the first politician, David Davis, to gain access to his email account. After compromising Davis's email account, researchers gained immediate entry to his PayPal account—Davis used the same login credentials for both Gmail and PayPal. In response to the attack, Davis stated, "Well, it is pretty horrifying, to be honest. What [the researchers] have extracted was a very tough password, tougher than most people use. It is certainly not 'Password.'"

Next, the researchers sent a phishing attack to the second politician's laptop, which mimicked a Facebook login page. Mary Honeyball signed in using the malicious page, allowing the "bad actors" to take control of her Facebook account.

Finally, the third politician, Lord Paul Strasburger, made a complimentary Voice over Internet Protocol (VoIP) call (which uses Wi-Fi to make phone calls) from his hotel room phone. The researchers were able to listen to and record his conversation.[2]

The British politicians bluntly learned the risks of using public Wi-Fi, including making phone calls over VoIP.[3]

The following are the cyberattacks commonly used against public Wi-Fi users:

Man-in-the-Middle (MitM) Attacks This is where a bad actor intercepts the communications between two parties (for example, between you and a website or email contact). During a MitM attack, a bad actor gets in between the network transmissions to snoop on, modify, or block communications. If you're using a website that isn't encrypted, it is wise to assume bad actors can see everything you're doing. And if you're using public Wi-Fi, anyone on the network can see your browsing history. Even if it's encrypted, bad actors can still see what websites or services you're using.

Fake Wi-Fi Networks Earlier in the book, I talked about how a bad actor can create a Wi-Fi hotspot, naming it something like "Starbucks Guest," which could be very similar to Starbucks' legitimate Wi-Fi network. By allowing anyone to connect, bad actors can monitor everything you do, as well as infect and compromise your system. Watch out for multiple, similarly named networks and alert the staff where you are located of the potential malicious "evil twin" network hotspot.

Packet Sniffing Bad actors can use free tools, like Wireshark, to analyze the network to which they're connected so they can spy on what other people are doing in hopes to obtain login credentials, sensitive information, and more. It is safe to assume that anyone on the Wi-Fi network you're on can see everything you're browsing. Packet sniffing may not be illegal if there is no banner before logging into a public Wi-Fi network that says so. This is why using a VPN when using public Wi-Fi is so essential. I discuss VPN usage more in the upcoming recommendation list for general travel security.

Session Hijacking (Sidejacking)   Bad actors use packet sniffing to take over your web browsing sessions to gain access to your account. Session hijacking works if the website you are browsing allows for sessions to be active in more than one location. All a bad actor needs is your session ID, which they can replicate in their browser to gain entry to your account. To combat this, again make sure to use a VPN and also log out of all of your sessions when you stop using the public Wi-Fi network. Later, log in to your accounts at home to verify the active sessions are only yours, with no bad actors lingering. You can also get alerted if there is a session in an unrecognized location or on an unauthorized device.

Shoulder Surfing   This is a simple attack, but it can be efficient. Try to sit in a position in public where a lot of people don't have a clear view of your device's screen. Avoid accessing or filling out personal information. If you can't avoid it altogether, purchase a privacy screen, which has a darker tint that prevents others from clearly seeing your display while you can see it just fine.

In addition to public Wi-Fi threats, the following are some general travel dangers to look out for when you're out adventuring.

General Travel Dangers

DON'T GET JUICE JACKED CHARGING YOUR PHONE

Kieran was at the JFK airport waiting to board his flight to see his family in California. He decided to charge his phone before he hopped on the plane. Kieran found a USB charging station nearby and plugged his phone in to charge. What Kieran didn't realize was that a bad actor was using the USB port to "juice jack" his information from his phone, as well as download malware and tracking programs to his device. Because USB ports do more than just charge, it is easy for bad actors to pull information from a device, as well as mirror the screen to see passwords and PIN codes entered. Not all USB charging stations at airports, rest stops, hotels, and other public spaces are malicious, but it is better to be safe and protect your device integrity and information than to be very sorry.

The following are specific recommendations to avoid *juice jacking* cyberattacks while traveling and charging your devices:[4]

- Instead of using a USB charging station, look for an electrical outlet where you can plug in your phone to avoid any possibility of data transfer.
- Purchase a USB cord that can only charge and doesn't have the technology to provide data transfer.
- Carry a fully charged extra portable device battery or power bank with you instead of using an outlet.
- Turn off your phone completely if you need to use a USB charging station. This may prevent data transfer.

Another mainstream risk when traveling is the *tourist scam*, which could result in your stolen identity, information, and money. There are a wide variety of scams targeting travelers, and most schemes are after your money through the use of pick-pocketing tactics, fraudulent transactions, and clever social engineering.

Be careful when interacting with the locals in an area you are visiting. Always make sure what you purchase is valid and not a fraudulent item or ticket. Be cautious of anyone who tries to distract you while other bad actors pick-pocket you and steal your devices, cash, and more. Think carefully before deciding to hand over your information.

The following are common tourist scams found around the globe:[5]

Fake Take-Out Menus   Watch out for phony food menus stuffed under your hotel room door. Your order may never arrive, and your payment information is now stolen.

Taxi Drivers Bad Actors   Keep an eye on your luggage when traveling. Some taxi drivers moonlight as bad actors and could drive off with one of your bags while you're in a hurry to get to your destination.

"Good Samaritan" Pickpockets   Often masquerading as helpful locals, pickpockets will warn you about others who they've "seen" get pickpocketed when, really, they are waiting to see where you check for your valuables so they can more easily steal your belongings later.

Photography Gone Awry   Scam artists can pretend to be a group of friends who want their photo taken. They'll ask you to take their photo with their camera, and when you realize it doesn't work, they grab it and drop it, causing it to smash and demand money from you for "repairs." They can also pickpocket you during the commotion. Bad actors can also run away with your phone or camera if you ask them to take a photo. Use your best judgment before saying "yes" to helping others out or asking someone to help you take a photo.

Fake Front Desk Call   If you receive a call from the hotel's "front desk" asking you to verify your payment information, a mental red flag should go up. Instead of handing over your credit card number, physically go down to the front desk to inquire about the call.

Now that you've gained insight into various travel scams and cyberattacks, you'll learn specific recommendations to protect your devices and, as a result, your identity and finances when traveling.

Recommendations: Protecting Your Information When Traveling (General)

The following are the fundamental recommendations to protect your data when traveling, either to a local café or to another country:

1. **Don't Leave Your Devices Unattended**: Always take note of the location of your devices and belongings. If you are driving, keep laptops in your trunk. If you are in a café, bring your computer with you when you go to the bathroom. Consider purchasing a device cable lock to secure your device to a nonmoving/hard-to-move piece of furniture. When flying, always store your devices in your carry-on bag.

2. **Ensure Security Software and Antivirus is Updated**: Prior to traveling and connecting to public Wi-Fi, verify your system firewall and anti-virus programs are up-to-date.

3. **Disable "Auto-Connect" to Available Wi-Fi Networks**: Auto-connect can accidentally connect you to malicious networks automatically. Disable this feature by searching your device manufacturer and *disable auto-connect* in a search engine for instructions on how to turn it off.

4. **Turn Off Device Wi-Fi When Not in Use**: By turning off the Wi-Fi on your devices, you'll prevent your laptop or smartphone from connecting to unsuspecting networks, and you'll conserve your battery life when traveling.

5. **Turn Off Sharing Services Before Connecting to Wi-Fi**: If your device shares any of its services, you will need to disable these prior to connecting to a public Wi-Fi network. In a search engine, search for your device information and *turn off sharing services* for detailed instructions.

6. **Verify the Network Before Connecting**: As you learned, bad actors can create "evil twin" Wi-Fi networks, which look similar to legitimate ones. Verify the correct network before connecting to it and make sure to follow the next step and use a VPN service when using public Wi-Fi.

7. **Use a VPN When Using Public Wi-Fi, Even In-Air**: When you connect to public Wi-Fi, anyone else who is also connected can see your browsing history. Using encrypted (HTTPS) websites is a proper precaution for protecting your information. In addition, it's vital to use a VPN service to adequately defend yourself by encrypting and encapsulating the emails you send, the websites you visit, the credentials you input, and more. There are many trusted VPN services you can install for your laptop and mobile device. One I've mentioned before is Tunnel Bear, which provides an easy-to-use interface, is simple to set up, and gives you a monthly data allowance for free.

8. **Avoid Performing Sensitive Actions and Transactions**: When traveling, avoid making online purchases or checking your bank account while using public Wi-Fi. Use your cellular service, if available. If you need to use Wi-Fi, make sure to follow the previous step and use a trusted VPN service. Always make sure the site into which you are inputting data is encrypted. You can determine this by looking for `https` at the beginning of the URL address. Also, make sure never to change your account passwords when connected to public Wi-Fi.

9. **Don't Use Free VoIP Calling Services**: As you learned from the story about the British politicians who got hacked using public Wi-Fi and free hotel VoIP calls, bad actors can use MitM attacks to intercept your transmissions and steal your personal information. Instead of using public VoIP calls, use a secure service on your phone instead, while using a VPN to protect what you're saying.

10. **Beware of Social Engineering Attacks**: Watch out for social engineering scams, such as tourist scams and phishing attacks, when traveling. Carry only the necessary payment information and personal ID documents required for travel. Keep an eye on your belongings, and remain vigilant to any unsolicited phone calls, texts, or emails asking you for personal info, such as credit card numbers.

11. **Don't Post Photos of Your Boarding Pass**: Most boarding passes include just enough information for a bad actor to gain access to your flight reservation page, cancel future flights, view/edit passport numbers, citizenship, date of birth, expiration date, and more.[6] Don't post photos of your boarding pass and other travel materials, like your passport.

12. **Don't Post Information About Your Trip**: As you learned in Chapter 15, "Protecting Your Social Media," bad actors look for publicly available travel information to send you phishing attacks, rob you on-site, and more. Keep information about your trip private, and don't use location tracking on social media, such as Instagram.

Now that you're prepared to keep yourself and your family safe during general travel, in the following section you'll learn about tailored travel recommendations when visiting nation-state countries abroad.

Nation-State Travel Dangers

BEWARE OF STATE-SPONSORED CYBERCRIME WHILE TRAVELING

Niko traveled to Russia for the FIFA World Cup. He was stoked to experience the inspirational event live. While venturing around and using public Wi-Fi at his hotel and public spaces, bad actors sponsored by the nation-state were targeting FIFA visitors to steal their information, download malware/spyware on their devices, and track their behaviors. Niko didn't realize he had no expectation of privacy when traveling to Russia since it has a surveillance system in place, known as System of Operative Investigative Measures, which allows the Kremlin to intercept phone calls and telephone networks operating within Russia legally. The government endorses cybercriminals in Russia because they help channel billions of dollars into the Russian economy.[7] The seemingly harmless and fun sporting event was turning into a bad cyber dream— malware-infected devices, compromised accounts, and stolen personal information.

According to the FBI, when you travel overseas, you can become a target of a foreign country's efforts to obtain information or technologies to increase a nation-state's market share, gain an economic advantage, and modernize warfare. Bad actors use attack methods such as luggage inspections, detailed questioning, and unwarranted examination and downloading of information from your laptop. The FBI also warns there is no expectation of privacy in most countries' Internet cafés, hotels, airplanes, offices, and public spaces—bad actors can intercept any data you send electronically. If bad actors find information of yours that may be useful to the government or a nongovernment organization (NGO), they will confiscate it from you. Bad actors in nation-states can track your location through your mobile device, as well as turn on the microphone without you noticing.[8]

By following the next travel recommendations, you will help protect your identity, finances, and personal information when traveling abroad to foreign nation-states.

Recommendations: Protecting Your Information When Traveling Abroad

The following are critical recommendations to protect yourself—your personal information, finances, and devices—while traveling abroad:[8]

1. **Before You Travel**:
   a. **Research Country-Specific Travel Advisories and Local Customs**: Some technologies, such as encryption, can be considered illegal in certain countries. Review specific travel advisories, as well as area cultural norms, so you can do your best to protect your information and blend in with locals.
   b. **Take Only the Minimum Identification and Payment Cards Needed**: The more money and forms of identification you bring, the more at risk your identity and finances are. Only bring the necessary forms of identification, credit card, and so forth.
   c. **Establish Emergency Contacts**: After registering your trip with the State Department, obtain the phone number and address for the U.S. embassy or consulate in the country that you plan to visit. Make sure to notify family members of your decision to make them your emergency contacts and to be aware of your communications with them while abroad.

d. **Perform Backups**: If your device gets stolen when traveling, your chance to recover your data is dependent upon you storing backups in the cloud.

e. **Update Your Devices**: Ensure your devices are up-to-date, as well as the software programs, such as antivirus. Only keep the minimum programs needed.

f. **Sanitize Your Devices**: Ensure there is no personal, sensitive information lingering on your devices before you take them abroad. Also, clean out your voicemail to ensure there is nothing sensitive.

g. **Create Travel-Specific Email Account**: Consider using a unique email account just for when you're traveling. This will prevent your email account from being hacked by bad actors while abroad.

2. **Protect Your Mobile Device**:

a. Take only a "burner" phone, purchased in the United States, into the country, and do not take your phone for everyday use. Don't purchase devices, or software, abroad.

b. If you are in a particularly sensitive meeting, power off your phone and remove the battery (if possible).

c. Use a complex password/pin to log in to the phone.

d. Disable the camera if not needed and/or place a piece of black tape over the lens when not in use.

e. Beware of phishing attacks through in-person social engineering, texts, emails, and phone calls.

f. Keep an eye on customs agents to make sure they keep your devices in a location within direct view.

3. **Lock Down Your Laptop**:

a. Use a strong, complex, and unique password to log in to the laptop. Save it in your password manager. Use your password manager to autofill your login credentials instead of typing them in. This prevents bad actors from seeing what you type.

b. Don't allow foreign electronic storage devices to connect to your laptop (such as thumb drives, and so on).

c. Keep sensitive data in a secure cloud storage location and not locally on your computer.

d. Use full disk encryption.

NOTE   Some countries have legal restrictions on using encryption. Check the country's travel warnings to see if it's allowed.

    e. Disable automatic login for any applications.

    f. Configure your laptop's firewall to allow only a small set of defined, trusted outbound connections.

    g. Don't use administrative access on your computer.

    h. Install only minimal, necessary applications.

    i. Disable microphone and camera if not needed. Use a camera lens cover when not in use for protection.

4. **While You Travel:**

    a. **Assume All Conversations Are Being Intercepted and Your Devices Monitored**: Unlike the United States, most countries don't have any legalities restricting surveillance. According to the FBI, foreign security services have methods of screening incoming visitors to identify individuals of potential intelligence interest. Foreign security services have established contacts with hotels that attempt to assist in monitoring you. You can be digitally monitored on airlines, in hotel rooms, in taxis, and also in meeting rooms.

    b. **Don't Leave Your Devices Unattended**: Keep your devices on you at all times. According to the FBI, laptop theft is especially prevalent at airports. Don't place your devices in checked baggage or hotel room safes. If it's been left unattended, even in a hotel room, assume it's been tampered with, putting your information at risk.

    c. **Immediately Report Lost or Stolen Devices**: When you are abroad, it is important to notify the U.S. embassy or consulate if you suspect your device is lost or stolen.

    d. **Protect Your Network Access**: The FBI states in some countries that Wi-Fi networks are controlled and surveilled by security services, and in all cases Wi-Fi abroad is insecure. Ensure you take the following precautions on the network:

        i. Use a VPN with robust encryption to connect to the Internet. A VPN will ensure your web traffic is protected and will allow you to circumvent any Internet censoring that may be in place.

        ii. Use a private web browsing window or make sure to clear out your browsing history after each use.

        iii. Be aware that standard consumer anti-malware programs may not catch nation-state malware.

        iv. Disable Bluetooth and Wi-Fi when not in use (for example, Bluetooth earpieces, and so forth).

5. **When You Return:**
   a. Wipe the burner phone, remove and recycle the battery, and securely dispose of the phone.
   b. Do not connect the computer or phone to your network at home or at work.
   c. Change all your passwords, even for your voicemail.
   d. Treat the laptop based on the assumption that it is fully infected with malware—maintain strict isolation—and remove and securely dispose of the hard drive. Replace it with a new hard drive.
   e. Report any unusual travel situations to the FBI.

You've learned about the risks of cyberattacks while onboard on a flight, the hazards of using public Wi-Fi and USB charging stations, common tourist scams, and how to protect yourself from perils while traveling. You also gained insight into the necessary precautions to take to protect yourself when visiting nation-state locations abroad.

Congratulations on now being prepared to outsmart bad actors by keeping your identity, personal information, and life's savings protected!

Notes

1. https://www.wired.com/2015/05/feds-say-banned-researcher-commandeered-plane/
2. https://thehackernews.com/2015/07/unsecure-public-Wi-Fi-hacking.html
3. https://www.makeuseof.com/tag/5-ways-hackers-can-use-public-wi-fi-steal-identity/
4. https://learningenglish.voanews.com/a/public-usb-hubs/3937860.html
5. www.relativelyinteresting.com/40-tourist-scams-avoid-travels/
6. https://krebsonsecurity.com/2017/08/why-its-still-a-bad-idea-to-post-or-trash-your-airline-boarding-pass/
7. http://thehill.com/policy/cybersecurity/392182-security-experts-warn-hackers-will-target-americans-traveling-to-russia
8. https://travel.state.gov/content/dam/NEWTravelAssets/pdfs/FBI%20business-travel-brochure%20(2).pdf

Index